British History in Perspective
General Editor: Jeremy Black

PUBLISHED TITLES

FORTHCOMING

Walter L. Arnstein *Queen Victoria*
Ian Arthurson *Henry VII*
Toby Barnard *The Kingdom of Ireland, 1640–1740*
Eugenio Biagini *Gladstone*
Peter Catterall *The Labour Party, 1918–1945*
Gregory Claeys *The French Revolution Debate in Britain*
Pauline Croft *James I*
Eveline Cruickshanks *The Glorious Revolution*
John Davis *British Politics, 1885–1939*
David Dean *Parliament and Politics in Elizabethan and Jacobean England,
. 1558–1614*
Colin Eldridge *The Victorians Overseas*
Richard English *The IRA*
Alan Heesom *The Anglo-Irish Union, 1800–1922*
I. G. C. Hutchison *Scottish Politics in the Twentieth Century*
Gareth Jones *Wales, 1700–1980: Crisis of Identity*
H. S. Jones *Political Thought in Nineteenth-Century Britain*
D. E. Kennedy *The English Revolution, 1642–1649*
Carol Levin *The Reign of Elizabeth I*
Roger Mason *Kingship and Tyranny? Scotland, 1513–1603*
Hiram Morgan *Ireland in the Early Modern Periphery, 1534–1690*
R. C. Nash *English Foreign Trade and the World Economy, 1600–1800*
Robin Prior and Trevor Wilson *Britain and the Impact of World War I*
Brian Quintrell *Government and Politics in Early Stuart England*
Stephen Roberts *Governance in England and Wales, 1603–1688*
David Scott *The British Civil Wars*
John Shaw *The Political History of Eighteenth-Century Scotland*
Alan Sykes *The Radical Right in Britain*
Ann Wiekel *The Elizabethan Counter-Revolution*
Ann Williams *Kingship and Government in Pre-Conquest England*
Ian Wood *Churchill*

Please note that a sister series, *Social History in Perspective*, is now available. It covers
the key topics in social, cultural and religious history.

British History in Perspective
Series Standing Order
ISBN 0–333–71356–7 hardcover
ISBN 0–333–69331–0 paperback
(outside North America only)

You can receive future titles in this series as they are published by placing a standing
order. Please contact your bookseller or, in case of difficulty, write to us at the address
below with your name and address, the title of the series and the ISBN quoted above.

Customer Services Department, Macmillan Distribution Ltd
Houndmills, Basingstoke, Hampshire RG21 6XS, England

SIR ROBERT PEEL

T. A. JENKINS
Research Officer
History of Parliament Trust

First published in Great Britain 1999 by
MACMILLAN PRESS LTD
Houndmills, Basingstoke, Hampshire RG21 6XS and London
Companies and representatives throughout the world

A catalogue record for this book is available from the British Library.

ISBN 0–333–68753–1 hardcover
ISBN 0–333–68754–X paperback

First published in the United States of America 1999 by
ST. MARTIN'S PRESS, INC.,
Scholarly and Reference Division,
175 Fifth Avenue, New York, N.Y. 10010

ISBN 0–312–21639–4

Library of Congress Cataloging-in-Publication Data
Jenkins, T. A. (Terence Andrew), 1958–
Sir Robert Peel / T.A. Jenkins.
p.   cm. — (British history in perspective)
Includes bibliographical references and index.
ISBN 0–312–21639–4
1. Peel, Robert, Sir, 1788–1850.   2. Great Britain—Politics and
government—1837–1901.   3. Great Britain—Politics and
government—1830–1837.   4. Conservatism—Great Britain–
–History—19th century.   5. Prime ministers—Great Britain–
–Biography.   6. Conservative Party (Great Britain)   I. Title.
II. Series.
DA536.P3J46   1998
941.081'092—dc21   98–6881
    [b]   CIP

© T. A. Jenkins 1999

This book is printed on paper suitable for recycling and made from fully managed and sustained forest sources.

10   9   8   7   6   5   4   3   2   1
08   07   06   05   04   03   02   01   00   99

Printed in Hong Kong

CONTENTS

INTRODUCTION

To study the career of Robert Peel (1788–1850), who became Sir Robert in 1830 when he inherited his father's baronetcy, is in effect to study the main developments in British political history between 1810 and 1850. Peel became a junior government minister at the age of only twenty-two, and he was appointed to the demanding post of Irish Chief Secretary two years later. Before reaching his 34th birthday he had entered the Cabinet as Home Secretary, and from 1828 until 1830 he combined this office with the Leadership of the House of Commons. Peel was thus an increasingly prominent figure in the Tory administrations of Spencer Perceval, Lord Liverpool and the Duke of Wellington, which virtually monopolised the government of Britain in the early decades of the nineteenth century; but he also played a key role in the acrimonious collapse of Toryism at the end of the 1820s. In opposition to the Whig governments of 1830–41, he seemed to enjoy considerable success in rebuilding the party which he now led, adopting the new name of 'Conservative', and as Prime Minister from 1841 to 1846 he embarked upon a revolution in commercial and fiscal policy, establishing Free Trade as the guiding principle followed by all subsequent governments until the 1930s. However, Peel moved much too quickly for the comfort of most members of the Conservative party, and his government was brought down in 1846 as the result of a rebellion by his own back-benchers.

It should be clear already that Peel was not only an outstanding presence in British public life, but also a highly controversial one, whose actions aroused strong feelings amongst his contemporaries, whether they were for or against him. On two occasions, in 1829 over the question of Catholic Emancipation, and in 1846 over the repeal of the Corn Laws, he faced accusations of having betrayed fundamental principles which he was expected to uphold. In the case of Catholic Emancipation, Peel assisted Wellington in carrying this measure of religious equality despite the fact that for more than a decade he had been the recognised spokesman of those who wished to maintain an exclusively 'Protestant Constitution'. As Prime Minister in 1846, Peel's abandonment of the system of protective tariffs for British agricultural producers, known as the Corn Laws, provoked intense bitterness on the part of many Conservative MPs, who denounced him for sacrificing the perceived interests of that section of the community which had elected them to prevent just such a change of policy. At both of these critical junctures in his career, Peel was forced to rely upon opposition Whig support in order to secure the safety of his measures. Indeed, during the last four years of his life, following the Corn Law crisis, when he occupied an independent position in the House of Commons, he used his influence to prop-up a *Whig* government and so ensure that his old party could not return to office. And yet, while Peel was driven into political exile and execrated by his former supporters, the extraordinary display of grief at the time of his death demonstrated that he had become a hero in the eyes of the British people, for having put the national interest above the interests of his party and his own government.

Peel's conduct in 1829 and 1846 raises important questions about his political judgement, and also about his character. It was unfortunate, to say the least, that as a rising young Tory politician he should have boxed himself in on the Catholic question, to the extent that he felt obliged to go on championing the Protestant cause even after he had realised that this was an untenable position to take. Peel may have been the victim, in this instance, of his own ill-judged ambition, although political fate undoubtedly played its part too. With regard to the Corn Law issue, whatever the merits of Peel's policy, the Conservative party was certainly entitled to think that it was pledged to maintaining agricultural protection, and it was quite unprepared for the abrupt change of course which Peel recommended in 1846. This led to hysterical accusations that he had been deviously planning to betray the landed interest all along. Perhaps the most extraordinary feature of Peel's attitude, both in 1829 and 1846, was the impatience and contempt which he exhibited towards those who adhered to principles which he had only just relinquished.

There is a central paradox in Peel's character, that a man who was anything but moderate or conciliatory in the pursuit of his chosen policies, was, at least in the 1830s and 1840s, committed to a moderate and conciliatory strategy aimed at accommodating the interests of different classes in British society. In his personal manner, Peel was notoriously cold and austere, and recent research has stressed how inflexible and dogmatic he tended to be in his thinking. Nevertheless, his objective, as leader of the Conservative party, was to construct an alliance between the traditional ruling élite, whose authority rested on aristocratic privilege and landed wealth, and the increasingly powerful urban middle classes created by the industrial, commercial and financial revolutions. Peel wanted to unite the interests of property owners, rural and urban, in the belief that this held out the best hope of preserving the status of the traditional élite and of the institutions associated with it – the Crown, the Church and the House of Lords. For this strategy to succeed, it was also necessary that government policies should be directed towards improving the material well-being of the unenfranchised labouring classes, since no political structure could be stable which ignored their concerns. The fact that Peel's family roots were in the Lancashire cotton textile industry, where his father had made a fortune, but that this manufacturing wealth enabled him to receive a conventional élite education at Harrow and Oxford, and proceed at once into a political career, suggested that he might be personally well-equipped to broker a compromise between the social forces of land and industry.

Ultimately, the greatest obstacle to Peel's ambition of governing for the benefit of the whole nation proved to be the inexorably pressing demands of party connection. His experience as a Tory official in the 1810s and 1820s shaped Peel's notions of 'executive' government, according to which ministers were the servants of the Crown rather than of their parliamentary supporters, and their responsibility was to promote the welfare of the kingdom, not just one section of it. It was by no means anachronistic for Peel to retain this view of his political role after 1832, as the Crown was still a potentially formidable influence; but the enhanced authority of parliament, resulting from the Great Reform Act, meant that in practice ministers depended on support from an organised political party. This situation inevitably produced tensions between the competing claims of an 'executive' government, requiring the loyalty of a parliamentary party in order to survive, and a parliamentary party which felt that its loyalty conferred an obligation on ministers to protect and further those interests with which the party was specially identified. As we shall see, it was Peel's inability – or rather, unwillingness – to square this political circle, which led to the destruction of his ministry – but not of his policies – in 1846.

1

THE TORY ADMINISTRATIONS, 1809–30

The Peel Family and Toryism

The election of Robert Peel to the House of Commons, as member for the tiny Irish borough of Cashel, at the age of only twenty-one in April 1809, marked an important stage in the social and political ascent of one of the most spectacularly successful families of the early Industrial Revolution. Although Peel was educated at Harrow and Christ Church, Oxford, and embarked immediately upon a parliamentary career, he had been born in Bury, Lancashire, in February 1788, the son of a wealthy cotton textile manufacturer. Like many business families of the late eighteenth century, the Peels were staunchly Tory in their politics, and the fact that they were able to rise so rapidly to a position of great prominence, supplying the country with a future Prime Minister, testifies to the relative openness of the British political élite. Indeed, the achievements of the Peel family exemplify the cultural resilience and adaptability which helped Britain to come to terms with the pressures of industrial transformation without experiencing a complete collapse of the social order.

Robert Peel's grandfather, also named Robert (1723–95), was a Lancashire yeoman farmer, owning land near Oswaldtwistle, who in the 1760s became involved in the embryonic cotton textile industry.[1] He acquired the nickname 'Parsley Peel', after the famous parsley-leaf design associated with the calico printing factory which he had set up in partnership with his brother-in-law, Jonathan Haworth, and William Yates. The firm quickly expanded, through vertical integration, incorporating the carding, spinning and weaving processes. Parsley Peel himself subsequently moved to Staffordshire, and established new cotton mills there, but his son, another Robert (1750–1830), the father of the Prime Minister, entered into partnership with Haworth and Yates, and their business emerged as the dominant force in the Lancashire cotton industry.

During the course of the 1790s, Robert, the son of 'Parsley', ambitious to raise the social rank of his family, purchased land and other property in Staffordshire including the Tudor manor of Drayton Bassett, which he demolished and had rebuilt to provide a new family home. His recently acquired landlord influence enabled him to be elected as one of the MPs for the borough of Tamworth, in 1790. In the House of Commons, his support was given to the Prime Minister, William Pitt the Younger, a leader whom Peel admired for his loyalty to King George III and commitment to policies of commercial expansion and administrative reform. With the outbreak of war against revolutionary France, in 1793, it was natural for Peel to back a Pittite administration which was now specially identified with the crusade in defence of monarchy, aristocracy, religion and property in general. Peel had already been active in founding an Association for Preserving Constitutional Order, in Manchester, designed to intimidate local radicals sympathetic to revolutionary ideas, and he later helped to raise volunteer forces both in Lancashire and Staffordshire. In 1797, Peel's firm also made a voluntary contribution of £10,000 to the Exchequer, to assist in meeting the cost of the war effort. These tangible signs of loyalty to the existing regime helped to secure Peel his reward, in the form of a baronetcy in 1800.

Peel's eldest son, Robert, the subject of this book, was, as has already been mentioned, born in Bury, and it was not until he was ten or eleven years old that the family settled permanently at Drayton Manor. Young Robert was therefore obviously conscious, through direct childhood experience, of his family's Lancastrian, industrial origins, even though he never had to work in the textile business himself. In February 1800 he was sent to Harrow, one of the traditional public schools, where he remained until Christmas 1804. Before going up to Oxford, in the autumn of 1805, young Peel spent several months in London, during which time he regularly visited the House of Commons, witnessing what proved to be the final session of the epic parliamentary duel between Pitt and the Whig leader, Charles James Fox. At Oxford, Peel clearly flourished: he is recalled as being tall, an elegant and fashionable dresser, and a good athlete, keen on rowing and cricket. His academic record was outstanding, culminating in the formidable achievement of a double first class degree in *literae humaniores* (essentially the Classics) and mathematics. Peel was fortunate to have been a student at a time when the university was undergoing reform, in an effort to raise academic standards, and at Christ Church, generally regarded as the top college, he was profoundly influenced by men such as the Dean, Cyril Jackson, who inculcated the values of strict diligence and scholastic excellence. In addition to many other things, Oxford taught Peel how to work.

Within a month of leaving university, Peel was elected as MP for Cashel (electorate twenty-four), thanks to his father's financial support. The general situation, at the time of Peel's entry into political life, was alarming both for the Tory government of the Duke of Portland and the country. Britain's military effort to combat revolutionary France had continued, with one short interval, for sixteen years, but apparently to little effect. In 1809, Napoleon Bonaparte was master of the European continent, and while Britain's naval strength protected her from the threat of an immediate invasion, the country now faced an alternative form of warfare as Napoleon sought to cripple her commercial power by shutting British traders out of European markets.

The strains and pressures of protracted warfare were undoubtedly a contributory factor in the fragmentation of Pittite Toryism, which took place during the early years of the 1800s,[2] although personal rivalries and antipathies were at the root of the problem. After Pitt's death in January 1806, the leaders of two of the Tory splinter groups, Lord Grenville and Lord Sidmouth, had participated with the Whigs in the short-lived 'Ministry of all the Talents'. Portland took office with the main body of Tories in March 1807, but the process of disintegration could not be halted, owing to the friction between the Secretary for War, Lord Castlereagh, and the Foreign Secretary, George Canning – the latter described by one unadmiring colleague as 'Vanity in a human form'.[3] Canning's impatience with Castlereagh's management of the war led him to intrigue behind the latter's back for his removal, and when this came to light, at the time of the dying Portland's retirement, in September 1809, Canning and Castlereagh both resigned and treated the country to the spectacle of a duel. Spencer Perceval endeavoured to carry on the government, but various attempts over the next couple of years to reinforce it, by re-admitting either Canning, or Castlereagh, or Sidmouth, and their respective groups of followers (the Grenville party seemed irrevocably lost to the Whigs), all ended in failure. The political conundrum facing Perceval was how to obtain urgently needed additional support for his Ministry, when any offer made to one set of Tory renegades was likely either to upset his existing colleagues or else to complicate his plans for reconciling the other renegades.

In an assessment of the confused state of public affairs, prior to the start of the parliamentary session in 1810, the Speaker of the House of Commons, Charles Abbot, wrote in his diary: 'The Public not much disposed to confidence in the present Government, yet unwilling to harass the King. Ministers weak and uncertain of support. Opposition eager and confident, but not popular.'[4] It was at this point that Peel was invited by ministers to second the Address to the Crown, a significant compliment to the young MP and one which provided the occasion for his first set-piece speech in the Commons. Peel's task was to speak in general defence of the government's policy, and he did so by justifying the aid given to Austria and Spain, despite the fact that this had yet to produce the desired military results. He also expressed confidence in the country's ability to withstand the Napoleonic embargo on its trade with Europe, and ended by calling for national unanimity in support of a great cause, trusting that Britain would continue to 'ride in safety through the storm that had destroyed the rest of Europe, and that we should still stretch forth a hand to succour those who were yet struggling for life against the angry waves'.[5] The Whig politician Thomas Creevey acknowledged in a letter to his wife that Peel had 'made a capital figure for a first speech. I think it was a *prepared* speech, but it was a most produceable *Pittish* performance, both in matter and manner.'[6]

Peel's speech on the Address, and a subsequent oratorical effort in defence of the ministerial attempt to open up a new military front against Napoleon in the Low Countries – the ill-fated, disease-ravaged Walcheren expedition of 1809 – made a sufficiently favourable impression for him to be offered a junior government post. In June 1810, therefore, he was appointed Under-Secretary of State for War and the Colonies. As the Secretary of State was a peer, the Earl of Liverpool, it fell to Peel and his fellow Under-Secretary, Colonel H. E. Bunbury, to represent their department in the House of Commons. Peel's specific responsibility within the department was for the colonial business, which meant that he was engaged in a heavy routine correspondence with overseas governors and others on a variety of military and civil matters. Somewhat surprisingly, Peel's side of the work also involved administering the government's Secret Service money, most of which was spent on annual allowances to French royalists, although spies were occasionally employed to bring back intelligence from the continent. When Bunbury was on leave, Peel did his colleague's work as well, affording him the opportunity to follow the progress of Wellington's military operations in the Iberian peninsula. This was to be the subject of Peel's next notable parliamentary speech, in March 1811, during the debate on a proposed vote of £2 million to maintain a body of Portuguese troops in the British government's pay. His object was not only to vindicate Wellington's peninsular campaign, which he argued had succeeded in tying down a large part of the French army, but to denounce the 'venal abuse', the 'tongue of envy', and the 'cavils of party animosity', displayed by the Whigs in their carping criticisms of the great British commander. It was, in fact, a polemical attack on the fatalistic attitude of opposition members, who seemed to believe that Napoleon's 'march was irresistible', and that Europe had no choice but to 'crouch before the usurper', a mentality which Peel considered to be 'deserving only of contempt'.[7] The Prime Minister himself reported to the Prince of Wales that Peel had made 'an extremely good speech', and others were even more enthusiastic. One delighted government minister, Robert Plumer Ward, recorded in his diary that the Whigs had been 'answered and pulled to pieces in one of the most beautiful, as well as argumentative, speeches ever delivered in the House, by young Peel; who gave another proof that there was ability on our side of the House. He was applauded almost as much by the opposition as by us at the end of his speech.'[8]

Fate played its part in Peel's ministerial progress when John Bellingham, a deranged businessman, assassinated Spencer Perceval in the lobby of the House of Commons, in May 1812. Liverpool eventually emerged as Perceval's successor, and his appreciation of his young subordinate's work at the War and Colonial Office prompted him to recommend Peel to the Duke of Richmond, the Lord Lieutenant of Ireland, as a suitable man for the post of Irish Chief Secretary. Peel duly accepted a new appointment, in August 1812, which was to significantly shape the course of his future political career.

The Protestant Constitution: Ireland, 1812–18

The office of Chief Secretary for Ireland was an unusual one, in many respects, requiring the 24-year-old Peel to undertake an enormous administrative workload and yet, at the same time, imposing restrictions on his political authority to act.[9] Peel had a dual role to play. When in Ireland, he was accountable to the King's representative, the Lord Lieutenant, who resided permanently in Dublin and performed the functions of an active constitutional monarch. The Chief Secretary was, in effect, the Lord Lieutenant's Prime Minister, and he was therefore directly responsible for the whole range of governmental activities, including finance, trade, law and order, and defence (he had two Under-Secretaries to assist him, as well as civil servants). But the Chief Secretary only spent part of each year in Ireland, for it was also his duty to be in London, during the parliamentary session, to act as the spokesman for the Irish administration. The long road journeys and hazardous sea crossings, involved in travelling from London to Dublin and back, were sometimes a major ordeal in themselves.[10] In addition to speaking on Irish affairs in the House of Commons, Peel had to press Ireland's claims for consideration within the British government, a task that was made more difficult by the fact that the Chief Secretary did not have the rank of a Cabinet minister. Instead, he had to negotiate with the Cabinet via the Home Secretary, who, in Peel's time, was Lord Sidmouth, a man who took little interest in Irish matters. One of the most frustrating parts of the Chief Secretary's work, as Peel discovered, was the difficulty in obtaining adequate parliamentary time for Irish legislation, which often tended to be left until the dying days of the session.

From a positive point of view, Peel's six year spell as Irish Chief Secretary provided him with a unique opportunity to gain an excellent, wide-ranging training in all areas of administration. This obviously had a beneficial effect, in helping to prepare him for his eventual role as Prime Minister, though it may also have been disadvantageous, as the experience of running the government of Ireland almost single-handedly encouraged an excessive degree of self-reliance. In later years, he always found it difficult properly to delegate work to his colleagues.[11] Peel's time in Ireland certainly enabled him to indulge what was probably a natural, bureaucratic habit of mind. One of his characteristic practices, then and later, was to gather as much information as possible on any given subject. Early in 1816, for example, he had detailed questionnaires sent out to all the magistrates in County Tipperary, in order to acquire a better understanding of the state of the peasantry: among other things, he wished to know about the land held by peasants, the rents they were paying, their daily wage rates, the kinds of food they ate, the quality of their housing, the price of fuel, the age at which they typically got married, their attitude towards their social superiors, the extent of their mobility, and so on.[12] At a time when governments, both in Britain and Ireland, were often hampered by a lack of reliable statistical information about the population, and the conditions in which people lived, Peel's painstakingly thorough approach was comparatively efficient, and highly commendable, even if it betrayed an essentially mechanical intellect, obsessed with facts and figures.

It is impossible to fully appreciate the long-term significance for Peel of his tenure in Ireland unless it is set in the context of the chaotic state of Tory politics in 1812. Peel's appointment drew him, unavoidably, into engagement with a controversial issue which had been at the heart of Tory internal disputes since 1801. At that time, Pitt the Younger had wished to accompany the Act of Union, incorporating Ireland into the United Kingdom, with the concession of Catholic Emancipation, so that the Roman Catholic Irish majority would be eligible for the higher civil and military offices in the State. This plan met with resolute resistance from King George III, however, and had to be dropped. An anomalous situation was thus created in which Catholics had the right to vote – if they possessed the requisite property qualification – but could not sit in parliament itself, could become barristers, but not King's Counsel or judges, and could serve in the army and navy, but not attain the rank of general or admiral. Consequently, an automatic Catholic grievance was built in to the new constitutional relationship between Ireland and Britain, creating conditions which were all too likely to erupt into serious conflict. At Westminster, meantime, a division existed between 'Protestant' Tories such as Perceval and Liverpool, who were determined to maintain the Anglican monopoly of key public offices, and pro-Catholic Tories favourable to the removal of religious disabilities. The most formidable of the Tory pro-Catholics was Canning, whose support for Emancipation became a badge of Pittite honour, distinguishing him, in his own mind, as the purest of the great leader's disciples.

Spencer Perceval's government, formed in September 1809, operated on the basis that Catholic Emancipation was an open question, but it remained vulnerable to attack from Tory factions, led by Canning, Castlereagh and Sidmouth, which, as we saw earlier, had been alienated from ministers and from each other by a compound of personal jealousies and ideological differences (only partly related to the Catholic question). Further complications arose, after October 1810, when King George suffered what proved to be a permanent breakdown of his mental and physical health. On the face of things, this greatly improved the political prospects for supporters of Catholic Emancipation. In February 1811 the Prince of Wales was named as Prince Regent, albeit with restricted constitutional powers for the first year, and it was widely assumed that in due course Perceval and his colleagues would be removed from office and the pro-Catholic Whig opposition, with whom the Prince had been closely associated in earlier times, installed in their places.

Anticipating imminent changes, the ambitious and imperious Tory Foreign Secretary, Lord Wellesley, resigned from Perceval's government in January 1812, declared his support for Catholic concessions and aligned with the outcast Canning. Evidently, the calculation behind this move was that when the Regent acquired full constitutional powers he might turn to Wellesley and Canning to form a 'broad-bottom' pro-Catholic administration, including the Whigs. In the event, Prince George, who had become increasingly conservative and indolent with middle-age, chose to retain Perceval's services. The Prime Minister was even able to strengthen his position by recruiting the Castlereagh and Sidmouth groups, shortly before his assassination in May 1812. Lord Liverpool then attempted to continue with the same ministerial team, but he was compelled to resign when the House of Commons carried a motion declaring that a strong and efficient government was needed – which was tantamount to a censure of the present arrangements.[13] At this point, the Prince Regent invited Wellesley to take the premiership, but the unwillingness of the Whig leader, Lord Grey, to allow his party to be absorbed into a 'broad-bottom' administration headed by politicians with whom he had little in common,[14] put an end to Wellesley's hopes. Eventually, Liverpool and his friends returned to office (agreeing to leave the Catholic question open again), which was probably the outcome desired all along by the Prince. In an ominous move, however, Canning, from his position outside the government, easily carried a motion in the Commons calling for the Catholic claims to be considered early in the next session.

This account of recent political events may appear bewilderingly complex, but it helps us to locate the precise situation in which Peel found himself when he became Irish Chief Secretary in August 1812. Lord Liverpool's government was in a desperately insecure position, being menaced from without by the Wellesley and Canning Tory groups, whose chief battle-cry related to Catholic Emancipation – an issue for which Peel was now the minister directly responsible. More provocatively still, Peel's appointment was made after the previous incumbent of the post – none other than Wellesley's brother, William Wellesley Pole – had been unceremoniously removed. Peel was therefore well aware of the political dangers ahead of him, but, as he remarked in a letter to his close friend, John Wilson Croker, 'I hope we may fight out this battle as we have fought out many others...there never was a time when I felt more determined to do all I could to support the Government on its present footing and on the principles on which it will meet Parliament.'[15] A general election held late in the summer brought gains for the Liverpool administration, on paper at least, though the Prime Minister reckoned that Wellesley and Canning between them commanded the allegiance of some twenty-five MPs, while there were others whose loyalty to the government could not be entirely trusted to. Thus, Liverpool advised Peel in November that:

> Our danger is not from Opposition, but evidently from the third parties headed by Lord Wellesley and Canning, who will represent themselves as holding the same opinions as we do on all popular topics, who will say that they have as much right to be considered as the successors of Mr Pitt's party as ourselves, and whose object will consequently be to detach as many of our friends as possible.[16]

The crucial question, as far as Peel's subsequent career is concerned, is whether his immersion in Irish affairs, at such an early age, caused him to harden his stance against Catholic Emancipation to a degree which was politically advantageous in the short-term, but which also stored up considerable difficulty and embarrassment for the future. After all, it is noticeable that in his first parliamentary speech on Ireland, made in February 1812 before he became Chief Secretary, Peel was careful not to pledge himself irrevocably against the Catholic claims, even though he clearly entertained serious doubts about the use the Catholics were likely to make of their power if fully emancipated.[17] In May 1813, on the other hand, when Peel was obliged to respond, as Chief Secretary, to Henry Grattan's Emancipation Bill, he declared his total opposition to a measure which would have allowed Catholics – whose allegiance was to an external authority (the Pope), and who were unwilling to offer adequate guarantees for the security of the Established Protestant Churches of England and Ireland – to sit in a parliament exercising legislative control over those churches. Furthermore, Peel feared the consequences for the Union between Britain and

Ireland if unrestricted opportunities were granted to Catholics, since they outnumbered the Irish Protestants by around four to one. He therefore reasoned that the Protestant ascendancy in Ireland, an essential bulwark of the London government's control in that country, would simply become untenable if the Catholics were emancipated.[18] Like most British politicians, Peel was not prepared to accept the alternative conclusion that the preservation of a 'Protestant Constitution', in a predominantly Catholic country, was an absurdity. Unable to trust to the good intentions of Irish Catholics, Peel believed that the only answer was to continue excluding them from their due share of power.

Following the narrow defeat of Grattan's bill, by just 251 votes to 247, Peel sent an optimistic report to the Lord Lieutenant expressing his opinion that 'I should not be surprised if the tide in favour of the Catholics had reached its height, and will begin to subside.'[19] In strictly parliamentary terms, this was an accurate assessment, as Canning's ambitions had suffered a severe blow and he responded by disbanding his small group of followers. One of his protégés, William Huskisson, joined the government in 1814, along with William Wellesley Pole, while Canning himself accepted an ambassadorial post in Lisbon. He finally returned to England, and the Cabinet, in 1816. The direct threat posed to the survival of Liverpool's government by Canning and his pro-Catholic associates, had thus been contained.

There is no reason to suppose that Peel's instincts were anything other than those of a sincere Church and King Tory, causing him to doubt the possibility of ever reconciling the Catholic demand for emancipation with the maintenance of an Anglican State. It may nevertheless be true that the force of political circumstances prompted him to express his 'Protestant' principles in a more exaggerated and uncompromising way than would have appeared prudent, or necessary, had he held some other ministerial post unconnected with Ireland. The extent to which personal opportunism played a part in dictating Peel's course is far more difficult to gauge, but one has to be aware that the effect of his speeches was to mark him out as the champion of the Protestant cause. Peel's definitive statement on the Catholic question came in May 1817, in answer to a motion by Grattan, when his powerful speech was probably decisive in swaying opinion in the House of Commons against the emancipationists (the motion was defeated by 245 votes to 221). He now confirmed that he was opposed to Catholic Emancipation *at any time*, rejecting as he did the argument of pro-Catholic colleagues such as Canning that concession would promote tranquillity in Ireland, persuading the Catholic majority to acquiesce in the country's Protestant institutions. Instead, Peel professed to stand by the *status quo*, which deserved the benefit of the doubt on a matter of such grave importance, more especially when there was so much uncertainty about the consequences of change. In a classic re-statement of 'Protestant' principles, founded on the belief that the religion of the British people was connected with the progress of the nation, Peel declared: 'Let us recollect that, under the constitution which we have derived from our ancestors, we have enjoyed more liberty, we have acquired more glory, we possess more character and power, than has hitherto fallen to the lot of any other Country on the globe.'[20]

Even a Tory MP sympathetic to the Catholic claims admitted, privately, that Peel had made an 'excellent anti-Catholic speech...really quite capital. He said all that could be said on that side, and said it as well as possible.'[21] Supporters of the 'Protestant Constitution', naturally enough, were delighted to have found such an outstanding spokesman for their cause.[22] Less generous in their appreciation of Peel's efforts were members of Canning's circle of friends, who saw the speech as a deliberate move intended to strengthen his hand in the eventual struggle for the Tory succession. This cynicism was only reinforced when Oxford University decided to invite the Irish Chief Secretary, rather than Canning, to fill the vacancy in its parliamentary representation left by Speaker Abbot's retirement – a prestigious tribute, indeed, from a largely ecclesiastical constituency to a politician who was still only twenty-nine years old. One of Canning's cronies, almost exploding with wrath and jealousy, wrote: 'This Peel has been wonderfully impudent and aspiring, unquestionably it was a most masterly speech of his, that upon the Catholic claims...it raised him instantly pegs innumerable, and I don't know how many people have been saying ever since "that young fellow will ere long be at the head of affairs in this Country, etc etc". Well, my youngster sees his vantage and is determined to push it...'[23] Perhaps it was unjust to accuse Peel of acting in quite such a calculating way as this, but the end result of his May 1817 speech, all the same, was to secure for himself a powerful position in Tory politics.

Despite Peel's increasingly rigid stance on the Catholic question, it would be wrong to suppose that his approach to Ireland's wider problems was characterised by an absence of imaginative understanding. On the contrary, he demonstrated an impressive grasp of the historical roots of a situation which currently required the presence of some 25,000 troops to help keep the peace. Responding to a motion on the state of Ireland, brought forward by Sir John Newport in April 1816, Peel recognised that the 'causes of the evils which afflicted Ireland' could be 'traced back to a very remote period in some respects'. The piecemeal way in which Ireland had been conquered in the middle ages, by various 'parties of adventurers', rather than by 'a sovereign at the head of an aimy', had produced a defective system of rule from the outset, and this had taken centuries to be rectified. In more recent times, the harmful effects of the policy of 'imposing commercial restrictions' on Ireland were accepted by Peel, who admitted that Britain had thereby 'curtailed the capital of Ireland, and lessened her means of industry'. It was Peel's view that this policy had also been the unintentional cause of Ireland's agrarian crisis, as the stifling of native industry had encouraged a more intensive cultivation of smaller and smaller plots of land by the surplus labour force. Dependence on the high-yielding potato crop was a mixed blessing, because it meant that 'the immediate means of supporting a family were more within the reach of the poorer classes of Ireland than of similar classes in this country', permitting the rapid expansion of the Irish population (from about four million in the 1780s, it reached seven million by the 1820s) which was desperately vulnerable to the vicissitudes of the harvest. On top of all this, there was the deep-seated religious animosity between Protestants and Catholics, fuelled by a licentious press caring nothing for the truth and apparently determined to 'keep alive and foment discord'.[24]

When it came to immediate solutions to the endemic state of disorder in many parts of Ireland, however, Peel did not pretend that there were any at his disposal. The 'difficulties and evils which encompassed Ireland formed a Gordian Knot', he told the House of Commons, which could not simply be cut, and all he had to suggest was that 'Time alone, the prevalence of a kind and paternal system of government, and the extension of education, were the remedies which must be chiefly relied on.'[25] In other words, the emphasis of Peel's policies as Chief Secretary was invariably placed on the need to contain those forces which threatened an ever-fragile social order, and there were never to be any bold measures of constructive reform. Two pieces of legislation carried in 1814, after Peel had managed to persuade a hesitant Cabinet, provided the Irish administration with special sanctions to combat lawlessness. Under the Peace Preservation Act, the Lord Lieutenant was empowered to proclaim districts where the situation was particularly bad, which meant that a superintending magistrate and special constables could then be imposed on these districts at their own expense. The Insurrection Act (renewed in 1817) allowed night-time curfews to be enforced in proclaimed districts, and it authorised local magistrates to impound arms. As a result of these measures, Peel expressed his satisfaction, in the autumn of 1814, that much had been done to improve the enforcement of law and order. Ireland, in Peel's time, was seldom free for long from alarms about impending serious disorder, but in practice the emergency powers with which he had equipped the administration were only required in a few disturbed areas.[26]

The campaign in Ireland for Catholic Emancipation had been co-ordinated, since 1811, by an organisation known as the Catholic Board, whose members included the lawyer Daniel O'Connell. Fortunately for Peel's administration, the Board was left in a state of confusion after the failure of Grattan's Bill, in 1813, opinions being divided as to the most appropriate tactics to pursue in the circumstances. In June 1814, therefore, the government was able to get away with banning the Catholic Board altogether, without provoking any serious display of resistance. For the remainder of Peel's time in Ireland, he was not troubled by the presence of any effectively organised Catholic political body. This did not save him, though, from vituperative personal attacks in the Irish press and on the public platform, and O'Connell was particularly fierce in his denunciations of 'Orange Peel'. One such attack so infuriated Peel, by impugning his integrity, that he was stung into challenging O'Connell to a duel. He even travelled to Ostend, ready to vindicate his honour on neutral soil, but the British authorities intervened by preventing O'Connell from following him.

It is hardly surprising to find that six years spent in the post of Chief Secretary induced a despairing attitude on Peel's part towards the Irish people. For example, he pointed to the 'enormous and overgrown population of Ireland' as presenting a 'great obstacle in the way of general improvement', and he only regretted that those who chose to emigrate tended to be Protestant Ulstermen, whom the country could ill-afford to lose.[27] Peel was exasperated, too, by what he considered to be the peculiarly Irish habit of looking to the government to do everything, including, apparently, clearing the snow. On one occasion he condemned the 'monstrous impolicy' of maintaining a Foundling Hospital in Dublin, at public expense: 'Really to make the Government of Ireland a nurse is painfully ridiculous . . . it is wrong, radically wrong, in principle.'[28] Moreover, the continuous flow of reports of agrarian outrages, including the murder of landowners and magistrates, filled him with a sense of the 'sheer wickedness and depravity' of the Irish peasantry.[29] The Roman Catholic priests, he believed, bore a heavy responsibility for the crimes that were being committed. In December 1816, at a time when conditions in Ireland were comparatively calm, Peel reported to the Speaker of the House of Commons that:

There is, no doubt, the average proportion of murders and burnings and other atrocities, the acts of a set of human beings very little advanced from barbarism, unaccustomed to regard the law either as the protector from or as the avenger of outrage, and subject, so far as the interests of society are concerned, to the pernicious influence of the religion they profess. It is quite impossible for anyone to witness the remorselessness with which crimes are committed here, the almost total annihilation of the agency of conscience as a preventive of crime, and the universal contempt in which the obligation of any but an illegal oath is held by the mass of the people, without being satisfied that the prevailing religion of Ireland operates as an impediment rather than an aid to the ends of Civil Government.[30]

If the conduct of the enemies of British rule in Ireland was such as to disgust the young Chief Secretary, it must often have appeared that the government's allies were, in their own way, equally contemptible. The paramilitary activities of the Orange Lodges were a frequent source of concern for Peel, who had no wish to ban these loyalist organisations but feared that their aggressive Protestantism might alienate sections of public opinion in Britain. Then there was the unrelenting pressure of applications, from Irish peers, MPs and other territorial magnates, for the bestowal of patronage on themselves and their clients, which occupied so much of the Chief Secretary's time. 'I am in the midst of all the Vultures', Peel informed his Under-Secretary in one letter, 'and must throw a little food among them occasionally.'[31] Distributing government favours was never going to be a pleasant task for someone as personally fastidious as Peel, and the post-war pressure on the Liverpool government for retrenchment in expenditure meant that the resources available to the Irish administration were being diminished. The Irish demand for patronage, on the other hand, showed no sign of following suit. Peel was therefore confronted with requests for the award of titles, or the grant of pensions, or the preferment of certain individuals in the Irish Church, of the appointment of other individuals to posts in the army and navy, the Customs Board, the Excise Board, the Navigation

Board, the Board of Stamps, the Fisheries Board, the Board of Works, and so on. It was not unknown for such requests to be accompanied by threats that parliamentary or electoral support might be withdrawn if satisfaction was not given.[32] The granting of patronage was obviously a thoroughly distasteful business, but no government could afford to ignore its value for securing and consolidating Irish politicians' voting fidelity at Westminster: quite simply, it was an indispensable part of Britain's system for governing Ireland.

In one respect, at least, Peel may have counted himself fortunate, in that his spell as Chief Secretary was not marred by a famine crisis. After the partial failure of the potato and cereal crops in 1816, because of wet autumn weather, there was a very real danger of widespread starvation if things did not improve the following year. In the early months of 1817, Peel was busy arranging emergency supplies of seed, for sowing that year's crops, while a total of £37,000 was distributed to local famine relief funds. However, these measures would have amounted to nothing like an adequate response if hunger had really taken a hold on Ireland. Thankfully, the harvest of 1817 turned out to be a good one, and the price of food subsequently fell. Peel was therefore lucky that a disaster was averted which would otherwise have exposed his powerlessness to protect the Irish population. Nearly thirty years later, when famine did finally strike in Ireland, Prime Minister Peel was only slightly better placed to render effective assistance.

Tory Reconstruction, 1818–22

Peel left Ireland in August 1818, as soon as the task of supervising the general election contest was completed, and he never visited the country again. There is no doubt that he was tired of his post, after six years, and frustrated that no offer of promotion to the Cabinet had been forthcoming. In these circumstances, he preferred to resign and enjoy a welcome break from ministerial routine. On returning to Britain, he headed immediately for his beloved Scottish Highlands, where he spent five weeks relaxing, slaughtering the local wildlife, and rhapsodising on the 'wildness and magnificence in the scenery'.[33] Surprisingly enough, this was to be the beginning of a period of more than three years spent out of office, which only ended when Peel became Home Secretary in January 1822. During this time of freedom, in June 1820, he married

Julia Floyd, the daughter of an army general, and his new domestic life provided a purely personal motive for his apparent lack of urgency about rejoining Lord Liverpool's government.

Some further explanation is, nevertheless, required for the fact that Peel was allowed to remain unharnessed for so long. The gossip of the time abounded with rumours of imminent ministerial reconstructions, in which Peel's name always figured prominently, and it was widely agreed that Liverpool's government was in desperate need of an infusion of political strength.[34] Part of the reason for the delay in re-enlisting Peel's services was that there was no concept, in the nineteenth century, of the periodic Cabinet 'reshuffle' carried out by the Prime Minister in order to rejuvenate his front-bench team. Consequently, Liverpool had to rely on patience, and maybe some subtle persuasion, before Cabinet members either died, retired or moved aside, creating vacancies for rising younger men to fill. But Peel's position only really makes sense when it is examined in the context of the confused state of British politics at the close of the Regency period and the beginning of George IV's reign,[35] and with reference to the complex and changing relationship between Crown, parliament and government.

Shortly after the general election of 1818, it was reported that the Whig leader in the House of Commons, George Tierney, had calculated that there were now some 172 or 173 'decided Opposition' members. Given that the total number of MPs was 658, this would seem to imply that Liverpool's government was in an overwhelmingly dominant position, but in reality the situation was much less favourable. Tierney's estimate 'did not take into consideration, on either side, the doubtfuls or uncertains, which might operate both ways, and make a calculation questionable'. Added to this, one had to make allowance for 'the activity of new members, and the state of public opinion', and it was therefore reckoned that in the new parliament there was likely to be 'an Opposition which, if well managed, must break-up any Government'.[36]

The Tory administration, to put it another way, did not command the support of an organised 'Tory party' comprising the majority of MPs. In fact, Lord Liverpool and his colleagues, many of whom had served their apprenticeships under Pitt the Younger, still conceived of themselves essentially as servants of the King,[37] who had appointed them, rather than as leaders of a political party which had placed them in power. It was within this Pittite tradition of government, devoted to the dispassionate pursuit of the national interest, that Peel, too, had received his political education. Identification with the Crown, rather than with party, was also politically advantageous, when George III was still alive, as the aged monarch (even if he was mentally incapacitated) attracted immense public respect and affection. Unfortunately, the same could not be said of the Prince Regent, later George IV, a slothful, vain, extravagant and spiteful individual, who was disliked by his own ministers as well as by the public. The result was that while Liverpool and his friends remained loyal to the monarchy as an institution, they did not feel the same sense of reverence towards the person of the King once George III was dead.

Important underlying changes had also been taking place which were gradually eroding the material basis on which the King's government had hitherto rested. Since the 1780s, successive instalments of 'Economical reform', designed to make the system of government cheaper in deference to public opinion, had meant the abolition of some of the patronage previously used by ministers to build political support in parliament. Between 1807 and 1818, for instance, the number of MPs classifiable as 'placemen' or 'pensioners' was cut by one-third, from 120 to seventy-nine,[38] and further reductions were achieved during the 1820s. One of the main resources available to eighteenth century prime ministers, for the purpose of constructing a parliamentary majority *after* their appointment by the King, was therefore no longer sufficient for the task in Liverpool's day.

The other chief source of support, on which governments had always relied, came from the 'independents' or 'country gentlemen' in the House of Commons, men who normally voted with ministers because they were the King's chosen ministers, and who were not in any formal sense 'members' of a governing 'party'.[39] Once again, however, long-term developments were slowly altering the situation. Pitt and his disciples enjoyed an almost unbroken tenure of office between 1783 and 1830, and during this time the country gentlemen were being imperceptibly transformed into *general* supporters of the Tory governments because of their common ideological concerns. A Tory political philosophy was evolving, focused on an attachment to the traditional governing institutions of the country – the Crown, the aristocracy and the Church – all of which felt menaced by the spectre of the French revolution. From this perspective, Pitt and his successors had gallantly pledged themselves to a patriotic struggle to resist, and finally eliminate, the contagion of revolutionary ideas in Europe and at home. (Incidentally, prolonged warfare also brought higher cereal prices and therefore higher rents for landlords.) But it was clear, especially after the conclusion of peace in 1815, that the process of converting the country gentlemen into a dependable voting bloc, or 'Tory party', was far from complete, and Liverpool and his colleagues regularly found themselves in precarious parliamentary situations where they were unsure of receiving support or else unable to procure the necessary attendance by MPs. Thus, pressure from the country gentlemen for drastic retrenchment in post-war government expenditure forced ministers to abandon the income tax, in March 1816, against their better judgement, and to make further cuts in spending on the army than were already proposed. The sessions of 1819 and 1822 were similarly traumatic ones for the government, facing as they did further threatened rebellions by the country gentlemen over the retrenchment issue.[40] If there was any comfort to be drawn by ministers, it was that the country gentlemen were evidently unwilling to bring down the government, because they feared the consequences of letting-in the Whigs, given the opposition's Foxite record of antagonism towards the Crown, religious indifference, 'unpatriotic' behaviour during the Napoleonic wars, and leanings towards 'democratic' reform.[41] As a Tory supporter observed, on one occasion in 1819, 'The Ministry is in a strange state. The majority of the House of Commons seems equally determined upon two points, first, that it shall always stumble, second, that it shall not fall.'[42]

To summarise this analysis of the foundations of government in Lord Liverpool's day, a corps of professional administrators, legatees of the tradition of Pitt the Younger, were running the nation's affairs. Officially, they still considered themselves to be the King's servants, although in reality there was a widening emotional distance between themselves and George IV. Their standing as the Ministers of the Crown was also being undermined by the fact that the quantity of patronage at their disposal for political purposes was continually diminishing. Liverpool and his colleagues could normally expect the independent country gentlemen to rally to their defence, especially on the critical law and order issues of the turbulent post-war years, and there was an increasing tendency for ministers and back-benchers to identify with the same 'Tory' principles. On the other hand, these independents had yet to be fully integrated into an organised 'Tory party', with a life of its own separate from its connection to the King's government. The implications of the underlying development of a party-based system of politics would only become apparent in the 1830s, after the Tories' monopoly of government had been broken.

It is now possible to consider the relevance of this fluid state of politics for the progress of Peel's career after 1818. The insecurity of Lord Liverpool's position, both in terms of parliamentary support and of royal favour, meant that there were various possibilities for the replacement or reconstruction of his administration, and many possible permutations of the individuals involved. In other words, the question was not simply whether Peel would rejoin the government, and in what capacity, but rather, whether he would join *a* government, and what his part in that might be.

To be fair to Peel, it should be emphasised that his general loyalty to Liverpool's government was never in doubt. If he had not remained close to ministers, it is unlikely that he would have been asked to move the re-election of the Speaker of the House of Commons, at the opening of the new parliament in 1819. Nor would Liverpool have invited him, soon afterwards, to chair a committee of inquiry into the currency question (see Chapter 2). Significantly, Peel also gave ministers his full support when they were attacked by the Whigs, in December 1819, over the so-called 'Peterloo massacre' – the deaths of fourteen people, and injury of hundreds of others, involved in a parliamentary reform demonstration near Manchester which was forcibly dispersed by the local magistrates. Speaking in defence of the notorious 'six acts', introduced by the government to curb public meetings and the activities of the press, Peel reportedly 'deviated from his usual discretion in rejoicing at the issue of the Manchester meeting; alleging that more blood must have been spilt hereafter if none had been drawn upon that occasion'.[43]

All the same, freed from the restrictions of office, Peel was advantageously placed to cultivate a personal following within the 'Tory' parliamentary ranks. Charles Arbuthnot, the Parliamentary Secretary to the Treasury (responsible for organising the government's parliamentary supporters), observed to the Leader of the House of Commons, Lord Castlereagh, in March 1819, that, while he could never suspect Peel of behaving dishonestly, 'it is in human nature to be pleased with the sort of following which he must observe is now attaching to him. He has dinners without end, & this he is enabled to have throughout the week, not only by his own great means, but also by his never being fixed to the House when we are obliged to be attending the debates.' Believing that a ministerial reconstruction was urgently required, Arbuthnot continued: 'We may imagine what is passing in Peel's mind, & it is ever to be recollected that to Peel there are belonging some persons who on their own accounts are boiling over with impatience at his not being already in high office.'[44] At the end of 1820, Charles Wynn, a member of the Grenville connection, now gravitating towards the government, wrote of Peel that 'Talent, independent fortune, official habits and reputation, and, above all, general character both in and out of Parliament have, I am persuaded, disposed more men to follow and more to unite with him than any person whom you can name among us.'[45]

Contemporaries were certainly struck by the way that, during the 1819 parliamentary session, Peel spoke in favour of an increase in the civil list allowance for the Prince Regent's brother, the Duke of York. This seemed to have a double significance, for not only was the Duke now the heir presumptive to the throne after the Regent (whose only child, Princess Charlotte, had died in 1817), but he was also a vehement opponent of Catholic Emancipation and determined upholder of the 'Protestant Constitution'. Peel's move could therefore be interpreted, as it was by friends of Canning, as a blatant attempt to curry royal favour.[46] Indeed, across the political spectum in 1819, it was rumoured that the next government was likely to be an avowedly anti-Catholic one, possibly led by a combination of the Duke of Wellington (who had joined Liverpool's Cabinet the previous year) and Peel.[47] In May, Peel played a prominent role in the debate on Grattan's Catholic Emancipation motion, which was rejected by MPs, and the following month, at the anniversary meeting of the Pitt Club in London, a leading 'Protestant' Tory noted of the proceedings: 'The Duke of Wellington in the Chair. Protestant ascendancy was drunk, Mr Peel's health, &c.'[48]

On the accession to the throne of the Prince Regent, as King George IV in January 1820, the political situation became exceptionally complicated, and it has to be admitted that it is far from easy to discern a coherent pattern in the subsequent negotiations and manoeuvrings involving Peel. The principal difficulty arose from the question of what should be done about the King's estranged wife, Caroline of Brunswick, whom George utterly despised, but who proved determined to assert her right to be crowned as Queen. In reluctant deference to the King's demands, Liverpool's government introduced into the House of Lords a Bill of Pains and Penalties, which would have granted George a divorce (on the grounds of adultery) and also deprived Caroline of her royal status. This proceeding served to transform Caroline into a popular heroine, a wronged woman, in the eyes of a general public unaware of her sordid private life and having little respect for the King. The agitation in Caroline's favour even led to rioting in London. Liverpool and his colleagues loyally persisted with their bill, but the thin majority in its favour among the peers, who passed it in November, showed that there was no chance of carrying it in the House of Commons. To the King's fury, the bill was therefore dropped. Shortly afterwards, Canning, an old friend (and lover?) of Caroline's, resigned from the Cabinet in protest at the way she had been treated.

The government's plight in December 1820 created a dilemma for Peel, whom Lord Liverpool turned to as the best replacement for Canning. Acceptance of this offer would undoubtedly have strengthened Peel's future claims to the premiership, *vis-à-vis* Canning, provided the government was likely to survive. But with the relations between King George and his ministers so strained, and the parliamentary position so fragile, many observers judged that Peel would have to be mad to agree to join a government whose early demise seemed probable.[49] The pretext which Peel used to justify his refusal of Liverpool's offer was that he disapproved of the way ministers had initially behaved towards Caroline, removing her name from the royal liturgy before her adultery had been proved.[50] An impression appears to have been conveyed, though, that Peel's refusal was only a temporary one, leaving open the possibility that if the government managed to withstand the forthcoming parliamentary attacks by the Whigs, over the Caroline affair, then his position might be altered.[51]

In the event, ministers did weather the storm at the beginning of the 1821 session, and signs were detected that Peel was moving closer to the government – literally – with his 'abandonment of Pitt's old Hill Fort, which he had occupied, and returning to his former position in the rear of the Treasury Bench'.[52] During the next few months, he might well have been appointed Chancellor of the Exchequer, but for the jealous objections from Castlereagh, who feared that Peel would become too powerful a rival to his own authority as Leader of the House of Commons.[53] When an offer did come, in June, of Canning's old post of President of the Board of Control (responsible for India), this was insufficiently tempting for Peel, who turned it down, to Liverpool's obvious annoyance.[54] Peel's return to the ministerial fold was thus delayed again, until in November he finally agreed to serve as Home Secretary – although he did not receive the seals of office until January 1822. Around the same time, the Grenvillite, Charles Wynn, was also brought into the Cabinet, while Lord Wellesley, allied to the Grenvilles since 1818, became Lord Lieutenant of Ireland. Against all the odds, Liverpool had not only survived as Prime Minister, but he had also succeeded in reuniting all the elements of Mr Pitt's party. It was arranged that Canning, who the King had not forgiven for his conduct over the Caroline affair, should eventually succeed Lord Hastings as Governor General of India, thereby removing him from the British political scene altogether.

One further – unforeseen – development impinged upon an otherwise satisfactory outcome, from Peel's point of view. In August 1822, just weeks before Canning was due to depart for India, Castlereagh (now Lord Londonderry) committed suicide, apparently succumbing to the accumulated pressures of a decade spent as Foreign Secretary and Leader of the House of Commons. The King would have preferred to see Peel succeed to the Leadership of the Commons, but Liverpool pressed for the appointment of Canning, who was unquestionably the foremost parliamentary debator of his day, as well as being eighteen years Peel's senior. Peel felt unable to object to Canning's elevation, in the circumstances, although Liverpool understood that he was ready to take the Leadership if the royal objection to Canning persisted.[55] The King, however, gave way, and Canning was saved from political oblivion. It is hard to believe that, privately at least, Peel did not consider himself unlucky that the timing of Londonderry's death so narrowly deprived him of the second position in Liverpool's government.[56]

Home Secretary

Peel assumed charge at the Home Office in January 1822 and remained there until Liverpool's retirement from the premiership in April 1827. He was out of office during the short lifetimes of the Canning and Goderich Ministries, for reasons to be discussed in Chapter 2, but held the Home Secretaryship again in Wellington's government of 1828–30. It is convenient, for the purpose of analysing Peel's achievements as Home Secretary, to treat the period 1822–30 as a single entity.

Historians writing before the 1970s tended to look upon the measures implemented by Peel as shining examples of the phenomenon known as 'Liberal Toryism'. More recently, however, his record has come under severe scrutiny, and a number of scholars have challenged the view that he deserves to be hailed as a great reformer. There is a real danger, on both sides of this argument, that anachronistic assumptions may be made, or anachronistic standards of judgement applied. In the account that follows, the emphasis will be placed on trying to understand how Peel himself perceived the nature of the problems confronting him, and what he thought he could do about them.

Peel's chief responsibilities as Home Secretary covered the maintenance of law and order and the regulation of the criminal justice system. In a society experiencing the disturbing and disorienting effects of rapid population growth, industrialisation and urbanisation, where the inequalities between the prosperous classes and the poor were increasingly visible, the task of preserving the peace was always likely to be a challenging one. There was, unsurprisingly, an upward trend in criminal convictions relative to population during the early decades of the nineteenth century, and the peak was not reached until 1842.[57] For the seven year period ending in December 1825, convictions in England and Wales totalled 63,418, which was more than double the figure for the seven year period ending in December 1816 (29,361). More worrying still was the fact that the machinery available for the enforcement of law and order, and the dispensing of justice, was entirely inadequate for its purposes. Not only was there no efficient network of locally managed, professional police forces, but there was strong resistance to such an arrangement from people at all levels of society, who took pride in Britain's freedom from the authoritarian systems found in many European states. When faced with outbreaks of violent industrial unrest, such as those in Monmouthshire and the Forest of Dean in 1822, or in the Lancashire textile districts in 1826, the Home Office therefore had no alternative but to order troops to be sent in to regain control. As for the criminal law itself, this consisted of an increasingly incoherent mass of statutes, accumulated over the centuries, much of which was either obsolete or contradictory. Approximately two hundred offences carried the death penalty, but the decision as to whether or not someone should hang was often arbitrary, depending on the whim of a jury – which might refuse to convict an obvious criminal because of the possibly fatal consequences of a guilty verdict – or on the judge's inclination to recommend that a condemned person's sentence be commuted.

In many ways, Peel's bureaucratic temperament was perfectly suited to the long overdue task of rationalising and clarifying the criminal law. He may well have derived some psychological satisfaction from cutting out large quantities of useless or unhelpful legislation, and leaving behind a simplified arrangement (there is, perhaps, a parallel here with his Free Trade measures of the 1840s). The first major exercise in consolidation came in 1825, with the Juries Regulation Act, which replaced eighty-five old statutes relating to aspects of the procedure for empanelling juries. It was now made clear what qualifications jurors were required to possess and how the selection process was to be conducted. In 1826 and 1827 a total of seven acts were passed, some dealing with the procedure in criminal justice cases, and others disentangling and pruning the statutes in specific areas such as theft. Further legislation in 1828 tackled the procedure for giving evidence in the courts, and consolidated into a single statute the law relating to offences against the person. As a result of Peel's labours, between 1825 and 1828 no less than 278 statutes were repealed and eight consolidated statutes put in their place. By the time he left the Home Office, in November 1830, more than three-quarters of all criminal offences were covered by legislation introduced since 1825.

The approach taken by Peel to the question of capital punishment provides a good indication of the spirit that lay behind his 'reforms'. His immediate object was to clear away from the statute book those capital offences which were rarely, if ever, enforced, so as to enhance the credibility of the laws that remained. It was necessary, he declared, to 'add to the solemnity and efficiency of the laws'.[58] Thus, in an early spate of statute-culling in 1823, Peel disposed of the death sentences for larceny to the value of 40 shillings in shops and ships, breaking river banks, cutting down hop vines, and impersonating Greenwich pensioners. Similarly, in his final year at the Home Office, a number of obsolete capital sentences relating to forgery were abandoned, although he significantly left in place those penalties attached to the offence of coining – which was still causing the authorities grave concern. The fact is that Peel may have succeeded in simplifying the criminal law, but the way in which it was applied was no more lenient than in the past. In the years between 1822 and 1828, the annual number of executions carried out in England and Wales averaged sixty-three, remarkably similar to the figure of sixty-seven executions per annum in the comparable period 1805–12. It is only through a misleading comparison with the exceptionally disturbed, economically depressed post-war years, 1815–21, when an average of 105 executions took place annually, that Peel can be made to look like a humanitarian reformer.[59] The task of systematically reducing the death toll by abolishing many capital penalties still in use, such as those for coining, livestock theft and housebreaking, fell to the Whig ministers of the 1830s, notably Lord John Russell. Whereas in 1830 there were forty-six executions in England and Wales (an unusually low figure, it had been seventy-four the previous year), of which fourteen involved people guilty of murder, by 1840 just nine convicts were hanged, all of them murderers. These statistics have prompted Derek Beales' crushing verdict that 'on the criminal law, Peel tinkered, while Russell made drastic reforms'.[60]

According to Boyd Hilton, the real reason for Peel's dissatisfaction with the justice system, as he found it in 1822, was not so much that it was too harsh, but that there was an excessive degree of uncertainty regarding the penalties which criminals could expect to face. So long as the imposition or enforcement of the death penalty remained a lottery, dependent on the mood of the jury or the judge, it was impossible for a person to weigh in advance the consequences of committing a criminal act. Peel therefore wanted to inject more consistency and certainty into the way the criminal law was applied: absurd capital penalties, that were never carried out anyway, had to be removed from the statute book, but those that remained should be enforced where appropriate. It is important to realise that Peel held a pessimistic view of human nature, and believed that retributive punishment formed an essential part of God's dispensation on earth, being necessary for the 'moral discipline' (a favourite phrase of Peel's) of corrupt humanity.[61] Judged by his own criterion, however, it has to be added that Peel's record as Home Secretary was one of complete failure. In his first year, 1822, 1016 death sentences were imposed, of which ninety-seven were carried out; but in 1830 the respective figures were 1397 and forty-six. Far from creating a more predictable administration of justice, Peel seems to have left behind a system that was even more capricious than before.

Much of the extraordinary disparity between the numbers of death sentences passed and those actually enforced can be accounted for in terms of judges using their discretion and recommending that sentences be commuted. If there was no such recommendation, it was open to the families of condemned prisoners to petition the King, pleading for mercy, and these appeals were usually successful. In 1828, of 175 cases reviewed by the King and the Privy Council, only twenty-one capital sentences were confirmed. There were certain occasions, though, when Peel felt compelled to make a stand against George IV's disposition to favour clemency for largely sentimental reasons. V. A. C. Gatrell has recently highlighted these episodes in order to justify his depiction of Peel as a bloodthirsty defender of the *ancien régime* in Britain.[62] Within a few months of taking office, for example, Peel engaged in a lengthy battle with the King over the fate of eight men condemned for non-violent burglary, eventually securing the execution of six of them. The following year, he successfully resisted the King's wishes in the case of a man guilty of forging a £5 note. While Gatrell's view of Peel as a resolute hanger seems rather melodramatic, given the large numbers of petitions for leniency which were accepted, there is no doubt that the Home Secretary was determined, as far as possible, to prevent exceptions to the law being made solely because of a capricious whim on the part of King George.

Peel's streamlining of the criminal law represented only a portion of his labours as Home Secretary, of course. In the sphere of prison reform he was also highly active, and bureaucratic efficiency and uniformity once more seem to have been the defining characteristics of his regime. The Gaols Act of 1823 required, for the first time, that prisons be maintained in every county and each Riding of Yorkshire, as well as in London and seventeen major provincial towns. Prisons were to be inspected on an annual basis by local Justices of the Peace (JPs), who were obliged to submit reports and completed questionnaires to the Home Office. Another act in 1824 extended this system of prison supervision to cover some 150 smaller towns. These measures provided no new powers for JPs, but were designed to put an end to the old practice whereby it was left to the initiative of the JPs themselves to carry out inspections. Official standards for prison discipline, and for the provision of medical and educational facilities, were now to be uniformly enforced. The new legislation provided a means by which the Home Office was able to gather detailed statistical information about prison conditions, and paved the way for greater control by the central government in the 1830s.[63] Peel's concern was less with making prison life in general more comfortable, than it was with ensuring that standards did not vary arbitrarily, according to the attitudes of the officials in each locality.

The Home Secretary was a firm believer in the efficacy of having a graduated range of 'secondary punishments' (i.e. non-capital) available for dealing with convicts. It was on these grounds that he defended the use of the whip, arguing that flagellation was not as bad a punishment as – for example – keeping prisoners in solitary confinement.[64] Another device, the treadmill, was described by Peel as 'an admirable contrivance', for similar reasons.[65] Transportation to the colonies was always an option in cases where prisoners were guilty of more serious crimes. In fairness to Peel, his efforts to extend the scale of secondary punishments, particularly for lesser offences against property, may well have reflected a long-term ambition to reduce the number of executions

taking place, rather than being proof of a desire for savage retribu-
tion.[66] Whatever the intention may have been, Peel confessed to one of
his correspondents on prison reform, in 1826, that 'The real truth is the
number of convicts is too overwhelming for the means of proper and
effectual punishment. I despair of any remedy but that which I wish I
could hope for – a great reduction in the amount of crime.'[67]

Preventative measures were something to which Peel attached great
importance from the beginning of his term at the Home Office. Influenced, no doubt, by his experience in Ireland, Peel was convinced of the
need for rationally organised police forces, without which penal reform
and the consolidation of the criminal law could achieve little. As early as
March 1822, he secured the appointment of a Select Committee to
inquire into the lax, chaotic and often corrupt system of policing in
London (where the population had reached 1.5 million), but to his
disappointment the Committee's report merely reiterated the traditional libertarian arguments against a co-ordinated police force under
the government's control. By the end of 1826, however, Peel was ready
to try again, and a letter of this period to a junior Home Office Minister,
Henry Hobhouse, contains the sketch of a plan for reorganising the
London police which is very similar to the measure implemented in
1829. Clearly, Peel knew already what he was aiming at, even though he
recognised that it was necessary to have another inquiry first, in order to
demonstrate the defects in the existing arrangements.[68] In February
1828 he justified his request for a Select Committee by reference to the
alarming increase in the incidence of crime in the metropolis, where
commitals had jumped from 2621 to 3457 between 1824 and 1826,
mainly involving offences against property.[69] On this occasion, the
Committee reported in favour of a decisive restructuring of police
resources in London, enabling Peel to proceed with his bill, the following year, to establish a single Metropolitan Police Force with jurisdiction
over the entire area within a ten mile radius of central London (except
in the City of London itself). The new force was headed by two commissioners, appointed by the Home Secretary, and an entirely fresh body of
uniformed policemen was recruited. Significantly, Peel expressed the
hope that it would now be possible to combat the activities of a hardened
criminal class, responsible for a large proportion of the offences committed in London, whose behaviour he attributed not to poverty but to
the temptations created by the growing wealth of the country. Once the
increase in crime had been checked, this might ultimately permit steps
to be taken 'to mitigate the severity of the criminal code'.[70] Writing to

the Duke of Wellington in November 1829, Peel felt confident enough to declare that the Metropolitan Police Force was already working well: 'I want to teach people that liberty does not consist in having your home robbed by organised gangs of thieves, and in leaving the principal streets of London in the nightly possession of drunken women and vagabonds.'[71] Over the next quarter of a century police forces were set up in large towns and counties throughout the country, adopting many of the features of the metropolitan model, and Peel's private correspondence, while Home Secretary, shows that this was what he wanted to see happen. 'It has always appeared to me', he told Hobhouse in February 1828, 'that the Country has entirely outgrown its police institutions. The difficulty in this, as in ten thousand cases, is to devise any general rule which shall apply to a society so varying in its subdivisions as ours is.'[72]

One of the most notable features of Peel's reforming activity, at the Home Office, is the ease with which he managed to steer his measures through parliament. For instance, George Canning's report to the King on proceedings in the House of Commons, in March 1826, mentioned a Criminal Law Consolidation Bill introduced by Peel 'with a speech of rare ability, temper, & information', which was 'received with unanimous approbation & applause' by MPs.[73] This facility in carrying legislation becomes easier to understand when we recognise that Peel was not attempting a radical transformation of the system for apprehending, trying and punishing criminals, but was seeking to make that system work more efficiently and in a consistent way. Peel's aims, in other words, were essentially 'conservative', and therefore uncontroversial from a parliamentary point of view. Even the Metropolitan Police Bill, ostensibly a highly contentious proposal, enjoyed a fairly smooth passage, as Peel had prepared MPs' minds for it in advance by convincing them that there was a rising tide of crime in London which demanded a bold remedy. It is to Peel's credit, nevertheless, that he provided the vital impetus for reform by making such questions as prison inspection and the removal of superfluous capital penalties matters of government policy, rather than leaving them in the hands of crusading back-benchers such as Mackintosh, whose initiatives could easily be obstructed by a determined minority. A perfect illustration of the skilful way in which Peel endeavoured to work with the grain of professional opinion, and so carry vested interests along with him on the path of reform, is provided by the legislation of 1825 relating to Scottish law court procedures (Scotland, of course, having a separate legal system). Rather than trying to impose reforms upon a reluctant and suspicious professional body, Peel encouraged the judicial authorities to examine for themselves, through participation in a Commission of Inquiry, possible ways of improving the Scottish system, presenting this procedure as the most effective means of deflecting radical criticism and thus preserving the essence of the existing arrangements. During a visit to Scotland in 1822, he informed Lord Liverpool that he had 'tried to convince them [the Scottish lawyers and judges] that it was the best policy to take to ourselves the credit of the reform, and that by being the authors of it we should have the best chance of prescribing limits to the innovation'.[74]

Peel's general responsibility for upholding law and order naturally meant that he was required to deal with a variety of awkward and interesting practical issues, and perhaps the most bizarre of all related to the use of human corpses for the purposes of medical teaching and research. A notorious practice had developed, whereby the graves of the recently dead were being robbed in order to supply the needs of the anatomical schools. One solution to this gruesome problem, put forward by Jeremy Bentham and other utilitarian radicals, was for the bodies of paupers to be given over for dissection, if they were unclaimed by relatives. Peel's response to Bentham's suggestion showed that he was well aware of the situation, but also disinclined to introduce legislation for fear that publicising the subject might raise a public outcry against existing methods and so restrict the supply of cadavers still further. He suspected that many of the bodies of patients dying in public hospitals were already finding their way into the medical schools, and, since there was no authority for this practice, it seemed best not to 'provoke too much inquiry'. The whole matter, in fact, was one not 'fit...for legislation, or even for public discussion'.[75] Other discreet measures were authorised by Peel, however, to facilitate a regular supply of bodies, as is shown by a letter to a ministerial colleague in December 1828:

> Directions were privately given some time since, by my request, to permit the import of dead bodies from France without minute inquiry, or at least without exposure.
>
> It is, of course, a very delicate subject to write upon, as it involves a connivance at a statuteable offence. But what can be done, if repeated murder is the consequence of an obstruction to the supply of bodies by other means?[76]

Peel was referring here to the recent horrific events in Edinburgh, where Messrs Burke and Hare had taken to killing people in order to satisfy the demand from their medical clients. It would have been hard to imagine a more effective way of attracting public attention to the issue, and in 1829 Peel announced his personal support for Henry Warburton's Anatomy Bill, incorporating the Benthamite solution of allowing the use of paupers' bodies for dissection (this was eventually passed in 1832).[77] In Peel's case, at least, recognition of the need for legislative action had less to do with any hardening in his attitude towards the poor, so much as with the purely pragmatic consideration of how to secure a legitimate source of human material to meet the growing demands of medical science.

2

THE CRISIS IN CHURCH AND STATE

The Limits of 'liberal' Toryism

There is a paradox surrounding the latter phase of Lord Liverpool's administration: that in its years of greatest outward strength, and of constructive achievement in domestic politics, alarming symptoms were also manifested of acute internal stress. Peel's appointment as Home Secretary was part of a general revitalisation of the government front-bench in the House of Commons, in 1822–3, which included Canning's accession to the Foreign Office, the promotions of Frederick Robinson and William Huskisson to be Chancellor of the Exchequer and President of the Board of Trade respectively, and the sidelining of the politically redundant Sidmouth connection.[1] These changes certainly augmented the government's debating power in the lower House, although the main reason why ministers appeared in an increasingly favourable public light was that the economy had finally recovered from the appalling depression of the immediate post-war years. The 1820s, taken as a whole, were a period of economic growth and comparative social calm, which saw a dramatic decline in popular agitation for radical parliamentary reform. In these auspicious conditions, most of the earlier repressive legislation was allowed to lapse, and it seemed permissible for ministers to adopt a more relaxed approach to policy than would previously have been considered safe. Peel could hardly have spoken of his wish to mitigate the severity of the criminal law had he been in charge of the Home Office at the time of the Peterloo massacre. Similarly, Robinson's and Huskisson's efforts to promote freer trade, by reducing the level of many import duties, were only possible because there was already a healthy budget surplus to work with, thanks to the revenues generated by a booming economy. And yet, despite so many encouraging signs for the government, the reality was that Liverpool's Cabinet, after 1822, was a more divided body than it had ever been during the desperate Peterloo years. Consequently, when ill health forced Liverpool to retire in 1827, a process of disintegration began which culminated in the collapse of Tory rule in 1830, and the advent of a Whig administration bent on reconstructing the political system to its own advantage. The part played by Peel in these dramatic events was, as we shall see, highly complicated and ambiguous.

Historians in recent years have tended to discount the notion that there was a distinct era of reformist 'Liberal Toryism', following the Cabinet reconstruction of 1822–3, in which ministers distanced themselves from the repressive measures implemented by their predecessors and consciously adopted new policies better attuned to the expectations of an increasingly sophisticated, urbanising society.[2] Instead, greater emphasis is usually placed on the elements of continuity, both in personnel and policy, between the early and later stages of Liverpool's administration.[3] After all, Peel, Canning, Robinson and Huskisson had been connected with the government before 1822–3, and were therefore implicated in steps such as the suspension of Habeas Corpus and the Six Acts,[4] while the ideas behind many of the commercial and Home Office reforms were germinated by the reports of Select Committees of inquiry appointed during the years of repression.

Nevertheless, a case can be made for the view that the Cabinet changes in 1822–3 did mark a watershed, leading to the promotion of policies recognisable to contemporaries as 'liberal' (with a small l), even if the use of the collective label 'Liberal Tories', to describe the ministers involved, is an anachronism. The rise to prominence of these 'liberal' policies indeed supplies the key to an understanding of the fissures within Liverpool's Cabinet.

The new direction in administration was associated with the growing political status of Canning, and it was in his particular sphere of responsibility, foreign affairs, that the idea of applying 'liberal' principles had greatest contemporary resonance. When Tory propagandists such as Sir Walter Scott and Robert Southey employed the term 'liberal', they meant it in a pejorative sense, and were aiming at radicals and advanced

Whigs who sympathised with national liberation movements on the European continent.[5] Lord Byron, the poet, who died on his way to fight for the Greeks in their struggle for independence from the Turkish empire, was a conspicuous example of this 'liberal' type. Canning's foreign policy can reasonably be described as 'liberal' in its leanings, because he was convinced that Britain had no further role to play in the Congress System, alongside autocratic powers such as Austria and Russia, who claimed a right of intervention in other countries to uphold the political order restored by the Vienna peace settlement of 1815. Britain, in Canning's view, should take an independent course, pursuing her own interests, and standing out as the exemplar and champion of the causes of constitutional government and national self-determination. The military support despatched to the Regent, Isabella, in Portugal, to help counter French and Spanish interference, and the decision to grant diplomatic recognition to the newly emergent republics of South America, which had thrown off European imperial control, are classic illustrations of the Canningite approach to foreign policy. In terms of style, Canning showed much greater appreciation than his predecessor, Castlereagh, of the value of publicity, and of the advantages to be gained by enlisting British public opinion in support of his diplomacy. Crucially, however, certain other members of the post-1822 Cabinet, notably the Duke of Wellington and Lord Chancellor Eldon, were disturbed by the Foreign Secretary's conduct, regretting as they did Canning's apparent eagerness to contradict and insult the European autocracies (which represented established authority), and deploring his more open, flamboyant and demagogic methods. Thus, it is possible to identify divergent strands of thought within the Cabinet regarding the objectives of foreign policy and the way in which it ought to be conducted.

It is true that the commercial reforms implemented by Robinson and Huskisson – cutting import duties, modifying the Navigation Laws governing shipping access to British ports, and negotiating Trade Reciprocity Treaties with various countries – were far less controversial, but even so there was perceived to be a link with 'liberal' principles. For a start, the leading theoretical advocates of trade liberation were the classical economists and utilitarian radicals, whose general political sympathies were certainly closer to those of Lord Byron than of Lord Eldon. More ominously, from Eldon's point of view, Huskisson, the real driving force behind the commercial reforms, was a protégé of Canning's. In fact, Canning's support for the South American republics was partly motivated by the consideration that this would create opportunities for British traders to expand their operations into Latin American markets. Foreign and commercial policy were therefore connected, and to traditionally minded Tory ministers they represented parts of a system of government identified with the detested Canning.

Of considerably greater concern to the anti-Canning school of Tories was the fact that Huskisson was known to favour a modification of the Corn Law introduced in 1815. This naturally caused alarm to many of the country gentlemen in the House of Commons, who were fearful of the effect on their rentals of a drop in agricultural prices brought about by foreign competition. Huskisson's analysis, which was gaining acceptance in ministerial circles during the 1820s, was that Britain's population was expanding too rapidly for a policy of agricultural autarchy to be feasible. The acute social distress of the post-war years had highlighted the dangers in a system of import duties fixed at prohibitively high levels, and it was now argued that a more flexible arrangement should be adopted, namely, a sliding scale of duties operating in accordance with variations in the domestic price of grain. In this way, it was hoped that greater price stability could be achieved and so speculation deterred. Lord Liverpool himself agreed with Huskisson's conclusion, and the government was preparing to act along these lines at the beginning of 1827, before the Prime Minister's stroke plunged the Tories into turmoil. It is noteworthy that, in Huskisson's scheme of things, a link existed between the proposed sliding scale and the wider 'liberal' policy of freer trade, as the promotion of British exports was deemed necessary in order to pay for the anticipated increase in agricultural imports.[6]

Peel was generally supportive of the foreign and commercial policies pursued by the government after 1822, although he was obviously not responsible for initiating any of them. The military intervention in Portugal and the recognition of the South American republics both met with his approval, and, in the years following Canning's death, Peel sympathised with the cause of Greek independence and the Belgian secession from the Netherlands.[7] He was also persuaded by Huskisson's arguments for the substitution of the fixed-rate Corn Law with a sliding scale.[8] Curiously, however, the measure directly associated with Peel's name which fits most readily into the 'liberal' model, had nothing to do with his Home Secretaryship. In 1819, when he was out of office, Peel agreed to chair a committee of inquiry into the state of the currency, which reported in favour of the phased resumption of cash payments; in other words, that the Bank of England's ability to issue paper money should be tied strictly to its reserves of gold (a 'sound money' policy, or 'convertibility'). Canning, Huskisson and Liverpool concurred with Peel's recommendations,[9] and these were duly implemented. Some of the strongest protests against this policy, on the other hand, came from the country gentlemen, who had benefited from the wartime inflation caused by the profligate issue of paper money. This had enabled them to borrow money cheaply – the real value of their repayments depreciating as prices rose – with which to invest in their estates and expand agricultural output, thus capitalising on the high wartime food prices. The deflationary consequences of the measure known as 'Peel's Act' meant that it stood out as a source of grievance for the landed interest for many years to come, being equated especially with the low agricultural prices of the early 1820s.

Boyd Hilton has proposed a broad ideological framework within which to comprehend the divisions of Tory opinion during the Liverpool era.[10] Ministers such as Castlereagh, Wellington, Eldon, Sidmouth and Vansittart can be categorised as 'High' Tories, who inclined towards an organic conception of society and favoured a managerial, even paternalistic, style of government. By contrast, 'liberal' Tories such as Liverpool, Canning and Peel, adhered to a more mechanistic view of society, and sought in various ways to create automatic, self-regulating systems. This distinction seems to be a helpful one, although we must be cautious about attempting to fit busy administrative politicians into intellectual pigeonholes. It is probably better to talk in terms of two competing *tendencies* in Tory thought, which were never entirely incompatible for the purposes of practical government. Peel himself, as Hilton acknowledges, represented something of an amalgam of 'liberal' and 'High' Tory instincts: 'inclination clashed with ability. He had the schematic intellect of the liberal Tory, but his talent was for management, for getting things done in the tangle of the early-nineteenth century bureaucracy.'[11] Nevertheless, the 'liberal' tendency in Peel's mind is discernible in his recommendations for currency reform, which aimed at establishing a self-acting machinery for regulating the money supply, so that governments would not feel compelled to intervene and try to manipulate the system. Similarly, Home Secretary Peel was keen to systematise the administration of criminal justice, reducing the amount of discretion available to judges and achieving a more consistent application of the law. In this way, individuals would know with greater certainty the likely consequences of their criminal actions. Had Peel succeeded in putting such a regime into place, it could theoretically have been left to work by itself.

In the realm of economic policy, as Hilton shows, 'liberal' Tory thinking betrayed the influence of the increasingly fashionable *laissez faire* doctrines of the time. The principal medium for transmitting these ideas to the politicians was the work of evangelical propagandists such as Dr Thomas Chalmers, who had absorbed the teachings of the classical economists but translated them into a distinctively Christian idiom. Peel could therefore regard the suffering caused by the wave of bankruptcies, during the financial crash of 1825–6, as a necessary and beneficial process, forcing men to learn the hard way the dangers of their greed and recklessness in business affairs. To many early nineteenth century minds, market forces were an instrument of Divine Providence. It would be wrong, though, to convey the impression that Peel was simply a rigid and unimaginative doctrinaire, devoid of all human feeling. He was well aware, for example, of the hardship inflicted on labourers who were being displaced through the introduction of new and more efficient machinery, but believed that it was misguided for governments to attempt to interfere – distorting the market for sentimental reasons. Tragically, there was no satisfactory answer to this problem: 'The national benefit of *sudden* discoveries which abridge manufacturing labour may be ultimately great, but the local and undeserved suffering which they produce is very lamentable, and I fear very irremediable.'[12] Interestingly enough, Peel was prepared to admit one exception to the rule of free market principles, as he recognised the legitimacy of workers combining in trades unions to negotiate with employers, provided there was no use of intimidatory tactics to deprive other workers of their free-will. 'Men who... have no property except their manual skill and strength', he wrote in 1825, 'ought to be allowed to confer together, if they think fit, for the purpose of determining at what rate they will sell their property.'[13]

From the point of view of rank-and-file MPs on the government side, restive over the direction being taken on the Corn Laws and other issues, Peel's general political orientation was deeply regrettable. In the words of an unfriendly Whig observer, Thomas Creevey, 'unhappily for Toryism, that prig Peel seems as deeply bitten by "liberality", in every way but on the Catholic question, as any of his fellows'.[14] This assessment was echoed by others, including Charles Wynn, a Grenvillite recruit to Liverpool's administration, who could see no effective House of Commons representative for those who were unhappy with the drift of government policy: 'the person whose opinions on the Catholic question would naturally point him out for that purpose, is upon every other subject, whether of foreign, commercial or domestic policy, disposed to participate to the fullest extent in the line of policy adopted by his colleagues'.[15]

It was the persistent obtrusiveness of the Catholic question in British politics, of course, which enormously complicated the situation, ensuring that a gulf would always exist between Peel and other 'liberal' Tory ministers, and that Liverpool's Cabinet, in its reformist phase after 1822, was a dangerously polarised body. One effect of the ministerial reconstruction of 1822–3, apart from strengthening the front-bench's debating prowess in the House of Commons, had been to enhance the influence of the pro-Catholic wing of the Tories. Canning, naturally, stood out as the champion of the Tory emancipationists, and this policy was regarded as part of his 'liberal' system by 'High' or 'Protestant' Tories such as Wellington and Eldon.[16]

Peel, too, made this association, complaining in 1823 that 'in this age of liberal doctrine, when prescription is no longer even a prescription in favour of what is established, it will be a work of desperate difficulty to contend against "emancipation".'[17] Canning, Huskisson and Robinson all supported the Catholic claims, as did the Grenvillite, Charles Wynn. In fact, Peel was the only senior minister in the House of Commons pledged to the defence of Protestant principles, and he felt his isolation on this issue acutely. Fortunately, the Prime Minister was a fellow 'Protestant', and his presence served as a guarantee that while, officially, Catholic Emancipation remained an open question within the government, in practice no hasty decisions, detrimental to the 'Protestant Constitution', need be feared as long as Liverpool was in charge. Wellington was one 'Protestant' Tory who accordingly took the view, expressed in a letter to Peel in 1824, that a broadly based Tory administration, with a Protestant head, afforded better prospects for blocking Catholic Emancipation than the formation of an exclusively 'Protestant' government.[18]

Peel's position as the sole representative of the Protestant viewpoint, amongst Cabinet ministers in the Commons, might have been tolerable had it not been for the fact that events in Ireland were creating a more formidable pressure for change than had hitherto existed since the Act of Union. Whereas in Peel's time as Irish Chief Secretary, the main organisation campaigning for emancipation, the Catholic Board, had been weak and divided, and was eventually suppressed with little difficulty, the Catholic Association, founded by Daniel O'Connell in 1823, proved to be a much more resilient and effective mouthpiece of Catholic opinion. O'Connell's movement operated on a national basis, funded by subscriptions (known as the 'Catholic rent'), and it attracted support even from members of the Catholic landed gentry, as well as from the influential Roman Catholic priesthood. Sidestepping an attempt by the government to ban it, in 1825, the Catholic Association was able to intervene decisively in several Irish county constituencies, notably Waterford, Roscommon, Louth and Westmeath, during the general election of the following year. Catholics were not eligible to sit in parliament, but they could vote in parliamentary elections if they possessed the necessary property qualification (a 40 shilling freehold, in the case of counties), and the election results in 1826 demonstrated that in some areas the Catholic freeholders were now beyond the political control of their Protestant landlords. At Westminster, meantime, Sir Francis Burdett's regular initiatives on behalf of the Catholic cause gained extra impetus from the O'Connellite agitation, and in 1825 he succeeded in carrying an Emancipation Bill through the House of Commons, compelling Liverpool to invoke his majority in the upper House in order to prevent the bill from becoming law.

The strain on Peel's nerves produced by the advance of the pro-Catholic case in the mid-1820s sometimes manifested itself in surprising displays of irritability. In February 1824, for instance, one MP related how Canning's inability to keep a diplomatic silence in the Commons, over his personal conduct on the emancipation question, 'brought up Peel, who, with some display of bad temper, made his declaration'. Later that month, according to the same source, Peel's frustration seemed to spill over into a 'very angry' outburst following an accidental defeat on a trivial Home Office issue: 'The question was of no consequence, but his temper would not brook it, and he showed it, as I hear, very much.'[19] When the Duke of Wellington had an interview with Peel to discuss the state of Ireland, in June 1824, he apparently found the Home Secretary 'in excessive ill-humour, saying he repented bitterly having taken office, that he was thwarted in every way, that all the Ministers in the H. of Commons were against him, & that it made him indignant to be obliged to remain silent when he heard Papists praised & Orangemen abused.'[20]

A rather different perspective on Peel's career, post-1822, thus begins to emerge, from which he appears not so much as the triumphant, reformist Home Secretary, but as an ambitious contender for the future premiership who all too frequently found his political position restricted and uncomfortable. His rivalry with Canning lay at the bottom of everything. In a private conversation with Charles Arbuthnot, Peel admitted that he disliked Canning personally: 'He [Peel] appeared to have the worst possible opinion of him, said he had no objection to do business in Cabinet with him & that they were very civil together in the H. of Commons, but that he was a sort of person he shd. be very sorry to have a tête-à-tête with.'[21] The constant state of tension between the two men is illustrated by an episode at the beginning of 1823, when Liverpool proposed that Canning should be allowed to occupy Number 11 Downing Street. Peel's under-secretary at the Home Office, Henry Hobhouse, commented in his diary that 'It is extraordinary...that Ld L. should not have reflected how much...[this plan] was calculated to excite Mr Peel's jealousy, since it would evince to the world a disposition in Ld L. as well as Mr C. that the latter should step into the Premier's place, whenever his Lordship quits it.'[22] The proposal was quickly buried. However, Peel continued to express his dismay at the extent to which the Prime Minister appeared to be under 'subjection' to the forceful Foreign Secretary, and he was also alarmed by the indications that Canning was beginning to rehabilitate himself with the King.[23] Indeed, by the summer of 1826, Peel was furious to discover that Liverpool and King George had allowed Canning to make nominations for peerages, and he declared to Arbuthnot that 'he quite felt for the state of degradation into which Lord Liverpool was fallen...but that he had no words to express his contempt and abhorrence of Mr Canning...his dirty intrigues with the King and Knighton [the King's private secretary] were disgusting'.[24] That Peel's suspicions of Canning were entirely reciprocated is suggested by Mrs Arbuthnot's comments on the idea broached by the Home Secretary, in December 1826, that he might succeed Robinson as Chancellor of the Exchequer: 'Mr Canning wd object most positively to Mr Peel setting his foot in the Treasury. He is excessively jealous of Mr Peel & always objects to anything that is to strengthen Mr Peel's party, which he considers as distinct from his own.'[25] Early in 1827, just weeks before Liverpool suffered the stroke which ended his premiership, Peel was predicting another row over the appointment of Wellington as Commander in Chief of the armed forces, his expectation being that Canning would press for the Duke to resign his Cabinet post, something which Peel could not allow to happen to his most powerful 'Protestant' ally.[26]

So long as the Catholic question continued to preoccupy political minds in Britain, it was clear that Peel would be at a considerable disadvantage *vis-à-vis* Canning. The harsh fact was that he had committed himself, irrevocably, to what increasingly looked like the losing side on this issue. Burdett's triumph in carrying an Emancipation Bill through the House of Commons, during the 1825 session, inevitably precipitated a ministerial crisis. Peel dutifully took the lead in opposing the bill, arguing that Burdett's plan would fail to tranquillise Ireland as the Roman Catholics were determined to overthrow the Protestant Ascendancy. Once the bill had passed, in May, Peel tendered his resignation, declaring that the isolated position he found himself occupying on the front bench was now untenable. Possibly, he was hoping that his colleagues would be able to settle the question without him, so that he might then return to office after a decent interval, without loss of dignity. If this was the case, however, Liverpool was going to have none of it, for the Prime Minister responded by indicating that, if Peel abandoned his post, he too would feel compelled to resign. Faced with the prospect of Canning's succession to the premiership, Peel was persuaded that it would be a mistake for him to break up the existing government. In the end, he agreed to remain in office until after the next general election, when he would be in a position to judge the feeling of the new parliament on the Catholic question.[27] Liverpool had thus succeeded in patching up his shaky craft for a little while longer, but, with the Irish election results in 1826 showing the progress made by the Catholic Association, the stage seemed set for another critical test of 'Protestant' Tory resolve early in the 1827 session of parliament.[28]

Catholic Emancipation and Tory Fragmentation, 1827–9

The sudden removal of two key players from the political scene, at the beginning of 1827, helped to accelerate the crisis that everyone expected to come, sooner or later. First, in January, there was the death of the Duke of York, the virulently anti-Catholic heir-presumptive to the throne, whose departure deprived the Protestant cause of a powerful weapon in its battle to block emancipation. Second, and much better known, came the incapacitation of Lord Liverpool by a stroke, on 17 February.[29] It suited all the leading political participants to prolong the ensuing state of confusion, ostensibly out of a sense of decency towards the stricken Prime Minister, but also because it enabled them to tide over the immediate problems posed by the Corn Law and Catholic question debates in the House of Commons. Only in late

March was Liverpool sufficiently recovered to be capable of submitting his resignation. King George IV's decision, at this point, to offer the premiership to Canning, with whom he had enjoyed vastly improved relations in recent years, finally brought matters to a head. Six Cabinet ministers, most notably Wellington and Peel, refused to serve in the new government. Canning was obliged, instead, to seek assistance from the opposition Whigs (who, as a party, had consistently advocated Catholic Emancipation), and Lord Landsdowne, Lord Carlisle and George Tierney were therefore included in his Cabinet. This marked the first stage in the disintegration of the 'Tory party' which had sustained Liverpool's government for fifteen years. Lord Eldon, one of the 'Protestant' Tory ministers who declined to remain in office under Canning, remarked that all of the conversation in London high society at this time seemed to be 'made up of abusive, bitterly abusive talk, of people about each other – all fire and flame. I have known nothing like it.'[30]

Peel's conduct during the ministerial crisis can only be explained in terms of his personal suspicion of Canning. After all, the new ministry was being formed on the same basis as Liverpool's – in other words, the Catholic question was left open. The King even offered himself as Peel's personal guarantee that he need have no apprehension of any action being taken on this subject.[31] Furthermore, Canning was prepared to be generous in the offers he made to Peel, which included the Foreign Secretaryship (albeit coupled with a peerage, to remove Peel from the House of Commons). Peel readily admitted that, excepting the Catholic question, he had no political differences with Canning – they were agreed, for instance, in opposing parliamentary reform – and he would have been willing to remain in office alongside Canning on condition that a 'Protestant' peer of sufficient weight held the premiership. His only sticking point, then, was that he could not contemplate serving under a Prime Minister whose personal views were known to be sympathetic to the Catholic claims, even though the government had no official line on this issue.[32] Peel's high profile public stance in defence of the Protestant Constitution meant that his refusal to join Canning's government was essentially dictated by an anxiety to maintain his 'character as a public man', and to act in accordance with 'my own impressions of what it is becoming for me to do.'[33] But it is unlikely that he would have felt it necessary to remain outside the government had he not been so profoundly distrustful of the motives and intentions of the new head.

It is hard to avoid the conclusion that Peel's association with the 'Protestant' wing of Toryism, dating back to his time as Irish Chief Secretary, had placed him in an increasingly artificial political position, but one from which it was impossible to escape with dignity. As late as 1825, he was being fêted at a Pitt Club dinner, after the House of Lords had thrown out Burdett's Emancipation Bill: 'The company was quite uproarious, they were in such high spirits upon the Catholic defeat... Peel was much gratified by their reception of him.'[34] Privately, however, there were signs of fatalism in Peel's attitude towards the Catholic question by 1826. His correspondence suggests that he realised that emancipation was going to be inevitable, eventually, and he even intimated that it might come as something of a relief to see the issue settled, if only he could bring himself to believe that religious equality really would put an end to the conflict between Catholicism and the Protestant Ascendancy in Ireland.[35] Given that these were his views, it can be argued that Peel and his Protestant colleagues made a serious mistake in allowing their personal dislike of Canning to affect their judgement in April 1827. They might have remained in office, without inconsistency, as part of an 'inclusive' Tory administration, provided there was no commitment on the Catholic question. By acting in the way they did, Canning was driven into the arms of the Whigs, and the forces of Toryism were fatally split. With the benefit of hindsight, it seems that if only the Tory leadership had remained united they might have fared much better when the force of circumstances compelled Wellington and Peel to concede Catholic Emancipation in 1829.

One of the great imponderables of early nineteenth century history is whether Canning could have consolidated his 'broad-bottom' ministry and perhaps settled the Catholic question before events in Ireland reached a critical point. In fact, he died in August 1827, after just four months as Prime Minister. There had already been tensions within his government, and the Whigs would certainly have demanded an increased share of Cabinet representation as the price for their continued participation. With Canning gone, the King might logically have been expected to turn to Wellington and Peel for an alternative government, but he chose instead to invite Lord Goderich (formerly Frederick Robinson) to try to keep alive Canning's Tory–Whig combination. Peel's own view was that the King had acted out of spite, because he was still offended by the Protestant Tories' unwillingness to accept his personal guarantee as an adequate basis for joining Canning's ministry.[36] Goderich's leadership, in the event, proved to be a pathetic failure, owing to his inability to assert his authority over disputatious Cabinet colleagues, and he was immensely relieved to be allowed to resign (January 1828) before he had even faced parliament as Prime Minister. Thus ended the coalition experiment initiated by Canning.

King George now commissioned Wellington to form a government, and it was natural for Peel to be appointed Leader of the House of Commons as well as returning to the Home Office. Significantly, though, Peel strongly urged upon the Duke the inexpediency of attempting to construct an exclusively Protestant administration, believing as he did that the best strategy was to 'reunite the most efficient members of Lord Liverpool's Administration'.[37] Writing to his former Christ Church tutor, Charles Lloyd, now Bishop of Oxford, Peel observed that:

> Of course Ultras will object to this, and all parties but moderate and reflecting men will be in some degree dissatisfied. Every blockhead is for the complete predominance of his own opinions, and generally with a vehemence proportional to their impracticability.
>
> I have the strongest conviction that the wise and generous part is to leave nothing untried that can unite those who differed, at least who separated, on no other account than a question about Canning's claim to be Prime Minister.[38]

In the new Cabinet, places were duly found for five men who had served under Goderich, the most prominent of these being William Huskisson, the acknowledged leader of the 'Canningite' strand of Toryism. Conversely, some of the staunchest 'Protestants' from Liverpool's government, including Eldon and Westmorland, were omitted, and the opportunity taken to bring forward some younger men, such as Aberdeen and Goulburn.

Paradoxically, bearing in mind his central role in the Tory schism of April 1827, Peel worked hard during the early months of Wellington's government to repair that damage by trying to smooth over the difficult relations between the Prime Minister and the Canningite section of the Cabinet. It quickly became obvious, however, that the suspicions and animosities generated by the earlier ministerial crisis had not been allayed. Catholic Emancipation, of course, had to be left as an open question once more, but Huskisson and his friends were distrustful of Wellington, and the Duke, in turn, resented the way that they acted together as a group within the Cabinet. Problems first emerged over the

question of what level of protection should be afforded to agriculturalists by the sliding scale of import duties, which replaced the fixed-rate
Corn Law of 1815. Peel's own sympathies were with Huskisson, who
favoured a lower level of protection than the Duke wanted, and a
compromise was finally reached, thanks largely to Peel's mediatory
efforts.[39] Nevertheless, Huskisson had been ominously close to resigning, and Wellington would have been glad to see him go. By the end of
May 1828, Huskisson and his associates, Palmerston, Grant and Dudley,
had indeed gone, much to the Duke's satisfaction, after an eminently
avoidable dispute concerning the redistribution of parliamentary seats
made available by the disfranchisement of the corrupt boroughs of
Penrhyn and East Retford.

Even before the Canningite secession, there were signs that Peel was
finding his role as Leader of the House of Commons an uncongenial
one. At a Cabinet dinner in March, he reportedly expressed frustration
with his position, complaining that he received little support from his
front-bench colleagues, and apparently declaring that he would be glad
to resign.[40] On the other hand, there were those who considered that
any blame for the unsatisfactory state of affairs in the Commons lay with
Peel himself, and that his reputation had diminished dramatically since
assuming the Leadership. Harriet Arbuthnot's diaries suggest that the
root cause of all the problems was Peel's manner, which she described at
different times as 'ill tempered and cowardly', or 'cold and arrogant'.[41]
On 20 May, she wrote that:

> Mr Peel is certainly the most unpopular leader a party can have. His
> low birth & vulgar manners wd be not only forgiven but forgotten if
> he wd practise the arts of conciliation, if he wd be kind & generous to
> those in office under him, & frank & good natured to his supporters
> in Parliament; but, instead of that, nothing can exceed his arrogance
> & ill temper &, if any of the official men speak to him or ask him what
> line the Govt will take on any particular question, he appears to think
> it an impertinence and will give no answer. He is detested by all the
> young men, and the House of Commons is, under his management,
> in a more wild, disorderly state than I ever remember it.[42]

Such a comment, if it existed in isolation, could perhaps be dismissed
as ill-informed, exaggerated gossip from a political bystander, but the
fact is that Mrs Arbuthnot was very well connected, being especially
close to the Duke of Wellington, whose views her diaries were often

reflecting. Nor was she alone in her assessment of Peel. Lord Ellenborough, a Cabinet colleague, was likewise convinced that 'Peel certainly has not the character suited to the leader of a party, or to the command of a popular assembly.'[43] Another Cabinet minister, Lord Bathurst, had evidently received similar messages about Peel: 'From what one hears... I doubt whether he will ever be a good head of a party. He is undoubtedly the first man in the H. of Commons, and his influence, back'd by a good character & a large fortune, must always be very considerable; but he seems to want that cordiality of manner, & that elevation of mind, one of which wins the affections, & the other commands the respect, of a popular assembly.'[44] Wellington, too, complained about Peel's 'confounded temper', following a dispute over the office of Lieutenant General of the Ordnance, which Peel wished to axe but the Duke was determined to preserve.[45]

One issue, more than any other, seems to have fuelled back-bench Tory discontent with Peel's leadership during the 1828 session. In February, the young Whig MP, Lord John Russell, successfully carried against the government, by forty-four votes, a motion calling for the repeal of the Test and Corporation Acts. These seventeenth century statutes, which theoretically barred Protestant nonconformists from holding public office, were regarded as a symbol of Anglican supremacy within the State. Peel was inclined to take the view that there was no practical grievance requiring a remedy, since annual Indemnity Acts allowed nonconformists to hold office with legal impunity, but the agitation in the country against the Test and Corporation Acts reflected the growing political self-confidence of the nonconformist sects. The government was not in a strong enough position in the House of Commons to stop Russell's motion, and, in the circumstances, the most realistic course seemed to be to facilitate a compromise settlement. At a conference with Church of England leaders in mid-March, Peel managed to secure their acquiescence in a new form of religious declaration, to be made by all office holders, and on this basis he gave the government's backing to a bill abolishing the Test and Corporation Acts. Undoubtedly, this was an adroit political move, given the government's parliamentary weakness, but it was hardly likely to be popular with Tory defenders of the Established Church.[46]

The mutual dissatisfaction apparent in Peel's relations with the Tory rank-and-file may well be relevant to our understanding of the subsequent tumultuous events, which ended in his notorious 'betrayal' of the Protestant cause when Wellington's government yielded to the mounting pressure for Catholic Emancipation. Following the demise of the Canningite–Whig coalition in January 1828, and the advent of a Pro-testant-led Tory administration, there had been renewed agitation in Ireland by O'Connell's Catholic Association. At Westminster, meantime, Sir Francis Burdett secured a small but significant majority (272 votes to 266) in favour of his emancipationist resolution, thus repeating the triumph achieved over Liverpool's government, three years earlier, and once again placing Peel in an exceptionally uncomfortable position. (As in 1825, Burdett's resolution was defeated in the House of Lords.) Matters were finally brought to a head in July 1828, when a by-election took place in County Clare, where the sitting Tory MP, Vesey Fitzgerald, was seeking his constituents' endorsement after accepting a Cabinet post (this was a legal requirement at the time). Fitzgerald was a pro-Catholic and an Irish landlord with a good reputation, yet he was challenged by none other than O'Connell, who captured the seat by a margin of more than two to one. O'Connell's victory posed an immediate challenge to the British government, because he was a Catholic and therefore legally barred from occupying his seat in the House of Commons. But the County Clare result also pointed to a wider dilemma for Wellington and Peel, as it confirmed (what the 1826 general election had already indicated) the potentially formidable power of the Catholic 40 shilling freeholders, now that traditional landlord influence was breaking down in Ireland and the Roman Catholic priesthood was exercising more control over voters' minds. In these circumstances, the option of doing nothing hardly seemed to be an option at all. If the government pre-vented O'Connell from taking his seat, they risked inflaming feelings in Ireland still further, and would probably only ensure that at the next general election large numbers of O'Connellites were returned by the counties.[47] Such a prospect was enough to persuade Wellington, not-withstanding his own Protestant sympathies, that it was expedient to grant Catholic Emancipation for the sake of preserving the authority of the King's government in Ireland.[48]

Although the growing momentum for a settlement of the Catholic question inevitably placed Peel in a predicament, any embarrassment he felt seems to have been outweighed by a sense of relief that events beyond his control were conspiring to remove an awkward political encumbrance from his back. In other words, he quietly welcomed the opportunity provided by the County Clare election to release himself from his obligations to the Protestant cause. As Lord Bathurst, a Pro-testant sympathiser, observed in August 1828, Peel had 'long been

strangely ashamed of the [Catholic] question, and of the eager Protestants'.[49] The big question was whether Peel could, with propriety, remain
a member of a government which had resolved to deal with Catholic
Emancipation. For several, months, between the summer of 1828 and
the beginning of 1829, he privately indicated that, while accepting the
Prime Minister's assessment that emancipation was now an 'executive'
matter which required a practical solution in the interests of national
security, irrespective of previous party loyalties and prejudices, the only
creditable course for himself was to give his support to the government
from the outside.[50] Eventually, however, Peel decided that it would be
wrong to abandon the government for the sake of his personal
consistency, when, by so doing, he was likely to create an 'insuperable
obstacle' to a settlement which he agreed was necessary.[51]

Peel was surely right in thinking that Wellington's government, supported on this occasion by the Whigs, was the only one capable of
overcoming the resistance to Catholic Emancipation from within parliament and from an unhappy monarch. He therefore concluded that he
had no right to allow selfish considerations to jeopardise a legislative
solution to the crisis in Ireland. In the early part of 1829, Peel immersed
himself in the Cabinet's efforts to work out the details of a scheme
which, in its final form, combined straightforward Catholic relief (without any compensatory securities for the Established Churches) with a
quid pro quo in the form of a higher franchise qualification for the Irish
counties – a £10 freehold in place of the traditional 40 shilling (£2)
freehold. The King, after making threats of abdication, was finally
compelled to give way and accept his ministers' plan, when it became
clear that Wellington and Peel would otherwise resign. On 5 March Peel
duly introduced the Catholic Relief Bill in a four and a quarter hour
speech to the House of Commons, which some considered to be the
finest oration he had yet delivered in that assembly.[52] He stated that, in
recommending emancipation, he was yielding to 'a moral necessity
which I cannot control', rather than admitting something that was
'right' in the abstract. Less optimistic than many advocates of Catholic
relief, about the future prospects in Ireland, he nevertheless expressed
the hope that the government's concession would encourage conciliatory sentiments amongst the Protestant and Catholic peoples. Implicit
in his reference to a 'moral necessity', which had forced ministers'
hands, was the recognition that what had made the agitation in Ireland
so formidable was its disciplined and orderly nature, achieved through
the influence of O'Connell's Catholic Association and of the Catholic

Church. The manifestation of *legitimate* Catholic force, at the County Clare by-election, was far more difficult for the government to combat than an outbreak of violence, which could always be suppressed using the army. It was the long-term challenge posed to Britain's political authority in Ireland that had caused Peel to change his mind about Catholic Emancipation, not the fear of an imminent civil war. Near the end of his life, Peel compiled a memoir in which he explained his perception of the situation in 1829:

> There is a wide distinction ... between the hasty concession to unprincipled agitation, and provident precautions against the explosion of public feeling gradually acquiring the strength which will make it irresistible.... In this case of the Clare election, and of its natural consequences, what was the evil to be apprehended? Not force – not violence – not any act of which law could take cognizance. The real danger was in the peaceable and legitimate exercise of a franchise ... [involving] a revolution in the electoral system of Ireland – the transfer of political power... from one party to another.[53]

Charles Greville, the celebrated Whig diarist who worked as clerk to the Privy Council, wrote that Peel's speech introducing the Relief Bill was 'said to be far the best he ever made. It is full of his never-failing fault, egotism, but certainly very able, plain, clear and Statesmanlike, and the peroration very eloquent.... The House was crammed to suffocation, and the lobby likewise. The cheering was loud and frequent, and often burst upon the impatient listener without.'[54] Crucially, the government's uncomplicated proposal satisfied Greville's Whig friends, and by the end of March it had been passed by the Commons (320 votes to 142 on the third reading), finally receiving the royal assent on 13 April.

Once Peel had resolved to remain in Wellington's government and assist in the implementation of the Catholic Relief Bill, he displayed a marked sense of personal release, amounting almost to a quiet euphoria, at having dissociated himself from a forlorn cause. In a typically self-righteous letter to a former colleague, from his days as Irish Chief Secretary, Peel declared that it had been essential for him to act as he was now doing, 'setting an example of sacrifice to others'; while) he assured a relative that 'I never took any step in public life with which I was so entirely satisfied as I am with that which I lately took.'[55] Boyd Hilton has detected in Peel's parliamentary language on the Relief Bill signs that he had now embraced a 'liberal' perspective on the Catholic question which was consonant with his general political philosophy. This is not to say that Peel had become any less hostile to Catholicism as a religious creed (indeed, he always considered it to be backward and intolerant), but he was convinced that discriminatory laws tended to strengthen Catholic solidarity and thus enhance the malign influence of the Catholic priesthood over Irish minds. It was actually in the Protestant interest to allow a free-play of spiritual forces – effectively, free trade in religion, a self-regulatory system – and Peel even hoped that this might conduce to the long-delayed progress of the Reformation in Ireland.[56]

Unsurprisingly, Peel's *volte face* over Catholic Emancipation meant that there was a heavy political price to pay with his erstwhile Protestant admirers. Before the Relief Bill was introduced, Oxford University, the constituency represented by Peel since 1817, had repudiated him. Perhaps it was a miscalculation on Peel's part to confront his constituents immediately, by resigning the Oxford seat and offering himself for re-election, but he was anxious to prove that his support for emancipation was not motivated by political self-interest. The outcome was defeat for Peel, by 755 votes to 609, at the hands of a Protestant candidate, Sir Robert Inglis. At the Oxford Convocation, there were 'Hisses and groans for Peel', and the whole affair presented 'a most disgraceful scene of riot and uproar.'[57] Lord Ellenborough thought that 'The violence of the parsons was beyond belief, and far beyond decency'; yet Peel seemed to be 'perfectly indifferent, and really I must confess that he has shown himself *a great man* by his equanimity in all that has taken place.'[58] For someone of Peel's great wealth, of course, it was a relatively simple matter to find another seat, and he was promptly returned for the small borough of Westbury, in Wiltshire, obligingly vacated by Sir Manasseh Lopes.[59]

While the Catholic Relief Bill was passed remarkably swiftly, its legacy for the Tories was more enduring, having provoked intense bitterness from those who felt betrayed by their own leaders. Both Wellington and 'turncoat' Peel were denounced as traitors to the Protestant cause, by so-called 'Ultra' Tories (Wellington even fought a duel with one of them, Lord Winchilsea). Consequently, the removal of the Catholic question from British politics, far from helping the Tories to overcome their differences and reunite, served to accelerate the process of disintegration begun in 1827. Huskisson and his Canningite friends were already so alienated from the Tory leadership that the concession of Catholic

Emancipation could not reconcile them now, and the fact that their resignations in 1828 had ostensibly been prompted by the dispute over a minor measure of parliamentary reform, offered potential common ground on which to combine with the opposition Whigs. Equally ominous for the future was the way that the Ultra Tory MP, Lord Blandford, brought forward resolutions in June 1829 calling for the abolition of the 'rotten' boroughs. This was an expression of the growing conviction, shared by many of the Ultras, that the great betrayal over Catholic Emancipation had been made possible by the corrupt system of parliamentary representation, which produced too many docile MPs obedient to the government's wishes. A system more accurately reflecting public opinion, it followed, would never have permitted such a shameful surrender. It would not be long before 'public opinion' itself joined in the clamour for parliamentary reform.

Parliamentary Reform and Tory Collapse, 1830–2

Wellington's government embarked upon the 1830 parliamentary campaign in an insecure position, unsure of its ability to command a working majority in the House of Commons. At an eve-of-session Cabinet dinner, Peel indicated to one of his colleagues that he was prepared, if necessary, to sit tight and face down the opposition: 'He is disposed to take a high tone, and thinks men will follow him better than when he temporises.'[60] In the early weeks of the session he made a number of spirited defences of the government against opposition attacks, successfully rallying many wavering MPs to his side,[61] and a well-qualified observer of the political scene like Charles Arbuthnot judged that Peel was doing a better job as leader than in previous years, allowing for the 'terrible difficulties' he had to contend with.[62] The problem was that the Ultra Tories remained disgruntled, and could never be relied upon for support, while the Whigs and their radical allies were taking advantage of the government's vulnerability by pressing hard on such issues as retrenchment in expenditure. It is interesting to note that Peel tried to secure Cabinet agreement for a bold initiative in fiscal policy, involving the introduction of a 'property' (or income) tax and the removal of duties on certain items of consumption, which some suspected to be an attempt to 'court the popular cry'.[63] In the end, he was unable to persuade his colleagues to adopt this proposal, but its long-term significance is that it foreshadowed the major experiment in fiscal and commercial reform launched during Peel's premiership in the 1840s (see Chapter 4).

As the 1830 session of parliament progressed, there were renewed complaints about Peel's allegedly secretive manner and reluctance to delegate responsibility, which was said to have had the effect of deterring the younger officials from showing any initiative in debate, for fear that they might say the wrong thing and be thrown over by their own leader.[64] According to Sir Henry Hardinge, Peel was 'cold and never encourages any one'.[65] The government was therefore over-dependent on the gallant solo performances from its House of Commons Leader, who took upon himself an excessive burden of labour. In the resulting climate of tension, which can only have been exacerbated by the personal strains arising from his father's death in May, Peel's general demeanour was described as '*sour* and dissatisfied ... morose and austere'.[66] Attending a Cabinet dinner in June, he reportedly spoke 'with much *ennui* of his position in the House of Commons', bemoaning the personal sacrifice required of him in attending for long hours in such an unruly assembly, where business was becoming almost impossible to conduct: 'He seemed not well, and thoroughly out of humour.' Two weeks later, the same Cabinet diarist thought that Peel was 'really ill, and quite broken down'.[67]

The most intriguing question about Peel's relationship with the Wellington administration, at this time, is whether he was expecting the Duke to stand aside and allow him to assume the premiership. Wellington's papers contain a memorandum of a letter to Peel, evidently written in the spring of 1830 while King George was dying, in which he expressed the opinion that Peel was better equipped, politically, to disarm the various opposition groupings ranged against the government, and also better placed to do this from his seat in the House of Commons. It is not clear, however, that the letter related to this memorandum was ever sent to Peel (there is nothing in his papers).[68] On the other hand, Tory diarists of this period were obviously aware of speculation regarding the Duke's intentions, and it is hard to believe that Peel knew nothing of this.[69] If Peel really had been put in a state of suspense in 1830, believing that the premiership might be about to fall into his hands, then this would help to make sense of his subsequent personal difficulties with Wellington, as we shall see.

George IV's death in June, and the succession of his brother as William IV, added a new dimension to the government's worries,

because of the legal requirement that a general election must be held
(this need not otherwise have taken place until 1832 or 1833). Unluckily
for ministers, the 1830 general election coincided with a recent revival
of popular agitation in favour of parliamentary reform, stimulated by
the effects of a bad harvest on food prices and cyclical unemployment in
the industrial districts. In many towns, the pressure for reform was
orchestrated by Political Unions, a new phenomenon drawing on support from the middle and artisanal as well as the lower classes in society,
and therefore possessing a degree of 'respectability' far greater than
that attached to earlier reform movements. It would be an exaggeration
to say that parliamentary reform was the decisive issue determining the
election results, or that Wellington's government 'lost' the general election, but the outcome undoubtedly weakened still further ministers'
already fragile control over the House of Commons. Peel received an
analysis of the election returns in September, prepared by the government 'whip', Joseph Planta, showing that the reliable supporters, or
'Friends', of the ministry numbered 311, in a House of 658 MPs. This
did not necessarily mean, though, that Wellington was at the head of a
minority administration, as the reality of the parliamentary situation was
far more complicated than a dichotomy between government and opposition members. Planta calculated that the government's 'Foes', consist-
ing of Whigs and a few radicals, totalled only 188, while another eleven
MPs were attributed to the 'Huskisson party' (i.e. Canningites). Of the
rest, twenty-five MPs were reckoned to be 'Violent Ultras', and thirty-
seven were described as 'Moderate Ultras': these, of course, were Tories
alienated (to a greater or lesser extent) from their own leaders since the
'betrayal' over Catholic Emancipation. In addition, thirty-seven MPs
were listed as 'Doubtful favourable', twenty-three as 'Doubtful unfa-
vourable', and twenty-four as 'very doubtful', which all serves to confirm
the bewilderingly fragmented and unpredictable state of opinion in the
new House of Commons.[70]

The implication of this parliamentary survey is that the potential still
existed for Wellington's government to buttress its position, provided
some of the disaffected Ultras and Doubtful men could be induced to
rally to its support. During the autumn of 1830, as the agitation in the
country gained momentum, the question at stake was whether ministers
should commit themselves to a moderate Reform bill in order to
appease public opinion and secure additional parliamentary votes. Huskisson's tragic death, at the opening of the Liverpool–Manchester railway in September, was actually a helpful development in this respect,

removing as it did an awkward personal element from the political equation. Contact was made with other leading Canningites, notably Palmerston, but no agreement could be reached. Early in November, Peel was still receiving reports that the Canningites were interested in doing a deal,[71] but Wellington's defiant statement in the House of Lords, about the perfection of the nation's existing constitutional arrangements, was a deliberate rebuff to these Tory renegades. With a Whig motion in favour of parliamentary reform impending, which looked set to attract Canningite and some Ultra Tory votes, and thus put the government in a minority, Wellington and Peel were grateful for the opportunity afforded by a defeat on a minor issue relating to the civil list (15 November), to justify resigning before the reform debate came on. In the fateful civil list division, the Whigs were joined by the Canningites and by thirty-four Ultras, while a further fifty-seven Ultras absented themselves.[72] Earl Grey, the Whig leader, proceeded to form a ministry pledged to introducing a Reform bill, and he included in his Cabinet four Canningites and the Ultra-Tory Duke of Richmond.

While it could be argued that Wellington's uncompromising stand on parliamentary reform was a disastrous mistake, which perpetuated the Tory divisions originating in the Catholic controversy and paved the way for the Whigs' return to office, the fact remains that Peel was equally determined to uphold the existing system of representation. This did not mean that Peel was unaware of the long-term changes in British society tending towards the creation of a more powerful 'public opinion' beyond Westminster. In a well-known letter to his friend, John Wilson Croker, dating from as far back as 1820, Peel had pondered on the implications for Lord Liverpool's government of the spirit of change that seemed to be in the air:

> Do you not think that the tone of England – of that great compound of folly, weakness, prejudice, wrong feeling, right feeling, obstinacy, and newspaper paragraphs, which is called public opinion – is more liberal – to use an odious but intelligible phrase – than the policy of the Government? Do not you think that there is a feeling, becoming daily more general and more confirmed – that is, independent of the pressure of taxation, or any immediate cause – in favour of some undefined change in the mode of governing the country? It seems to me a curious crisis – when public opinion never had such influence on public measures, and yet never was so dissatisfied with the share which it possessed. It is growing too large for the channels that it

has been accustomed to run through. God knows, it is very difficult to widen them exactly in proportion to the size and force of the current which they have to convey, but the engineers that made them never dreamt of various streams that are now struggling for a vent.[73]

By the beginning of the 1830s, the public mood in favour of reform was more insistent still, and it was being articulated in weighty and 'respectable' newspapers such as *The Times*, the *Morning Chronicle* and the *Leeds Mercury*. Political Unions were organising mass meetings, and petitions were sent to parliament – one from Bristol, for example, contained 12,000 signatures. In the final days of Wellington's administration, however, Peel seems to have resolved that he wanted nothing to do with any measure of parliamentary reform, even though some action on the issue was looking increasingly inevitable. Lord Ellenborough, recording in his diary the opinions expressed by Peel at a Cabinet meeting, on 14 November, suspected that 'obstinacy, and the fear of being again accused of ratting, lead to this determination to resist when resistance is, in his own opinion, fruitless'. Once the Whigs and their ex-Tory allies were installed in office, Peel apparently told a meeting of Tory leaders that he hoped to see the new ministers 'disembarrass us from the question of reform'.[74]

Peel's assumption was that the Whigs' Reform bill would turn out to be a modest affair, possibly confining itself to the redistribution of some seats from small boroughs in order to provide direct representation for rapidly expanding industrial centres such as Manchester, Birmingham and Leeds. In fact, the measure unveiled to the House of Commons by Lord John Russell, on 1 March 1831, went much further than any of the proposals made while the Whigs had been in opposition. A total of 168 seats were to be taken away from small boroughs, through the complete disfranchisement of sixty and partial disfranchisement of another forty-seven, and a uniform voting qualification for borough constituencies – the £10 household franchise – was to replace the existing mixture of franchises. According to one Whig observer, the House was left in a state of shock, so sweeping were the proposals announced by Russell, and even committed reformers were taken aback: 'They were like men taking breath immediately after an explosion. No-one, however, was less himself than Peel. He sat pale and forlorn, utterly at a loss how to act. His countenance at times looked convulsed. The workings within him were evidently beyond his controul.'[75] It now dawned on Peel that the Whigs had decided to attach to themselves the popular enthusiasm for reform in the country, as a means of strengthening their precarious foothold in the House of Commons. This consideration dictated that a comprehensive scheme must be introduced, with the intention of giving full satisfaction to the 'reasonable' demands of an impassioned populace.

On the third night of the ensuing debate, Peel delivered his first major speech condemning the Reform Bill. Emphasising the hazards entailed in tampering with a mechanism so complex as the British Constitution, he argued that this point was especially pertinent considering how uniquely successful the nation's political structure had been in promoting the liberty and prosperity of its people. Peel maintained that he was not opposed to the idea of reform entirely, but he made clear his total opposition to a measure which amounted to 'an entire reconstruction of the House of Commons', and which would assuredly lead to further demands for reform in the future. In defence of the small boroughs facing extinction, he relied upon the argument commonly used by anti-reformers – that these constituencies provided men of exceptional talent with opportunities to gain entry to the Commons. To prove his point, Peel recited a long list of distinguished MPs, including Burke, Pitt the Younger, Canning, Brougham, Romilly, Horner, Sheridan, Windham and Tierney, who had at some stage or other been returned by boroughs which the Whigs now proposed to abolish. Turning to the franchise provisions of the bill, Peel objected to the arbitrary nature of the £10 threshhold for householders, observing that the imposition of a uniform voting qualification for the boroughs was going to deprive working men of the right to vote in certain towns, such as Preston and Coventry, where a much wider franchise currently operated. Indeed, he declared that one of the fatal defects in the Whigs' Bill was the way 'it severs all connexion between the lower classes of the community and the direct representation in this House'. Finally, Peel denounced ministers for their irresponsibility in stirring up the 'fever of popular excitement' in the country, and encouraging the erroneous belief that reform was a panacea for temporary economic distress.[76]

Whereas Peel's initial attitude to the reform issue, on leaving office in November 1830, had been that it was preferable to allow Lord Grey's government to dispose of the problem, his reaction to the Bill of 1831 was that it was so much more radical than anyone had anticipated that the proper course was not merely to oppose it personally, but to work strenuously for its complete rejection. The Bill passed its second reading stage by just one vote, 302 to 301, in the largest division ever to have taken place in the House of Commons, and its opponents included most of the Ultra Tories who, after toying with the idea of reform in 1829–30 and assisting in the downfall of Wellington's ministry, were now utterly horrified and alarmed by the Whigs' plan. It seemed certain, therefore, that the Bill would be defeated during its committee stage, and an amendment put forward by General Gascoyne, opposing the reduction in the number of English MPs (extra seats were being given to Scotland, Wales and Ireland, at England's expense), was perfectly designed for this object. Peel appears to have been genuinely confident that the Whigs' reform scheme could be eliminated, writing to Croker in mid-April that, 'Give us another month and there is an end of the Bill, positively an end to it.' Reiterating his argument that the 'fatal error' in the Bill was its disfranchisement of working-class voters, who would be infuriated by the electoral power conferred on the middle classes, Peel went so far as to predict that 'One month hence, if the Bill is still in suspense, there will be an enforced natural union between aristocracy and disfranchised population against a vulgar privileged "pedlary".'[77] Significantly, when Gascoyne's amendment was carried against ministers, Lord Ellenborough heard from Sir Henry Hardinge that Peel was 'ready to undertake the Govnt'.[78] If this report was correct, it is of interest for two reasons: first, because it shows that Peel expected the Whigs to respond to their defeat by resigning and, secondly, because it reveals his assumption that *he*, not Wellington, should be the one to form the replacement government. Logically, we must suppose that Peel envisaged introducing a more sober Reform Bill of his own, in the hope of appeasing public opinion (his original speech in the Commons, after all, had not rejected reform outright), but any such calculations were rendered meaningless when King William acceded to the Whigs' request for a dissolution of parliament, less than a year after the last one.

The general election of May 1831 registered a decisive victory for the cause of reform. In the English counties, for instance, where the electorates were usually sufficiently large already to be capable of reflecting the popular mood, seventy-six out of the eighty-two successful candidates were pledged to support the Whigs' Bill. There was no doubt that in the new parliament Lord Grey's government would have little difficulty in carrying its resurrected Reform plan through the House of Commons, regardless of Tory opposition, and attention was now focused on the crucial question of what line was going to be taken by the Tory-dominated House of Lords. In October 1831 the answer came,

in the form of a direct negative, with the peers rejecting the Bill by a
majority of forty-one votes. This verdict provoked violent demonstrations in some of the larger towns, including Derby, Nottingham and
Coventry, whose alarming proximity to Peel's estate at Drayton, in
Staffordshire, obliged him, along with other landowners, to return
home and make preparations for the defence of their families and
property against possible mob attack.

In spite of the dangerously inflamed state of popular feeling, Peel
was determined to continue resisting the Reform Bill until the bitter
end. For this reason, he gave no encouragement to the attempt by a
group of wavering Tory peers, represented by Lords Harrowby
and Wharncliffe, to find a compromise solution acceptable to government and opposition.[79] Consequently, the Whigs proceeded to introduce their Reform Bill for a third time, substantially unaltered, in
December 1831. Peel was well aware that, in advising the Lords to
oppose the Reform Bill again, he and they were inviting the government to apply its ultimate coercive remedy, namely, to ask the King to
create a sufficient number of new peers to swamp the existing Tory
majority. Appalling as this prospect was, Peel argued that it would be
better for the long-term reputation of the upper House if it did force the
Whigs to resort to a mass-creation of peers. As he explained to Harrowby, in February 1832:

> I assure you that my great object in public life for the last six months
> has been to vindicate the authority and maintain the character of the
> House of Lords. I think that is the institution most exposed to danger
> from the short-sighted folly of the times, and also the institution
> which, if it remain erect in character, is most likely to serve us as a
> rallying point for the returning good sense of the Country.

If the government was allowed to have its own way simply by threatening to create more peers, Peel warned that there would be an irresistible
temptation for ministers to employ the same tactic in future:

> Why have we been struggling against the Reform Bill in the House of
> Commons? Not in the hope of resisting its final success in that House,
> but because we look beyond the Bill, because we know the nature of
> popular concessions, their tendency to propagate the necessity for
> further and more extensive compliances. We want to make the 'des-
> census' as 'difficilis' as we can – to teach young inexperienced men

charged with the trust of government that, though they may be backed by popular clamour, they shall not over-ride on the first springtide of excitement every barrier and breakwater raised against popular impulses.... Suppose that we had given way.... My firm belief is that the Country, so far from being satisfied with our concessions, would have lost all reverence and care for remaining institutions, and would have had their appetite whetted for a further feast at the expense of the Church, or the Monarchy.[80]

When the Reform Bill reached the House of Lords again, a sufficient number of Tory waverers were willing to endorse its principle for the second reading to be given. During the committee stage, however, Lord Lyndhurst succeeded in carrying an amendment, postponing the disfranchising clauses, which was expressly intended as the prelude to a fundamental re-casting of the Bill along more moderate lines. The infuriated Whig ministers tendered their resignations after the King – now thoroughly alarmed by the turbulent state of the country – refused their request for the creation of fifty new peers. Wellington, always a better soldier than a politician, was prepared to respond to his monarch's cries of distress by undertaking to form a government pledged to implementing an alternative Reform Bill, regardless of his previous opposition to any measure. From the Duke's point of view, this was an opportunity to prevent any further damage being done to the authority of the upper House. Peel, on the other hand, was adamant that he would have nothing to do with a Tory Reform administration, and his refusal to co-operate made it impossible for Wellington to proceed. In Peel's eyes, to accept a share of the responsibility for introducing a modified Reform Bill, after all his denunciations of the disastrous consequences of the Whigs' scheme, would have amounted to a 'personal degradation'. There was nothing for it, he concluded, but to let the Whigs return to office and complete their work.[81] Lord Ellenborough was not the only high-ranking Tory who felt indignant at Peel's refusal to serve, believing that his obsession with his own political consistency was quite discreditable, given the exceptional circumstances.[82] Deprived of other options, the distraught King was obliged to reinstate the Whigs and agree to their conditions regarding the creation of peers. It was only a small consolation that, in the event, he was not called upon to exercise his prerogative power: the mere knowledge that the King had promised to act in accordance with his ministers' wishes was enough to ensure that the Reform Bill was allowed to pass, on 7 June 1832.

The Last of Tory England

The Great Reform Act, for all its limitations, created an electoral dispensation that was sufficiently different from the old system to raise
serious concerns about the future political prospects of the 'Tory party'
of Pitt and Liverpool. While the Whigs could plausibly maintain that
they had acted in the national interest, by broadening the social basis of
the constitution, it was also true that their measure was designed to
erode the electoral base of Toryism and transfer influence to sections of
society more likely, on balance, to support Whig governments. In its
final form, the 1832 Act removed 144 seats from small English
boroughs, precisely the type of constituency in which the Tories had
flourished, and sixty-four of these seats were redistributed to create
twenty-two new two-member boroughs and twenty new single-member
boroughs, many of them northern and midland industrial centres.
Meantime, the uniform £10 borough householder franchise provided
a rough-and-ready device for confining the electorate to the industrious, respectable 'middling classes', with whom the Whigs claimed to be
identified, and it even deprived some working men of the right to vote
in a few places where the old franchise had been more generous.
Predictably, and ominously, the general election held in December
1832 yielded an overwhelming majority for supporters of Lord
Grey's government. Of the 658 seats in the reformed House of Commons, no more than about 150 were filled by members of the
Tory opposition.

Recent events were open to interpretation, by Tory pessimists, as
parts of a logical sequence which was undermining those institutions
of Church and State upon which the long Tory ascendancy of the reigns
of George III and George IV had rested. From this perspective, the rot
had set in when the opposition Whigs succeeded in carrying the repeal
of the Test and Corporation Acts, in 1828, thereby ending the Anglican
monopoly (in theory, at least) of public office. Wellington's and Peel's
dismal surrender over Catholic Emancipation, the following year, delivered an even more grievous blow to Tory principles by abandoning the
concept of a 'Protestant Constitution'. As a result, in the 1830s, there was
a bloc of Roman Catholic Irish representatives, led by O'Connell, who
were permitted to sit in a parliament exercising legislative authority
over the Established Protestant Churches of England and Ireland. At
the same time, the effect of the 1832 Reform Act in British constituencies was to enhance the power of certain social groups, such as artisans,

who were disproportionately associated with the Protestant nonconformist sects. Inevitably, therefore, more legislation was subsequently introduced as Whig ministers attempted to gratify the non-Anglican forces within the British and Irish electorates. For instance, the Irish Church Temporalities Act of 1833 reduced the number of bishoprics in the Church of Ireland, while the Municipal Corporations Act of 1835 broke the Anglican hold on local government in many of the chartered boroughs of England and Wales, opening them up to nonconformist participation.

Quite apart from the impact of these political and religious measures, the manner in which some of them had been carried was equally disturbing to Tory minds. This was particularly true of the passing of the Reform Act, which involved attacks on all the great institutions in the State. The Anglican bishops became targets for the infuriated mobs, because of their decisive role in the House of Lords' rejection of the second Whig Bill, in October 1831; the Lords as a whole were finally intimidated into acquiescence in the Whigs' third Bill, after it was made clear that a mass creation of peers would follow if they continued their resistance; and the hapless King William, though initially willing to support the Whigs' Reform crusade, was also humiliated in the end when an unwilling pledge to create the extra peers was extracted from him. In the new political order constructed by the Whigs, where the prestige and authority of the Crown, the Church and the House of Lords had been diminished, and a greater share of power placed in the hands of an expanded electorate, it was difficult to see how another Tory government, such as that of Lord Liverpool's, could hope to maintain itself in office. The pillars of the old Tory political hegemony had apparently been weakened beyond repair.

At the beginning of 1832, when the politicians and the public were still embroiled in the debate over parliamentary reform, the signs were that Peel had reconciled himself to the fact that the Whigs' Bill was bound to pass, and that he was already looking to the new political world ahead. His letter to Lord Harrowby, cited earlier, showed that Peel's thoughts were turning towards finding the best means of preserving what was left of the character and reputation of Tory institutions, in the belief that they might yet provide a 'rallying point' for the country once the reform fever had subsided.

With regard to Peel himself, there is a strong impression that the political and psychological ordeal which he had endured since 1827 substantially modified his public personality. Never again would he commit himself so unequivocally to a political cause, as he had to the 'Protestant Constitution' at the start of his career; nor would he be forced into another embarrassing withdrawal from a position rendered untenable by the course of events. After 1832, Sir Robert Peel – he had succeeded to his father's title and landed estate in 1830, reinforcing his sense of personal responsibility – was even more determined than before to act the part of the 'executive' politician, adopting a self-consciously detached view of public affairs, and preferring to look to the wider issues at stake rather than consulting the interests of a party or faction. The problem with this, as we shall see in the following chapters, was that party connections became increasingly indispensable, and party obligations more inescapable, in the post-Reform-Act era.

Shortly after Peel's death one of his protégés, W. E. Gladstone, was shown the unpublished memoir in which Peel had justified his conduct during the Catholic Emancipation crisis. Gladstone was very much struck with the personal transformation that had evidently occurred in his mentor: 'The Crisis of 1829', he noted in a memorandum, 'seems to have [at] once forced into expansion and ripeness Sir R. Peel's political character. Compare the tone, scope, and range of mind in his letters on accession to office in 1828 with his sayings during the agony of the next year. This process I should say was completed by the Reform Bill.' In consequence, as Gladstone went on to observe, by the time his own acquaintance with Peel began in 1833, 'he was already the profound Statesman'.[83]

3

THE NEW CONSERVATISM

Opposition Principles

Looking ahead, early in January 1833, to the opening session of the reformed parliament and the likely course of public affairs, Peel wrote to one of his closest colleagues that 'I presume the chief object of that party which is called Conservative...will be to resist Radicalism, to prevent those further encroachments of democratic influence which will be attempted (probably successfully attempted) as the natural consequence of the triumph already achieved.'[1] It is interesting to observe Peel making use of the new party nomenclature – 'Conservative' – which had only come into fashion since the collapse of the Tory regime in 1830. In a political world given its shape by the crisis over parliamentary reform, there was an evident desire, on the part of those hitherto content to be called Tories, to avoid a party label associated in the popular mind with a bigoted and selfish opposition to all proposals for improvement. The distinction between 'Tory' and 'Conservative' was essentially one of methodology rather than of ultimate purpose: whereas the former title conveyed the idea of an uncompromising defence of the privileges and monopolies enjoyed by institutions connected to the Anglican, landed élite, the latter allowed for the possibility of gradual, cautious change, designed to reconcile those institutions with the prevailing attitudes in the modern world. As Peel's career after 1832 demonstrates, the strategy of reforming in order to conserve frequently commended itself as the most effective way of resisting hostile schemes of radical reform which threatened to erode, and perhaps eventually destroy, the traditional ruling institutions of the country. Conservatism, in fact, represented an extension of the 'liberal' Tory reformist impulse of the 1820s.

Peel's prediction that the passing of the Reform Act would encourage fresh demands for drastic change, was based on the fact that Lord Grey's Whig government relied for its existence upon the support of a diverse alliance of interests in parliament and in the country. An analysis of the composition of the newly elected House of Commons, reported to Peel, put the Conservatives' strength at about 150, and the Whigs' at 320, but in addition to these there were 'thick-and-thin Radicals, Repealers from Ireland, members or friends of the political unions, and so on, not less than 190'.[2] The Whigs were therefore likely to be susceptible to pressure from the group of forty or so Irish MPs, led by Daniel O'Connell, whose ultimate objective was the repeal of the Act of Union between Britain and Ireland (hence their title, 'Repealers'), and who as a prelude were focusing their energies on the privileged position of the Established, Anglican Church of Ireland. Similarly, it was going to be difficult for the government to ignore the views of the large body of radicals on the backbenches, even if it was true that they were really a very heterogeneous bunch of politicians and dreamers. For many radicals, the Reform Act did not go far enough, and they advocated an extension of the franchise, the introduction of a select ballot for elections (to protect voters against intimidation), and triennial parliaments, so that MPs could be made accountable to their constituents every three years instead of every seven years. In addition to all this, radical antipathy towards the aristocratic and landed élite could be expected to manifest itself in demands for the reform or abolition of the House of Lords, and the repeal of the Corn Laws which helped to protect landowners' incomes. No-one could be entirely sure that the existence of the monarchy itself might not finally be called into question. At the same time, Conservatives were alarmed by the evidence that Protestant nonconformists were wielding considerable electoral influence in the constituencies, which suggested that in the reformed parliament there was going to be a powerful impetus for renewed assaults on the Church of England. The Test and Corporation Acts had already gone; the Municipal Corporations looked set to be re-modelled, breaking the monopoly of local control held in many boroughs by Anglicans; the future of Oxford and Cambridge Universities, as exclusively Anglican institutions, was in doubt; and an agitation was growing up in many towns against the Church's right to levy a local rate to pay for the maintenance of its parish churches.

It may seem rather surprising, in these circumstances, to find that Peel's preferred strategy was, as far as possible, to support rather than oppose the Whig ministers in parliament. For instance, he delivered a notable speech in March 1833 defending the government's Coercion Bill, brought in to combat agrarian unrest in Ireland, while in July of the same year great efforts were made to 'whip-up' Conservative MPs in order to save the Whigs from defeat on a radical motion for triennial parliaments.[3] On two occasions in 1834, the Conservatives came to the Whigs' rescue over the question of the pension list: some forty-five opposition MPs voted against a radical motion in February, which was only narrowly defeated by a majority of eight, and over 100 Conservatives helped the government to block another motion put forward in May.[4] Peel was determined to resist the temptation to enter into opportunistic alliances with the radicals or Irish MPs, merely for the pleasure of inflicting embarrassing defeats on the Whigs, choosing instead to shield ministers from the attacks launched by their own nominal supporters. In this way, as Peel explained to his friend, John Wilson Croker, the Conservative opposition was 'making the Reform Bill work; we are falsifying our own predictions, which would be realised but for our active interference; we are protecting the authors of the evil from the work of their own hands'.[5] Of course, the Conservatives were not precluded from *criticising* various aspects of the government's policy, nor of voting against it when a clear difference of principle existed, but there was to be no relentless opposition to everything the Whigs did.

We should not suppose that Peel acted in this way from feelings of benevolence towards the government. On the contrary, it suited his purposes very well to see ministers coming under attack from their own back-benchers. It was vitally important, however, that the opposition did not make the mistake of exploiting the Whigs' plight by remaining aloof and leaving them exposed to radical pressure, or, worse still, of engaging in their own gratuitous attacks on ministers. To do either of these things would inevitably have the effect of driving the Whigs closer into the arms of the radicals, thereby defeating the Conservatives' own objects. 'I am adverse to any course of proceeding on our part', Peel advised his colleague, J. C. Herries, 'which should justify the Government in the eyes of the Country in forming a cordial union with the Radicals. That I think would be tantamount to positive destruction, because it would be tantamount to the adoption of the views and principles of the Radicals, and their practical enforcement through the Crown and Government.'[6] In other words, Peel's policy of supporting the government, wherever possible, was designed to perpetuate the division between Whigs and radicals, and thus to prevent radical ideas from gaining ground in ministerial circles. Nothing could be more suicidal, from this point of view, than for the Conservatives to indulge in opposition for opposition's sake.

Peel's long-term aim was to promote subtly the gradual disintegration, and ultimate collapse, of the government's vast parliamentary majority. There was a widespread Conservative perception, even at the beginning of the 1833 session, that some Whig MPs were likely to be alarmed by the sight of their leaders coming under pressure from radicals and O'Connellites, and probably yielding to some of their demands. These moderate Whigs, it was reckoned, were potential future recruits to the Conservative cause.[7] Thomas Raikes, a Conservative diarist, therefore suspected that rational calculation lay behind Peel's display of statesmanlike forebearance towards the government: 'He has declared himself to be of no party; but his object is insensibly to make *one* of which he shall be himself the centre and the chief. He is an ambitious man; and to this great object his endeavours will inevitably tend.' In the reformed House of Commons, as Raikes noted, party connections were peculiarly weak, and there were many MPs lacking in any firm allegiance to a leader – 'loose Tories, loose Whigs, loose Conservatives, and loose Radicals' – who might well be persuaded 'that *Sir Robert Peel* is the fittest man to govern the Country'.[8]

It is necessary at this stage to clarify certain points about Peel's position in the House of Commons and his relationship with Conservative MPs. While he was, unquestionably, the dominant figure on the opposition front-bench, to whom most Conservatives automatically looked for leadership, he was not in any official sense the leader of the opposition party. According to constitutional practice, the power to appoint the Prime Minister still rested with the King, and for this reason it would have been improper for a political party to restrict the King's freedom of choice by electing its own leader. During the sessions of 1833 and 1834, then, Peel was merely the most conspicuous member of the opposition in the Commons, and it was not until he was commissioned by the King to form a government, in December 1834, that he truly became the leader of the Conservative party. This helps to make sense of Raikes's depiction of him, in 1833, as an independent politician rather than a party man. Likewise, it helps to explain why Peel could not always command the loyalty of opposition members, as was evidenced in March 1833 when more than one-half of the Conservative MPs present voted for a radical motion on currency reform which Peel strongly opposed. His problems with the Conservative opposition were also complicated by the fact that he was still at loggerheads with the 'Ultras', men such as Sir Richard Vyvyan, Sir Edward Knatchbull and Lord Chandos, who had been estranged ever since 'turncoat' Peel's abandonment of the Protestant cause in 1829. After the fall of Wellington's government, Peel made little effort to conceal his contempt for the Ultras, and in 1831 he rejected the suggestion of a rapprochement.[9] The continuing nuisance potential of the Ultras was demonstrated, in April 1833, by Sir William Ingilby's triumph over the government on the malt tax issue, which he achieved with radical assistance and contrary to Peel's wishes. For his part, Peel had no intention of building up an opposition party dependent on Ultra support, and his efforts to construct a broad, central coalition, by wooing moderate Whigs, was partly designed to neutralise Vyvyan, Chandos and their friends.[10]

By the spring of 1834 there were encouraging signs that Peel's general strategy was about to pay rich political dividends. Internal Cabinet disputes over Irish policy culminated in May, with the resignations of four ministers, Lord Stanley, Sir James Graham, Lord Ripon and the Duke of Richmond, raising Conservative expectations of a complete ministerial collapse. Peel's view of this crisis, as the events unfolded, was that it vindicated his decision to eschew factious alliances with the Radicals or Irish Repealers. It was far more likely, he argued, that moderate Whigs would be drawn towards the Conservatives if the latter had behaved responsibly as an opposition party. If the Whig government did indeed fall to pieces, and the Conservatives were called upon to take office, Peel believed that their only chance of survival lay in 'conciliating the goodwill, at least by mitigating the hostility, of many of the moderate and respectable supporters of the present Government'. This was not likely to be achieved if the fall of the Whigs had come about through Conservative aggression: 'If it [the government] breaks-up, or avails itself of the pretext of breaking-up, in consequence of a union between Radicals and Conservatives, in my opinion the Government which succeeds it will have a very short-lived triumph. For it will have opposed to it the adherents of the present Government and the Radicals.' On the other hand, if the Whigs' demise was the result of their 'own differences and misunderstandings', proving their unfitness to govern, then the Conservatives would be better placed to make 'a forcible appeal to the Country' with some hope of a favourable verdict.[11]

Peel's adoption of a non-partisan approach to opposition politics can be seen as a realistic response to the fact that, in the immediate aftermath of the Reform Act, the Conservatives were in a hopelessly small minority in the House of Commons. The situation in the House of Lords, however, was totally different and constituted a potential source of trouble for Peel. It is important to remember that the mass-creation of peers, threatened by Grey's government in 1832, had not been required, which meant that the Conservatives retained their substantial majority in the upper House. Their ranks included prominent Ultras such as the Duke of Newcastle, Lord Eldon and Lord Roden. Furthermore, the Reform crisis had left the constitutional powers of the House of Lords unaltered, and the Conservative majority were therefore capable of exercising an unrestricted right to veto legislation sent up from the Commons. Peel's constant worry was that the Conservative-controlled upper House might come into conflict again with the Whig-dominated elected Chamber. Consequently, he relied heavily upon the personal influence of the Duke of Wellington to dissuade Conservative peers from deliberately wrecking major items of government legislation. In the case of the Irish Church Temporalities Bill of 1833, for example, Peel decided to support the Whigs after they agreed to drop the controversial clause 147, which had proposed that the State should be allowed to appropriate surplus Church revenues for secular purposes ('lay appropriation'). This concession by the Whigs infuriated radical and O'Connellite MPs, confirming Peel's judgment that by assisting the government he was sowing the seeds of dissension within the ministerial majority.[12] Everything depended, though, on the ability of Wellington, who fully appreciated the dangers entailed in throwing out the government's plan,[13] to convince their Lordships that it was prudent to allow the amended Bill to pass.

It was remarkably fortunate for Peel that the Duke concurred in his assessment of the opposition's tactical position, because on a personal level the relations between the two men – respectful, rather than cordial, even in the 1820s – were frequently strained. This was a legacy of the mutual ill-feeling generated in May 1832, when Peel refused to serve in the projected Wellington Reform ministry (see Chapter 2). At that time, both leaders made speeches in parliament implicitly condemning the other's conduct, and their subsequent communications had been rather distant and cool. Peel may also have been partly actuated by resentment of what appeared to be the Duke's going back on earlier intimations that he, Peel, should be at the head of the next government. Further tensions were created in 1833–4 by Wellington's acceptance of an invitation to stand for election as Chancellor of Oxford University, a decision which he took without consulting Peel, who also happened to have received a requisition urging him to come forward as a candidate. Peel was left with no alternative but to decline to be nominated for a position which, in other circumstances, he would have been honoured and delighted to occupy. These accumulated resentments lingered on in both men's minds, and in May 1834, with the Whig administration apparently on the verge of disintegration, it was necessary for Charles Arbuthnot and others to act as intermediaries in order to bring about an improved understanding between Wellington and Peel. As a result, the Duke let it be known that, in his opinion, the Prime Minister ought to sit in the House of Commons, thus acknowledging Peel's superior claims to the first place in a future Conservative government.[14]

Notwithstanding the various tensions and suspicions which continued to dog Peel's relationship with the Conservative party, the early years of the Reformed parliament were probably, on balance, a satisfying time for him. Liberated from the shackles of his earlier commitment to the Protestant cause, and with the awkward question of parliamentary reform disposed of by the Whigs, he now had the opportunity to establish his leadership on terms acceptable to himself. It is true that he found the tone of the House of Commons depressing, at first, complaining to Raikes in February 1833 that 'there was an asperity, a rudeness, a vulgar assumption of independence, combined with a fawning reference to the people out of doors, expressed by many of the new members, which was highly disgusting'.[15] But contemporary observers were impressed by the speed with which Peel stamped his personal authority on the Commons. Charles Greville, a Whig diarist, considered Peel to be *'facile princeps'* among MPs, with Lord Stanley his only serious rival as an orator:

No matter how unruly the House, how impatient or fatigued, the moment he rises all is silence, and he is sure of being heard with profound attention and respect.... He speaks with great energy, great dexterity – his language is powerful and easy; he reasons well, hits hard, and replies with remarkable promptitude and effect; but he is at an immense distance below the great models of eloquence, Pitt, Fox and Canning; his voice is not melodious, and it is a little monotonous; his action is very ungraceful, his person and manner are vulgar, and he has certain tricks in his motions which exhibit that vulgarity in a manner almost offensive, and which is only redeemed by the real power of his speeches. His great merit consists in his judgement, tact, and discretion, his facility, promptitude, thorough knowledge of the assembly he addresses, familiarity with the details of every sort of Parliamentary business, and the great command he has over himself. He never was a great favourite of mine, but I am satisfied that he is the fittest man to be Minister, and I therefore wish to see him return to power.[16]

To Greville, it seemed that this was the 'enjoyable period' of Peel's life, which he would be well advised to make the most of.

Peel's First Ministry, 1834–5

In the early nineteenth century it was the normal practice for parliament to be in recess from mid-summer until the following January or February. No obvious reason therefore existed, in October 1834, to prevent Peel from taking his family to Italy for a prolonged holiday. While he was absent, however, the political scene in Britain was thrown into chaos by King William IV's decision to dismiss the Whig government (headed since July by Lord Melbourne), because of the worrying direction in which ministerial policy towards the Irish Church seemed to be heading. Wellington was summoned by the King, but, true to his earlier intimations, the Duke recommended that Peel should be invited to take the premiership. It was arranged for Wellington to hold all of the key offices of State in a caretaker capacity (except for the Lord Chancellorship, which had to be filled by a lawyer, hence Lord Lyndhurst's appointment), until Peel could be located and asked to return to London. There was bound to be a considerable delay involved, as there were of course no telephones, or a telegraph system, and a rider had to be despatched to discover Peel's whereabouts.

Peel was in Rome when the King's messenger found him on 25 November. In the absence of railways on the continent, Peel had to bring his family back to Britain by horse-drawn coach, travelling 'over Alps, precipices, and snow, eight nights out of twelve, in the carriage'.[17] Reaching London on 9 December, he accepted the King's commission to form a new government.

While Peel had little choice but to respond to the royal summons, there is no doubt that he privately regretted the King's hasty action. His strategy since the Reform Act had been to stand back and wait for the Whigs to discredit themselves, through the manifestation of internal differences. Now, instead, the indignity of being thrown out of office as the result of a royal coup, and replaced (albeit temporarily) by the soldier-statesman Wellington, was perfectly designed to stimulate the Whigs' historic antagonism towards the monarchy and thereby draw them close together. Even one of their own sympathisers, Thomas Creevey, recognised that 'The Whigs might have died a natural death...had they been let alone', but the manner of their removal from power had changed things completely.[18] In his anxiety to be rid of the Whigs, it appeared, the King had unwittingly forestalled the process of ministerial disintegration and deprived Peel of his best hope for the construction of a viable alternative government.

The King's premature move hampered Peel in other ways, too. It quickly became clear that Lord Stanley, and the other former Whig ministers who had resigned in May, were not prepared to risk their reputations by joining a government tainted, in the public eye, with the 'reactionary' Toryism of the Iron Duke (now Foreign Secretary) and Lord Lyndhurst.[19] This destroyed any chance that Peel might have had of building his government on the broadest possible foundations of parliamentary support, and compelled him to rely solely on the personnel of the Conservative party. A number of posts were therefore given to Ultras, notably Sir Edward Knatchbull, and, as one Whig diarist commented, Peel's ministerial team was characterised by an 'undiluted Toryism'.[20]

Set in this context, we can begin to appreciate the significance of the document known as the 'Tamworth Manifesto'. This was technically an address by Peel to his constituents at Tamworth (on taking office, he was legally required to seek re-election), but it had been approved in advance by the Cabinet and sent to the leading London newspapers for publication on 18 December. Peel's object was to reassure the country as to the intentions of his government, by providing 'a frank exposition of general principles and views'. He was anxious, above all else, to emphasise that he accepted the Reform Act of 1832 as 'a final and irrevocable settlement of a great Constitutional question'. There would be no attempt, in other words, to reverse the changes already made by the Whigs. Indeed, Peel claimed that the administration of which he was the head had its own moderate reforming intentions. No-one in the 1830s would have expected the Prime Minister to produce a detailed programme of policies, and Peel's main aim was to show that he was willing to give a dispassionate consideration to all practical suggestions for the improvement of laws and institutions, and all legitimate demands for the removal of proven abuses. Certain specific issues were touched upon: the inquiry initiated by the Whigs into the working of Municipal Corporations was to be continued, and another inquiry set up to look at the Church of England; the hope was also expressed that nonconformist grievances could be satisfied in such areas as Church rates, tithes, civil marriages and admission to the legal and medical professions. But while Peel professed to be open-minded in his approach to questions of reform, he was equally adamant that he had no wish to see the country convulsed by a 'perpetual vortex of agitation'. The encouragement of reform for reform's sake certainly did not commend itself to the Prime Minister. Through the Tamworth Manifesto, Peel was launching a direct appeal to middle-of-the-road opinion in the country – 'that great and intelligent class of society... which is much less interested in the contentions of party, than in the maintenance of order and the cause of good government' – in the hope of being given a fair trial, and of thus upholding the King's prerogative to choose his own ministers.[21] Thomas Raikes considered the Tamworth address to be 'a manly and sensible document, calculated to inspire confidence in the Country', and Charles Greville noted how it had 'made a prodigious sensation... nobody talks of anything else'.[22]

At the end of December the dissolution of parliament was announced, as everyone expected, and a general election followed in January 1835. If William IV had hoped that by this use of the royal prerogative he might emulate the triumphs of his father, George III, who had granted dissolutions in 1784 and 1807 in order to consolidate the position of his chosen ministers, the result of the 1835 general election was both a disappointment and a serious blow to William's authority. It was true that the Conservatives achieved a remarkable recovery from the nadir of 1832, gaining somewhere in the region of 100 seats in the new House of Commons, but this was still insufficient to counteract the combined Whig/Radical/O'Connellite forces, which looked set to cement their alliance and force their way into office regardless of the King's wishes.

Peel was not in power for long enough to implement any substantial measures of reform, although his government did announce plans to legalise nonconformist marriages and commute English tithes. An important piece of legislative machinery was also set into motion, which produced valuable results after the fall of Peel's ministry and exemplified the spirit of his 'Conservatism'. The Ecclesiastical Commission was a body comprised of senior churchmen and Anglican politicians, including the Prime Minister, whose task was to prepare bills ready for presentation to parliament, tackling the abuses and malpractices which had been shown to be widespread within the Church of England. For some years, the Established Church had been an easy target for radical attack, with publications such as John Wade's *Black Book* exposing some of the grossest examples of personal greed and nepotism. While it was certainly true that some individuals, particularly at the uppermost levels of the Anglican hierarchy, were amassing fortunes through the possession of several lucrative appointments, the other half of the picture was that the unequal distribution of resources meant that many Church livings did not yield an adequate income to support their clergymen. This was one of the reasons why the practice of pluralism had developed, whereby clergymen commonly held more than one Church living, and this inevitably led to the problem of non-residence. It had been found in 1815 that some 40 per cent of parishes in England and Wales did not have a resident vicar, and in a quarter of these there was not even a curate to act as caretaker.[23]

There is a strong sense of horror and indignation in Peel's correspondence of 1834–5 relating to the state of affairs in the Established Church. It seemed to him that the Church was concerned more with providing comfortable employment for 'men of birth' and 'men of learning', than with fulfilling its primary duty of spreading the word of God in every part of the land. The feeble Anglican presence in many of the rapidly expanding industrial towns was largely to blame, in Peel's opinion, for the regrettable progress made in recent decades by the nonconformist sects.[24] He therefore advised the recalcitrant Bishop of Exeter that the Ecclesiastical Commission afforded possibly the last opportunity for the 'true friends' of the Church to assist it by facilitating 'judicious reform'. The object in view was to give 'real stability to the Church in its spiritual character... I believe enlarged political interests will be best promoted by strengthening the hold of the Church of England upon the love and veneration of the community.'[25] Clearly, Peel was implying that unless something was done quickly the question of Church reform might fall into the hands of other politicians, less friendly to the Anglican cause, and perhaps jeopardise the future status of the Church as an Established body. By setting up a permanent machinery which involved the Church of England in initiating plans for its own reform, Peel sought to encourage a greater sense of responsibility amongst Anglican leaders and thereby overcome the vested interests hostile to change. In this way, hopefully, the Church could be shielded from further damaging attacks while helping it to restore its claim to be accepted as a truly national spiritual institution. It gave great satisfaction to Peel that the Ecclesiastical Commission survived the change of government in April 1835, and over the next few years it proceeded to bring forward a series of measures to re-organise Church dioceses and revenues, abolish many sinecures, and combat the evils of pluralism and non-residence.[26]

In the new House of Commons, which assembled at Westminister on 19 February 1835, around 290 of the 658 seats were filled by Conservative members (compared with 150 in 1832), thanks to by-election gains in 1833–4, some defections from the Whig benches, and the advances made at the recent general election. This was obviously not going to be enough to sustain Peel's government, unless it could attract additional support from wavering members of the opposition, or from neutral MPs – of whom there were still a few. It was an ominous sign, however, that a meeting of Whigs, radicals and O'Connellites held at Lichfield House the day before parliament met, had resolved to join in a concerted opposition effort to turn out the Conservative ministry. On the first trial of strength between government and opposition – the election of the Speaker of the House of Commons – the Whigs and their allies succeeded in replacing the Conservative incumbent, Charles Manners Sutton, with their own nominee, James Abercromby. More seriously still, the opposition carried an amendment to the Address, after the King's Speech outlining ministerial plans for the session, by 309 votes to 302, which indicated that the majority of MPs were not prepared to give Peel and his colleagues the fair trial they had requested. Further defeats occurred in the weeks that followed, confirming the inability of ministers to conduct even routine business, and the *coup de grâce* was finally delivered on 7 April when Lord John Russell carried a resolution in favour of lay appropriation of Irish Church revenues, by a margin of twenty-seven votes. Peel resigned the next day.

Some leading Conservatives, including Wellington, had consistently maintained that they were under an obligation to hold on to office for as long as possible, because they still possessed the King's confidence. Peel, on the other hand, concluded that there was no prospect of converting his Commons' minority into a majority, and that his government's position was therefore untenable.[27] In letters to William IV and to Wellington, he deployed various constitutional arguments in support of his view that resignation was unavoidable. Peel warned the King that

the succession of adverse votes suffered by ministers posed a grave
threat to the royal prerogative, as the weakness of the executive meant
that the House of Commons was being allowed to usurp many of the
functions properly performed by the King's ministers. If this were
permitted to continue, it might be impossible for future governments
to regain control over the Commons. Writing to the Duke, Peel was
more blunt about the dangers he saw ahead, arguing that it would be a
mistake for the Conservatives to cling to office, without hope of achieving a Commons' majority, as this would give their opponents 'time to
mature a new Government...independently of the King's consent'. In
other words, a protracted but ultimately futile struggle against the
Whigs and their allies would aggravate the situation by forcing them
to become a more cohesive body – in effect, an organised party – until a
point was finally reached where they were able to impose themselves
upon the King. The Whigs would thus 'virtually command a majority of
the House of Commons', and, once installed in power, they would give
'to the whole world the appearance of having been nominated by the
House of Commons, having been dictated to the King, and of continuing in office independently of his will and control.' If this was allowed to
happen, a disastrous blow would have been delivered against the
authority of the Crown.[28]

No doubt Peel's fears were genuine enough, as far as they went. He
conceived of himself as an 'executive' politician who, when in office,
served the King who had appointed him, not the House of Commons or
a political party. The prospect of an opposition building itself into a
disciplined party, in order to deprive the King of his freedom of choice
and compel him to appoint ministers he did not want, was repugnant to
Peel's principles of political conduct. In the circumstances of 1834–5,
however, it seemed that William IV had no real freedom of choice
anyway. Peel's reluctance to go on fighting to retain office until the last
possible moment, suggests that he was also anxious to extricate himself
from what he must have considered to be a false position. After all, he
had not wanted the King to dismiss the Whigs and install him in their
place; nor was he comfortable with the narrow basis on which he had
been obliged to construct his ministry. During the final days of the Peel
administration, Charles Greville recorded his impression that many of
the old-fashioned 'Tories', with their 'long-cherished maxims of exclusion and ascendancy', were angry with their leader because of his
'Liberal principles and Liberal measures'. This feeling, Greville
believed, was fully reciprocated by Peel, who realised that he was 'not

the Minister for them and they no longer the party for him'. Greville
suspected that Peel was therefore 'anxious to break-up this unmanage-
able force...he probably would rather trust to that increasing feeling
and opinion about himself, which is so apparent among all classes of
politicians, and place him by and by at the head of a party formed upon
Conservative principles and embracing a much wider circle of opinions.'[29] A return to opposition, it seemed, might give Peel the time and
space he needed to fully unfold his Conservative wings.

The Perils of Conservative Opposition, 1835–41

After the failure of his unintended experiment in minority government,
Peel was inclined to bide his time and avoid any precipitate action aimed
at securing an immediate return to office. He was particularly anxious
that William IV should not attempt another coup against the Whig
ministers whom he so transparently detested. Any such move, as Peel
observed to the Duke of Wellington, was bound to end in defeat for the
King, and would inflict yet further damage on the constitutional authority of the Crown.[30]

The future conduct of the House of Lords was a source of similar
concern for the Conservative leader. Now that the Whigs were back in
power, supported by the Radicals and the Irish Repealers, there was a
real danger that the intransigent attitude of the Ultras in the upper
House might set the Lords on a collision course with the House of
Commons – with disastrous consequences for the hereditary chamber.
This was precisely the scenario which confronted Peel in the summer of
1835, when rabid Ultras, such as Lord Lyndhurst, Lord Winchilsea and
the Duke of Newcastle, led the opposition in the upper House to the
government's Municipal Corporations Bill for England and Wales. Peel
had given his assent to this measure, recognising as he did the desir-
ability of establishing an efficient and honest system of local government
to help preserve law and order, especially in the rapidly growing manufacturing towns.[31] Unable to control the Conservative peers, Peel left
London altogether while they proceeded to carry a series of drastic
amendments to the Bill, and he declared that he would accept no
responsibility for what was being done.[32] From his vantage point at
Drayton Manor, Peel expressed alarm that the Lords seemed determined to try to drive ministers out of office. The danger was that

Conservative peers were playing directly into the government's hands, as the Whigs might well be tempted to seize the opportunity to tender their resignations and force on a constitutional crisis. In such an event, it was clear to Peel that 'The Conservative party cannot govern the Country with the present Parliament', and he had no confidence that another dissolution would improve the party's position. The Whigs might therefore be allowed to obtain a fresh mandate from the electorate, and the King would be obliged to take them back for a third time, enabling them to 'confirm their hold on power, and settle their relations to the King'. For this reason, Peel was convinced that there could be 'nothing but an aggravation of evil in fruitless attempts to dispossess the Government of office'.[33] To his immense relief, the Whigs proved willing to make some compromises, when the heavily amended Municipal Corporations Bill returned to the House of Commons, and this provided enough scope for a settlement to be reached.

Addressing a public audience in the City of London, shortly before the crisis over the Municipal Corporations issue erupted, Peel had indicated his willingness to support reasonable measures of reform proposed by the Whig government, and his determination to avoid Conservative alignments with the Radicals or Repealers simply for the purpose of embarrassing ministers.[34] Of course, this represented a renewal of the strategy pursued in 1833–4, of 'governing in opposition' by permitting acceptable reforms to be carried, while helping the Whigs to resist unwelcome pressures from their own allies. The objective was the same, to exacerbate the tensions between front-benchers and back-benchers on the ministerial side in the House of Commons, and so facilitate an eventual internal collapse. For instance, in the early months of 1837 the government was assailed by a series of radical motions in favour of the secret ballot, the abolition of the property qualification for MPs, the repeal of the Septennial Act, and the removal of the bishops from the House of Lords, and on each occasion the Whigs depended on Conservative support for their successful stand against the Radicals.[35] 'Tonight we have Canada', Peel wrote to his friend Croker in April of that year, 'we supporting, the Radicals violently opposing, the Government.' Indeed, it seemed as if 'All the convictions and inclinations of the Government are with their Conservative opponents', although 'Half their actions and all their speeches are with the Radicals.'[36]

The delicate balancing act performed by Peel, as leader of the opposition, is well illustrated by the discussions in January 1836 regarding the advisability of seeking a trial of strength with the government by moving an amendment to the Address at the opening of parliament. Peel was disdainful of the more 'flippant' of his many correspondents on the subject, 'all those who look on a party as a pack of hounds which must have blood', and who therefore looked upon an amendment to the Address as a useful 'bag fox', to provide Conservative MPs with some sport. At the same time, he recognised that aggressive action was sometimes required in order to maintain the morale and enthusiasm of his parliamentary supporters. The question he had to ask himself was exactly what purpose would be served by moving a 'premeditated amendment', on an abstract matter of principle, as distinct from making a specific protest against any contentious statements that happened to be included in the King's Speech. If there was a realistic chance of a 'premeditated amendment' helping to consolidate the Conservatives' alliance with Lord Stanley and his small band of ex-Whig followers, then such a course of action would be perfectly justifiable; but Peel doubted whether Stanley was ready to be drawn in this way. Another tactical difficulty, emphasised by Peel, was that of finding a suitable subject for the 'premeditated amendment'. In his opinion, a declaration of support for the constitutional rights of the House of Lords would be timely, but there was a risk that by ventilating such an issue, when the opposition in the Commons was likely to be defeated, the whole exercise could backfire: 'we may, and probably shall, appear by a voluntary and gratuitous act of our own...[to] put the House of Lords, its privileges and authority, in an actual minority of the House of Commons.'[37]

Consequently, as Peel informed a meeting of Conservative MPs, summoned to his London house on the morning of the day that parliament was due to assemble, no action was going to be taken on the Address. However, this advice was not heeded by the Conservative peers, who obstinately carried an amendment in the upper House on the subject of Irish Municipal Corporations, and an embarrassed Peel felt obliged to follow suit in the Commons. When the division was taken, ministers had a comfortable majority of forty-one, exposing the opposition's lack of preparedness for a fight. Thomas Raikes learned from a London correspondent that 'twelve Tories never came down to the House, and several more disregarded the summons to come from the Country'.[38] This unfortunate episode merely served to confirm Peel's wariness about launching synthetic attacks on the government, purely for the sake of keeping his followers in good spirits.

Despite these occasional setbacks, the sessions of 1836 and early 1837 were encouraging ones, on the whole, for Peel and his friends. The conservative feeling in the country seemed to be gaining in force, no doubt encouraged by the flourishing state of trade and agriculture; there was an evident want of cordiality between the Whigs and their allies; and the cohesion of the opposition was improving, with the recruitment of Stanley and his associates bringing the Conservative numbers in the House of Commons up to almost 300.[39] Peel and Wellington were managing to restrain the more fanatical Conservative peers from launching a suicide attack against the government, and King William appeared to have been persuaded of the merits of self-restraint, avoiding any rash attempt to rid himself of his unwanted ministers. Even a member of the Cabinet, Lord Holland, appreciated that what was happening was that the forces of Conservatism were holding back, and waiting for Whig support to drain away, before they delivered the fatal blow.[40]

Modern research has vindicated Peel's cautious strategy by demonstrating how successful he was in enticing moderate Whig MPs, unhappy with the drift of government policy since the Reform Act, to switch sides and enlist as Conservatives. It is not usually possible to pinpoint a precise moment at which an individual changed his allegiance, as there was no such thing as formal membership of a political party, and an MP might not publicly declare his defection until quite some time after his voting behaviour in the division lobbies suggested that he had done this. Robert Stewart's analysis nevertheless shows that between 1833 and 1837 at least thirty-one MPs who had supported the Reform Act joined with the Conservatives, and only about a dozen of these were connected with Lord Stanley. Another seventeen MPs crossed the floor at some stage during the parliament of 1837–41.[41] Peel would have been entitled to feel that these accessions of parliamentary strength testified to the wisdom of his policy of refraining from violent opposition to the Whig government.

In June 1837, the political situation was transformed by the death of King William. Admittedly, the ensuing general election – required by law – brought further Conservative gains, so that the opposition accounted for around 317 MPs (out of 658), but the Whigs' increasingly precarious parliamentary position was compensated for by another important element in the equation. Whereas it had been well known that the late King detested his ministers, and was only waiting for a suitable moment to dispense with their services, the new monarch, the 18-year-old Queen Victoria, held strongly pro-Whiggish opinions. Indeed, over the next few years she was to display a deep personal attachment to her Prime Minister, Lord Melbourne, which the Whigs were able to exploit for their own advantage. This naturally made Peel's role as leader of the opposition exceptionally awkward. In a memorandum dating from July 1837, surveying his recent problems in conducting a united opposition to the Whigs, Peel had stated that 'Opposition on Conservative principles' was 'almost a contradiction in terms', because 'the recourse to faction, or temporary alliances with extreme opinions for the purposes of faction', was irreconcilable 'with *Conservative* Opposition.'[42] It was going to become even more difficult to square Conservative principles with opposition methods now that it was clear that the monarch had no wish to be rescued from the clutches of her Whig ministers. As Charles Arbuthnot lamented, at the beginning of the 1838 session of parliament, the opposition seemed 'farther than ever' from removing the government:

> They have the Queen with them, heart & soul as it wd appear. Whenever the Radicals propose revolutionary measures we are obliged to support them [the government], & when we press them hard they are sure to be supported by the Radicals.... It is a most grievous state of things. If the late King had [lived] we might have turned them out; but with the young foolish Queen against us we can have but little hope.[43]

The most urgent issue on which the opposition had to determine its course, early in 1838, arose from the government's handling of the rebellion in Canada. Peel and Wellington were instinctively disposed to support the emergency measures, including the suspension of the Canadian constitution, taken by the Whigs in an effort to restore control over the colony. There were warnings from the Conservative party managers, on the other hand, that unless some hostile action was taken by the leadership, many back-benchers were likely to vote for the censure motion put down by a Radical MP, Sir William Molesworth. Peel fully concurred in the views expressed by Stanley and Wellington, who were echoing his own long-held belief that direct opposition attacks on the government were likely to be counter-productive, tending to forestall the process of internal Whig disintegration and making it harder for the Whigs' more moderate adherents to switch their allegiance to the Conservatives in the event of a change of government. But he was also persuaded that something had to be done in order to preserve the opposition's unity. In the event, a meeting of Conservative

MPs at Peel's house resolved to support an amendment to Molesworth's censure motion, pledging opposition co-operation in the measures necessary to suppress the Canadian rebellion, yet blaming ministers for allowing the rebellion to happen in the first place. This was tactically astute, from Peel's point of view, as it enabled him to attack the Whigs, to the satisfaction of his own back-benchers, while remaining safe in the knowledge that the government was sure to survive because Molesworth and his Radical friends could not, with consistency (given their sympathy with the Canadian rebels), vote for the amendment to their original censure motion.[44] The Whigs duly triumphed by a majority of twenty-nine votes, but the Conservatives achieved a strong showing in the division lobby, with only fourteen of their MPs absent without a pair.

All the same, the uncomfortable truth was that Peel had been forced into a show of hostility towards the government against his better judgement. Prior to the 1839 session, he refused to countenance another outright attack on ministers, through an amendment to the Address, and he also rejected the chief whip's advice that he should at least summon MPs to a meeting at his house on the opening day of the session, to explain the current situation to them. Sir Thomas Fremantle, the whip concerned, had argued that a preliminary meeting would help him to secure a good attendance of Conservative members at Westminster, and make it easier to keep his flock under control thereafter, but Peel's frigid response was that MPs ought to be aware of their duty without the need for him to call them together when he had nothing to say.[45] The dangers entailed in Peel's uncommunicative attitude became apparent in March, when sixty-five Conservative back-benchers, evidently working in conjunction with the Ultra peers, staged an open revolt against Peel's leadership by ignoring his advice to support the government's Irish Municipal Corporations Bill (the rebels were already angry because of the way Peel had backed the Whigs' Irish Tithes and Irish Poor Law Bills, during the previous session).[46] This act of defiance seems to have stung Peel into adopting a more aggressive line, and in April, for example, he defended the House of Lords after it had carried a censure of the Whigs' administration in Ireland. Conservative MPs displayed an impressive degree of cohesion when a corresponding motion was introduced in the Commons, with 298 turning up to vote against the government and only seven being absent unpaired. In May, Peel went on to condemn the Whigs for their handling of the crisis in Jamaica, where the constitution had been suspended, regardless of his earlier approval of an identical course of action in the case of

Canada. The glaring inconsistency in Peel's conduct can only be accounted for in terms of his need to be seen to be acting decisively in order to appease his restless back-benchers. His one consolation must have been the thought that, even with a few Radicals joining the Conservatives in the division lobby, it was unlikely that ministers would be defeated. However, while this expectation was correct, in the sense that the government survived by a majority of five votes, the narrowness of their victory provided the harassed and exhausted Whigs with an excuse for submitting their resignations.

On 8 May, Queen Victoria, having been advised by Wellington that the new Prime Minister should be in the House of Commons, summoned Peel to Buckingham Palace. At his audience, according to Peel's memorandum,[47] the Queen immediately made it plain that she regretted the loss of her Whig ministers, and in asking Peel to form a government she expressed her reluctance to grant him a dissolution of parliament. Later in their conversation, Victoria also stated that she must not be asked to cease all communication with Lord Melbourne. These declarations must have set the alarm bells ringing in Peel's mind. He replied that he was willing to do everything in his power to assist his sovereign, and that he would meet the Queen's wishes by attempting to govern with the existing parliament, while reserving the right to request a dissolution if this proved necessary. Peel went on to indicate that it was essential for him to have a mark of the Queen's confidence, in the form of changes to the Royal Household, since many of the most senior positions were held by women relatives of the outgoing Whig ministers. This latter stipulation was presumably intended by Peel as a test of the Queen's commitment, and at a meeting with some of his principal colleagues that evening, he stressed how much importance he attached to obtaining some concessions in this respect. Returning to Buckingham Palace the next day, with a list of proposed ministerial appointments, Peel learned of the Queen's refusal to make any changes at all to the personnel of her Household. In the face of Victoria's obstinacy, and after further consultation with his colleagues, Peel declined the commission to form a government. To the Queen's delight, her beloved Melbourne agreed to resume the premiership.

Peel's motives for refusing to take office, during the so-called 'Bedchamber crisis' of May 1839, are open to different interpretations. A cynical view would be that Peel did not consider the time yet ripe for him to take over the reins of government from the Whigs, and that he deliberately raised the issue of the Queen's Household attendants in the expectation that this would lead to the breakdown of negotiations. It is certainly true that the crisis prompted by the Whigs' resignation was not strictly of Peel's making, as he had never intended to bring down the government over the Jamaica question. On the other hand, we must recognise that the Crown still constituted a potentially negative, obstructive force in the British system of government, making it a legitimate matter of concern for Peel that the wilful and inexperienced young Queen must not be surrounded at Court by Whig ladies. Had Peel undertaken to form a *minority* government, with no guarantee that a dissolution of parliament would be allowed, and without obtaining a clear mark of royal confidence, he risked being undermined by the hostile influence of the Ladies of the Bedchamber, reinforcing the Queen's own prejudices against the Conservatives. The end result might easily have been a humiliating failure for Peel, and a speedy return to office for the Whigs. Peel only asked the Queen to make *some* changes to her Household, not to sweep out the entire staff, and it seems rather unlikely that he could have calculated on his request being rejected in such an uncompromising manner. The balance of probabilities is that Peel did make a genuine attempt to form a government, albeit reluctantly, and that the conditions he tried to lay down were perfectly reasonable, given the Queen's obvious Whiggish sympathies. He may well have felt a quiet sense of relief when he was compelled to abandon the project, but at the same time he must have been conscious of the dilemma facing a Conservative opposition now that its relations with the Crown were so frosty.[48]

From a positive perspective, it was true that Conservative MPs, ably commanded by the chief whip, Fremantle, continued to display their capacity for highly disciplined parliamentary action. In late May 1839, no less than 301 attended to vote for the Conservative candidate for the vacant Speakership of the House of Commons, and only eight could not be accounted for after pairs had been taken into consideration. But Conservative frustration at the sight of their leader's failure to take office also led to increasingly vocal demands, during the autumn recess, for the opposition to engage in systematic warfare against the Whigs in order to drive them from power. An article in the highbrow *Quarterly Review* was critical of Peel's forbearance towards the Whigs, and his apparent contentment to govern in opposition rather than seizing power for his party. Peel's reaction to these complaints provides an excellent illustration of his attitude towards the conduct of politics and government, as well as betraying a somewhat contemptuous view of the

depth of most Conservative MPs' political commitment. Writing to
Charles Arbuthnot early in November, Peel argued that:

> People very much mistake the constitution of the Conservative party
> who suppose that it will be held together under such a system of
> worrying and vexatious tactics as the article recommends. A Radical
> Opposition might pursue it: those might pursue it who wish to cut
> down the prerogatives of the Crown, and to introduce the House of
> Commons into every department of the State, at the expense – and,
> be it remembered, the permanent, everlasting expense – of the
> authority of the Executive. But such a system does not very well
> consort with Conservative principles. Even if it did, it would not be
> long practically acted upon with effect.
>
> When gentlemen complain, as they do now, that the division does
> not take place precisely at the hour which enables them to dine
> comfortably and be down by half-past-ten, they would soon get tired
> of a plan of operations which, to be successfully acted upon, must
> require incessant and general attendance.
>
> After you had deducted the idle, the shuffling, the diners-out, the
> country gentlemen with country occupations, and above all the mod-
> erate and quiet men disliking the principle of a factious Opposition,
> we should find the Conservative ranks pretty well thinned.[49]

Nevertheless, the pressure for hostile action by the opposition was
mounting, and during December the party leaders engaged in a lengthy
correspondence on the question of whether or not to initiate a direct
attack on ministers when parliament met. Wellington was cautious,
believing that the difficulties with the Queen, manifested at the time of
the Bedchamber crisis, presented a formidable obstacle to the construction of a Conservative government on a satisfactory basis. Sir James
Graham, the ex-Whig minister who was now a close confidant of Peel's,
maintained to the contrary that unless positive leadership was shown
there was a risk of the Conservative party becoming fatally demoral-
ised.[50] In the end, Peel acceded to the requests for a more belligerent
strategy, and a motion of no confidence was put down against the
government. To the disappointment of many who attended, however,
Peel's contribution in the debate was comparatively feeble, and seemed
to be concerned as much with defending himself as with criticising the
Whigs, whose main fault was deemed to be their reliance upon open
questions to mask their internal differences over the Corn Laws and the

secret ballot.[51] The government survived by the fairly comfortable margin of twenty-one votes, and though Conservative MPs again made a good showing in the division lobby, the opposition had less success than they had originally hoped for in attracting support from disaffected radicals.

Events during the remainder of the 1840 session of parliament revealed the continuing tensions within the Conservative opposition. Peel and Wellington had never had a great deal in common, personally, other than pride and diffidence, and their relationship was put under renewed strain by differences over the Whigs' Irish Municipal Corporations and Canada Bills. Whereas Peel was inclined to offer a bipartisan support, recognising as he did the advantages of having these troublesome issues settled before the Conservatives assumed the responsibilities of office, Wellington, along with many other peers, wished to reject both of the Bills. Arbuthnot and Graham were kept busy trying to encourage more communication between the two opposition leaders, fearing that the Duke might become totally estranged and refuse to serve in the next Conservative government. As Graham warned Peel, it would be lamentable if, 'on the eve of success, with power almost within our grasp', the difficulties with Wellington were disclosed, for the effect would be to 'destroy the Conservative party, and restore life and vigour to a Government which is now tottering to its fall'.[52] Some personal contact between Peel and the Duke was restored, and the latter finally gave ground on the Canada Bill, confining himself to a speech opposing the ministerial plan but at the same time recommending that it should be allowed to pass. No such concession was forthcoming over the Irish Municipal Corporations Bill, however, and Peel was powerless to prevent this from being completely emasculated by Lords' amendments. Further diplomatic work was required of Arbuthnot and Graham, during the autumn recess, to ensure that there was a better understanding between Peel and Wellington prior to the opening of what proved to be the final session of parliament before the general election.[53]

Happily for Peel and the Conservatives, the government was about to present them with an alternative set of issues on which it was possible to unite with great effect. Responding to the problem of a growing budget deficit, caused by declining revenue from indirect taxes at a time of acute economic depression, the Whigs brought forward proposals to cut the import duties on timber and on foreign (not colonial) sugar. The rationale behind this was that lower tariffs might stimulate the volume of trade and thus increase the tax yield to the Exchequer. It was also announced that a separate measure, the introduction of a fixed duty of eight shillings per quarter on wheat, in place of the sliding scale of 1828, would form an integral part of the new commercial package. The opposition seized upon the sugar duties as the item in the budget offering the best target for attack, believing that they were likely to win support from back-benchers on the ministerial side who were hostile to a plan which benefited foreign sugar producers – many of whom used slave labour – at the expense of colonial growers employing free labour (the slaves having been fully emancipated in 1838). Furthermore, it was predicted that some of the Whig agriculturalists, alarmed by the Corn Law scheme, would be tempted to use the sugar issue as an excuse for joining forces with the opposition.[54] When the division was taken on 18 May 1841, ministers suffered a devastating defeat, by 317 votes to 281, watching fifteen of their own MPs vote with the Conservatives and another eighteen stay away without pairing. A buoyant opposition followed up this triumph with a direct motion of no confidence, maintaining that the Whigs were no longer capable of conducting vital government business. On this occasion, the voting could not have been closer, but in the early hours of 5 June the opposition motion was carried by 302 to 301. Not a single Conservative MP was unaccounted for, whereas eight ministerialists were absent unpaired. As expected, the Whigs subsequently announced that parliament would be dissolved.

Although the Conservatives had finally succeeded in inflicting a mortal wound on Melbourne's government, forcing it to resort to a direct appeal to the electorate which resulted in a great victory for the Conservatives, it is much too simplistic to regard this outcome as the inevitable culmination of an increasingly well-orchestrated opposition campaign waged against the Whigs since 1835. As we have seen, the Conservatives had been beset by serious internal difficulties, up to and including the 1840 session of parliament, and Peel was often ambivalent about the very concept of a Conservative opposition to the ministers of the Crown, especially when it was known that those ministers enjoyed Queen Victoria's full confidence. It had placed a considerable strain on Peel's political principles, in other words, for him to have to act as the leader of the opposition at all, and he had always been reluctant to countenance hostile action merely for the sake of pleasing his supporters. Moreover, during the fateful 1841 session, Peel's leadership was unavoidably identified, to a greater extent than he must have wished, with issues close to the heart of his more unreconstructed back-benchers. A determination to uphold the Corn Laws underpinned the Conservatives' onslaught against the Whig government, even though it was not the direct issue at stake in the critical divisions of May and June. Protectionism served as a perfect unifying cause for Conservatives, after the Whigs obligingly pushed it to the forefront of political debate, but it would later become clear that fundamental differ-ences of opinion existed between Peel and the majority of his party, over the Corn Laws, which the excitement and enthusiasm of 1841 had only temporarily concealed.

Party Organisation and Electoral Recovery

The general elections of 1835, 1837 and 1841 brought about a remark-able transformation in the fortunes of the Conservative party. In the aftermath of the Great Reform Act, many Radicals had confidently predicted the imminent expiration of their political enemies, and some Conservatives had feared that the Radicals were probably right. But the reality was that the opponents of Reform, having once come to terms with the new dispensation, achieved a rapid electoral recovery. Substantial gains were made in 1835, though not enough to keep Peel's government in power; additional gains in 1837 lifted the Conservatives' numbers in the House of Commons well over the 300 mark (roughly double the figure of five years earlier), and in the summer of 1841 the party won a total of 367 seats, giving them a comfortable overall major-ity of more than seventy.

It does not necessarily follow, however, that the Conservative victory at the polls in 1841 should be interpreted as an overwhelming personal endorsement for Peel and the principles he had laid down in his Tam-worth Manifesto of 1834. Undoubtedly, Peel's reputation as a respons-ible, Statesmanlike opposition leader was a valuable political asset for his party, providing reassurance to middle-of-the-road public opinion that the Conservatives could safely be trusted with the government of the country. Yet the party built up by Peel in opposition was not so much a new political entity – despite the widespread adoption of the label 'Conservative' – as the resurrection, in a more perfectly developed form, of the 'Tory party' of professional administrators and country gentlemen which had been evolving in Lord Liverpool's day. The state of disarray resulting from the crises of 1827–32, including the revolt of the Ultras, had only temporarily halted this process of party development. Furthermore, we must not exaggerate Peel's role in encouraging the growth of party organisation during the opposition years. In fact, he was distinctly uncomfortable with the implications for the way politics was conducted, of relying on electoral machinery to assist him into office.

An analysis of the geographical basis of support for the Conservatives in the 1841 general election, makes it clear that the character of Peel's party was not fundamentally different from that of its Tory precursor.[55] The great preponderance of Conservative seats were won in English constituencies, which accounted for 279 out of the party's 367 MPs, and Table 3.1 shows how they were distributed.

Table 3.1   Conservative seats in England, 1841

Counties	124 (out of 144)
Small boroughs (under 1000 voters)	111 (out of 202)
Medium boroughs (1000–2000 voters)	29 (out of 63)
Large boroughs (over 2000 voters)	15 (out of 58)

Conservative support was strongest, then, in the counties and in boroughs with electorates of less than 1000. While it is technically true to say that the forty-four seats won in the medium-sized and large English boroughs were indispensable, giving the party its overall majority in the House of Commons, this ignores the rather obvious point that these constituencies only returned a small proportion of the Conservative total. The party's successes in the larger boroughs tended to be concentrated in the older commercial and financial centres, such as the City of London, Bristol, Liverpool and Hull, but these were not new constituencies and they had often returned Tory MPs prior to the Great Reform Act. Evidence from surviving pollbooks suggests that it was occupational groups such as bankers, merchants, lawyers and other professionals, who were most likely to vote Conservative. By contrast, there was a distinct lack of enthusiasm for the party in the industrial areas: of forty-five English seats covering the major centres of manufacturing, only thirteen were won by Conservatives. Looking beyond England, the Conservatives did well in the Welsh constituencies (twenty-three seats out of a possible twenty-nine), where voting patterns at this time were similar to those in England, and in the Scottish counties, where the party captured twenty out of the thirty seats. However, in overall terms the Conservatives still found themselves in a minority of nine in Scotland, having won just two burgh seats, while in Ireland they were left with a deficit of nineteen, failing to secure a majority even of the county seats.

The outcome of the 1841 general election was a tribute to the resilience of the landowning élite, which had quickly reasserted its influence in many constituencies after the partial and temporary loss of control experienced during the Reform crisis of the early-1830s. That this should have happened is less than surprising when we consider the limitations of the Reform Act, which may have swept away some of the most grotesque cases of borough representation, such as Dunwich and Old Sarum, but still left behind many boroughs with electorates of a few hundred which were largely rural in character. Furthermore, sixty-five of the seats taken from rotten boroughs for the purpose of redistribution were used to provide additional representation for the English counties, and in these constituencies the enfranchisement of £50 tenants-at-will created a new class of agrarian voters who, if not always under the thumb of their landlords, tended in any case to share a similar political outlook – especially on the question of agricultural protection. Thus, parliamentary representation after 1832 was still heavily weighted towards the counties and small boroughs – to put it another way, one-half of the total English borough population lived in the sixteen largest borough constituencies, which returned just thirty-three MPs – and in these circumstances it is hard to see how it could ever have been possible for Peel significantly to alter the character of the Conservative party. Even those ex-Whig MPs who had crossed the floor of the House mostly represented the same sorts of constituencies as their new-found Conservative friends.

If we look at the issues on which Conservative candidates campaigned in the three general elections between 1835 and 1841, there is plentiful support for the view that the party based its appeal mainly on the defence of traditional interests and institutions. In 1835 and 1837 the cry of 'the Church in danger' proved to be a potent weapon for the Conservatives, enabling them to attract moderate voters alarmed by the allegedly extremist propensities of the Whig/Radical/Nonconformist/O'Connellite governing alliance. The Whigs, it was claimed, were vulnerable to pressure from their allies, whose support they needed in order to remain in power, and this was leading them to adopt measures inimical to the Established Churches of England and Ireland, such as the abolition of Church Rates (a bill for this was introduced in 1837, but failed to pass) and the repeated attempts to assert the principle of lay appropriation of Irish Church revenues. There was a strong anti-Catholic flavour to the

Conservative attacks on the government for its connection with O'Connell and the Irish Repealers. Peel himself, in his rare public addresses at Glasgow (January 1837) and London (May 1838), confirmed that the *raison d'être* of the Conservative party was to uphold the settled institutions of the country, including the Protestant Churches and that great bulwark against insidious Whig legislation – the House of Lords.[56] The growing confidence of the Church of England, as the political reaction against the Whig government set in, is demonstrated by its successful campaign in 1839–40, using petitions and meetings, to compel ministers to abandon their plan for reform of the system of education grants, which if implemented would have directed State money away from Anglican schools and more towards nonconformist schools.[57]

By 1841, the Whigs' reforming energies were so enfeebled that the Church no longer seemed to be in any imminent danger. The Melbourne government's proposal to introduce a low, fixed duty on wheat, however, provided Conservative candidates at the general election with an ideal war-cry. Agricultural protection, an issue which united the interests of landowners and farmers, naturally dominated the county contests, but in many small and medium-sized boroughs, too, the maintenance of the Corn Laws was of paramount concern. In Essex, all ten borough and county seats were won by advocates of protectionism, one of whom was an ex-Whig. The electors of Canterbury were warned by the *Kentish Gazette* that the Whigs' budget plans, involving reductions in the duties on timber and sugar as well as wheat, were certain to 'overthrow the existing order of society, to trample down the agriculturalist and the farm labourer, and to pave the way for the downfall and destruction of all those great mercantile and commercial institutions by which the magnificence and superiority of Great Britain are maintained.'[58] Meanwhile, in certain northern industrial towns such as Blackburn, the Conservatives were arguing that the ruination of British agriculture, arising from the loss of protective tariffs, would lead to the urban labour markets being flooded with unemployed farm labourers, whose competition for jobs would force down wage rates.

Improvements had certainly been made to the Conservatives' organisational machinery, which contributed to the party's electoral revival, although it would be far beyond the scope of the available evidence to try to measure this contribution. It is probably fair to assume that party organisation played a valuable subsidiary role, enabling the Conservatives to capitalise on the shift of public opinion away from the Whigs after the Reform Act. Peel's direct involvement in organisational matters was minimal, as was only to be expected of an early nineteenth century parliamentary leader, and the initiative in the 1830s came from men with a previous track-record in the work of party management. Joseph Planta, William Holmes and Charles Arbuthnot formed the nucleus of the so-called 'Charles Street Gang', named after the address of the office they had established at the end of 1830, from which whips' notes were sent out to MPs and attempts made to manipulate the press. The Charles Street Gang were instrumental in founding the Carlton Club, in 1832, which quickly became recognised as the Conservative party's headquarters. In addition to providing a social and dining venue for MPs, the Carlton housed the *ad hoc* general election committees formed in 1832 and 1835. Shortly after the 1835 election and the fall of Peel's minority government, Francis Bonham persuaded the Conservative leader that a committee needed to be kept up on a permanent footing, and he thereupon became (in effect) the party's first full-time election agent. The functions of Bonham's committee were confined, in practice, mainly to gathering information from the various localities, for the guidance of the national leaders, and to disseminating information and advice to the constituencies, suggesting suitable candidates for constituencies in search of them, and providing modest subsidies to deserving candidates from a small, secret election fund. Bonham and his associates could hardly have expected to do much more, since any attempt at direct interference in constituency arrangements was sure to be deeply resented by local landowners and other activists accustomed to financing and controlling their own local affairs.[59]

Developments in party organisation at the constituency level inevitably counted for more than the tentative efforts of the central election committee. The impetus for change came from the new requirement, laid down by the Reform Act, that a register of electors must be compiled in each constituency and updated annually. It therefore made sense for local Conservatives to form what were, essentially, Registration Associations, employing a solicitor to conduct the annual battle over who should or should not be on the register. Care needed to be taken to ensure that the names of Conservative supporters were placed and retained on the electoral roll, while challenging the eligibility of known opponents. Associations of this kind emerged in many of the boroughs and also a few counties, during the 1830s, although it is impossible to state exactly how many there were.[60]

Peel's appreciation of the value of registration work at the local level, and of its long-term implications for the conduct of politics and government at the centre, is revealed in a letter to Arbuthnot dating from November 1839:

> The Reform Bill has made a change in the position of parties, and in the practical working of public affairs, which the author of it did not anticipate.
>
> There is a perfectly new element of political power – namely, the registration of voters, a more powerful one than either the sovereign or the House of Commons.
>
> That party is the strongest in point of fact which has the existing registration in its favour. It is a dormant instrument, but a most powerful one, in its tacit and preventive operation.
>
> What a check it is at this moment upon the efficiency and influence of the existing Government, backed as it is by all the favour and private goodwill of the Crown, and by a small majority of the House of Commons. It meets them every day, and at every hour. Of what use is the prerogative of dissolution to the Crown, with an unfavourable registry, and the fact of its being unfavourable known to all the world? The menace of dissolution is only laughed at.
>
> Then it is almost impossible to make any promotion, or vacate any office, for fear of sustaining a defeat.
>
> The registration will govern the disposal of offices, and determine the policy of party attacks; and the power of this new element will go on increasing, as its secret strength becomes better known, and is more fully developed. We shall soon have, I have no doubt, a regular systematic organisation of it. Where this is to end I know not, but substantial power will be in the Registry Courts, and there the contest will be determined.[61]

In the published edition of Peel's correspondence, this item is mistakenly attributed to the year 1838. Its true date is of some significance, for it means that Peel was writing *after* the parliamentary session in which the Bedchamber crisis had occurred. This suggests that Peel was being drawn, however reluctantly, towards the conclusion pressed upon him and others by Sir James Graham, that the hostility displayed towards the opposition by Queen Victoria, and her obvious desire to keep the Whigs in office, meant that the only way in which the Conservatives could now expect to remove the government was by winning a general election and compelling the Queen to take them as her ministers. Graham admitted that this decidedly un-Conservative strategy was a 'fearful one', but he could 'see no other means so safe or constitutional of bringing back the Crown to an accordance with the aristocracy and with . . . the elective body as now constituted'.[62] It was for this reason that Graham strongly supported the call for a motion of no confidence to be put down against the Whigs, when the 1840 session opened, as he wanted to defeat the government and force a dissolution of parliament. He presented this course of action to Peel as 'an honest effort to save the Crown against its will, and to avert the evils of the headlong course which hurries us to ruin'.[63]

The no confidence motion of January 1840 did not achieve its object- ive, as we have already seen, but it was a similar line of attack which brought about the dissolution of parliament in the summer of 1841, and thus paved the way for the Conservatives' decisive general election victory. Peel's old friend Croker, the editor of the *Quarterly Review*, in a letter that is often quoted by historians, remarked that 'the elections are wonderful, and the curiosity is that all turns on the name of Sir Robert Peel. 'Tis the first time that I remember in our history that the people have chosen the first Minister for the Sovereign.'[64] Obviously there was an element of sycophantic exaggeration in Croker's claim that the con- test had revolved around Peel's personal reputation, important though this must have been, but there was an uncomfortable truth that Peel, as the acknowledged leader of the Conservative party, had virtually been chosen as Prime Minister by the electorate. Ironically, Peel's accession to office in 1841 was achieved through means that ran contrary to his frequently expressed 'executive' ideal of government, according to which ministers were regarded as servants of the Crown, and custodians of the national interest, rather than as representatives of an elected parliamentary majority. This contradiction between Peel's theory of government and the reality of the circumstances which had placed him in power, was to make itself conspicuously apparent in the years that followed.

4

PRIME MINISTER, 1841–6

Peel's Government

When the new parliament assembled at Westminster on 19 August 1841, Lord Melbourne and the Whigs were still in office despite their recent general election defeat. In the eyes of the British Constitution, the Prime Minister was not appointed directly by the electorate, but was chosen by the monarch. Of course, it was necessary in practice for the monarch to give his or her confidence to someone capable of commanding majority support in the House of Commons, and the development of more highly organised political parties during the 1830s had effectively restricted the monarch's freedom of choice. Nevertheless, the result of the 1841 general election was unique in the way that it had converted a Commons' majority (on paper at least) for the governing party into a majority for the opposition party. This had never happened before, and it would not happen again until 1874. In these unprecedented circumstances, therefore, the Conservatives were obliged to carry an amendment to the Address, expressing a want of confidence in ministers, before the Whigs could properly tender their resignations. Melbourne advised the dismayed Queen Victoria that he and his colleagues were no longer able to conduct the government of the country with efficiency, and on 30 August Peel was duly invited to form a new administration.

The composition of Peel's Cabinet inevitably reflected his need to achieve a balance between the various sections of the Conservative party. Crucially for the new Prime Minister, the Duke of Wellington agreed to serve as Minister without Portfolio: increasingly deaf and somnolent as the Duke was becoming, his immense personal prestige made him an indispensable asset to the government. Lord Aberdeen took on the post of Foreign Secretary which the Duke had held in the minority administration of 1834–5. The retention of Lord Lyndhurst and Sir Edward Knatchbull from that earlier government provided some representation for the Ultra strand of opinion within the party, while the appointment of the Duke of Buckingham (formerly Lord Chandos), popularly regarded as the 'farmers' friend', was a calculated move to please the agricultural interest. On the other hand, key posts were given to two recent recruits from the Whigs, Lord Stanley becoming Secretary of State for War and the Colonies, and Sir James Graham being selected as Home Secretary. Lord Ripon (formerly Lord Goderich, formerly Frederick Robinson), also joined the government as President of the Board of Trade. Taking an overall view of Peel's Cabinet team, the most striking fact is that it was an almost entirely aristocratic body. Of the fourteen Cabinet ministers, eight were peers (including two dukes and three earls), Stanley was the heir to an earldom, and four others were baronets. Henry Goulburn, the Chancellor of the Exchequer, who owned property in the West Indies, was the only untitled member of the Cabinet, although he did have aristocratic connections through his mother and his wife.

At the lower levels of the government, Peel was nurturing the talents of a number of the Conservative party's brightest young men. The most important of these proved to be Lord Lincoln, Sidney Herbert and W. E. Gladstone, all of whom were Oxford educated and had been given their first brief taste of office in 1834–5. They were appointed to the junior ranks again in 1841, along with newcomers such as Lord Dalhousie, Lord Canning and Lord Eliot. Gladstone was the first to be promoted to the Cabinet, in 1843, but Lincoln, Herbert and Dalhousie attained this distinction in 1845. Another Oxford man of subsequent political eminence, Edward Cardwell, had been made a junior minister by the latter date. In the company of his protégés, who were 20–25 years younger than himself, Peel displayed a warm affection and a paternal concern which contrasted surprisingly with the cold and remote personality known to most of his contemporaries. There is an obvious similarity, in this respect, between Peel and Pitt: both leaders found it easier to relax their manner when dealing with much younger men, whom they sought to train for future high office, imbuing them with their own lofty principles of administration. In return, naturally enough, the chosen disciples became personally devoted to their political mentors.[1]

It was one of Peel's protégés, Gladstone, who identified the salient characteristic of his master's style of leadership – namely, the desire to control what was being done in every department of State. As he had shown in the past, Peel found it difficult to delegate responsibility to others, and this habit now led him to assume an impossibly onerous burden of work, with unfortunate long-term consequences. In February 1842 Gladstone recorded Sir James Graham's remark that ' "The pressure upon him [Peel] is immense – we never had a Minister who was so truly a First Minister as he is: he makes himself felt in every department and is really cognisant of the affairs of each." '[2] This was particularly true of business relating to the Treasury, where Goulburn was nominally the Chancellor of the Exchequer, but in reality it was Peel who devised the budgets and presented them to parliament. Irish affairs, too, occupied a great deal of the Prime Minister's attention, and he always worked closely in this area with the relevant Cabinet minister, Graham. Their task was made more burdensome by the political differences between the Lord Lieutenant in Dublin, Lord de Grey, whose sympathies were narrowly Protestant, and the more reformist-minded Chief Secretary, Lord Eliot. An intolerable situation thus developed in which, as Peel observed to Graham, 'We are invited, not only to govern Ireland in details, but to solve the difficulties arising from the discrepancies of opinion of those on the spot.'[3]

Close supervision from London of the administration of India was quite impracticable, given the slowness of communications between the two countries (messages took several weeks to reach their destination), but the erratic conduct of the Governor General, Lord Ellenborough, whose expansionist ambitions resulted in the annexation of Sind in 1843, meant that the home government was given considerable trouble. Peel and the Cabinet minister responsible for India, the President of the Board of Control, were involved in the attempts to curb Ellenborough, and to handle the problems created by the deteriorating relations between the Governor General and the Directors of the East India Company in London. Eventually, in 1844, arrangements had to be made for Ellenborough's re-call. Meantime, in the field of foreign policy, Peel exercised a close scutiny over Lord Aberdeen's work, often amending the drafts of despatches before they were sent to British ambassadors abroad. Indeed, Peel sometimes found it necessary to counter the pacific and conciliatory disposition of his Foreign Secretary, believing as he did in a more robust assertion of Britain's interests – especially in any dealings with France. Peel's suspicion of French intentions also prompted him to act decisively when calls were made for increased expenditure on the navy and on coastal fortifications. Consequently, during the summer of 1845, he was immersed in the discussions and correspondence regarding these and other military preparations, taking the work largely out of the hands of the relevant ministers.[4]

Before the 1842 session of parliament had ended, Peel was already feeling the effects of what he described to Lord Ashley as the 'constant unvarying demand upon sixteen or seventeen hours of the twenty-four for months together'.[5] On Christmas day of that year, he celebrated by spending six hours writing letters. Privately, he continued to complain about an excessive workload which involved not only dealing with administrative matters in the various government departments, but also some eight or nine hours of attendance each day as Leader of the House of Commons, when parliament was sitting.[6] Peel's burden of labour in the Commons was far heavier than it might have been owing to the fact that so many senior Cabinet ministers sat in the upper House. By the summer of 1845, he told Gladstone that he was suffering from brain fatigue – 'a physical sensation'[7] – and he excused his failure to communicate as regularly as he ought, with the Duke of Wellington, in the following terms:

> where are the means during the session of Parliament? The fact is that the state of public business during a session of Parliament is becoming in many ways a matter of most serious concern. I defy the Minister of this Country to perform properly the duties of his office – to read all that he ought to read, including the whole foreign correspondence, to keep up the constant communication which he must keep up with the Queen and the PRINCE – to see all whom he ought to see – to superintend the grant of honours and the disposal of civil and ecclesiastical patronage – to write with his own hand to every person of note who chooses to write to him – to be prepared for every debate including the most trumpery concerns: to do all these indispensable things – and also sit in the House of Commons eight hours a day for 118 days.
>
> It is impossible for me not to feel that the duties are incompatible and above all human strength, at least above mine.[8]

Shortly after leaving office, in 1846, Peel confided to Graham and Gladstone that his physical symptoms had become so bad, during the final months of his premiership, that he would have found it impossible to continue for much longer anyway. It appears that he had damaged his ears while firing a gun, many years before, and overwork made the noises and pain in his head almost unbearable at times. The pressure was only relieved by frequent nose-bleeds.[9] Clearly, statements made after the downfall of his government cannot automatically be accepted as reliable indicators of his real intentions when he was still in office, and it is possible that they were influenced by feelings of frustration and bitterness at the hostility displayed towards him by his own party. But there is little doubt that Peel's physical resources were being exhausted by the inexorable pressures associated with the premiership, and the effect was to make him increasingly careless of the opinions of ordinary Conservative MPs about his policies, an attitude which helped to bring about the disastrous schism in the party. Regarding Peel's position after 1846, it can be suggested that, quite apart from his sense of alienation from the bulk of the Conservative party, there were more purely physical reasons for his declared intention never to take office again.

The Queen's Minister

Peel's letter to Arbuthnot, cited above, mentioned the need to maintain regular communication with 'the Queen and the PRINCE' as one of the many time-absorbing responsibilities of his position. This, at least, was a task from which he derived considerable personal satisfaction. The influence of Victoria's husband, Prince Albert of Saxe-Coburg-Gotha (they married in 1840), enabled Peel to establish a far more cordial relationship with the Crown than could have been anticipated after the Bedchamber crisis. In the earnest young Prince, Peel found an invaluable ally who shared his own high ideals concerning the conduct of government.

In May 1841, with Melbourne's government evidently nearing its end, Albert had sent his private secretary as an intermediary to inform Peel that, in the event of the Conservatives taking office, he would be anxious to avoid a repetition of the difficulties over the Ladies of the Bedchamber.[10] This gesture obviously helped to place matters on a better footing, and when Peel's government was formed, three of the most senior Whig ladies, the Duchess of Bedford, the Duchess of Sutherland and Lady Normanby, retired voluntarily. Peel was delighted to find himself being 'met by her Majesty in a very fair and considerate spirit', in the business of making new Household appointments.[11] The Queen was similarly gratified by Peel's suggestion that her husband should become chairman of the Royal Commission on fine arts, which not only provided the Prince with interesting employment but also helped him to become better acquainted with many of the leading figures in British public life.[12] Initially, there were still some problems arising from Victoria's emotional reliance upon Melbourne, and her desire to maintain private contact with her former Prime Minister, but Melbourne's influence soon diminished as Albert took on the role of his wife's advisor and (effectively) private secretary. Within a few months, Peel was expressing his pleasure at the 'great kindness' shown to him by the Queen, as well as the 'perfect fidelity and honour' with which she acted. He was particularly impressed by Victoria's 'scrupulous and most punctual discharge of every public duty', and her 'exact understanding of the relation of a Constitutional Sovereign to her advisors'.[13] When a deranged gunman made an assassination attempt on the Queen, in July 1842, Peel reportedly burst into tears on arriving to find that his royal mistress was safe.[14]

Many more details can be given which illustrate the growing personal attachment between the Prime Minister and the royal couple. Accompanying Victoria and Albert on a visit to Scotland, in the summer of 1842, Peel reported with satisfaction that they had been greeted with displays of loyalty and good humour.[15] Shortly before Christmas 1843, the Queen and the Prince paid a private visit to Peel at Drayton Manor, which, as Albert noted, 'made the Premier very happy, and is calculated to strengthen his position'.[16] Victoria subsequently agreed to be the godmother of one of Peel's grandsons. The success of State visits by the King and Queen of France, and the Tsar of Russia, in 1844, were flatteringly described by Peel as 'signal proofs of the extent to which the interests and welfare of a great empire may be promoted by the personal character of its ruler'.[17] And it was the Prime Minister who recommended Osborne House, on the Isle of Wight, as a suitable royal retreat not too distant from London. In a typical specimen of his correspondence, dating from March 1845, Peel gushingly declared himself to be 'a true and faithful servant of your Majesty', who was dedicated to 'the maintenance of the honour and just prerogatives of the Crown, and the advancement of the public welfare'.[18] There was at least one Cabinet colleague, Lord Stanley, who considered that Peel devoted rather too much of his time to 'waiting on the Queen'.[19]

The quality that Peel found so admirable in Albert, apart from his fine private character, was the Prince's determination to use his influence over Victoria in order to enhance the personal and political prestige of the monarchy. Albert, in turn, was being guided by the advice of his old tutor, Baron Stockmar, and, behind him, of King Leopold of the Belgians, who was the uncle of both Albert and Victoria. Their belief was that it was essential for the Queen to be instructed in the importance of acting as a truly impartial, constitutional monarch, keeping herself above the political fray and avoiding identification with any particular party leader. In other words, she must not repeat the mistake that she had made before her marriage – of appearing to be a partisan supporter of Melbourne and his Whig government. Leopold and Stockmar also emphasised the need to raise the moral character of the Crown (quite apart from the scandalous conduct of Victoria's uncles, George IV and William IV, her own Court, prior to her marriage, had had a rather sordid reputation attached to it), through a strict adherence to truth and fidelity, 'high thoughts and noble purposes'.[20] The carefully cultivated public image of Victoria and Albert's idyllic family life, with their burgeoning offspring, was to be of immense value in this respect. By March 1845, Albert's report to Stockmar on a recent interview with the Prime Minister revealed that 'Peel regards my present position as extremely good, and thinks that, all in all, Monarchy never stood so well. He says, that despite the encroachments of democracy, "there was something (considering the sex of the Sovereign, the private character of the family &c) in the position, that worked strongly on the feelings of the nation".'[21]

Like Albert, Leopold and Stockmar, Peel recognised that a constitutional monarchy, elevated in the affections of the people and commanding the respect of politicians of all parties, still had an important role to play in the British system of government. Several years earlier, at the time of William IV's death, Peel had written a letter to Croker, the editor of the *Quarterly Review*, in which he was dismissive of the constitutional theory that the monarch's opinions were wholly subjugated to the wishes of his or her ministers. As he assured Croker, 'this, like a thousand other theories, is at variance with the fact. The personal character of the Sovereign...has an immense practical effect...his influence, though dormant and unseen, may be very powerful.' The King, according to Peel (his letter consistently used the masculine case), had one great advantage over his ministers, namely, that he was permanent whereas they were only temporarily in place; after ruling for a decade, therefore, the King ought to know more about the workings of government than anyone else. Consequently, 'He is the centre towards which all business gravitates.' George III was an excellent case in point: the knowledge of his opinions, on Catholic Emancipation and other issues, had materially influenced the conduct of politicians. In Peel's view, the presence of an experienced constitutional monarch was essential for the true interests of the country, because he provided 'so much ballast keeping the vessel of the State steady in her course, counteracting the levity of popular Ministers, of orators forced by oratory into public councils, the blasts of Democratic passions, the groundswell of discontent'.[22]

The practical relevance of this discussion of the political role of the Crown is that it helps us to understand Peel's philosophy of government. His warm relationship with Victoria and Albert reinforced Peel's instinctively 'executive' approach to the responsibilities of high office; that is to say, he perceived himself to be the servant of the Crown, devoted to furthering the interests of the whole nation, rather than the agent of a selfish, partisan majority in the House of Commons. He had made this view ominously clear during the parliamentary debate which forced the resignation of Melbourne's government, and the following month, with his own party freshly installed in power, he repeated his intention never to hold office by a 'servile tenure which would compel me to be the instrument of carrying other men's opinions into effect'. Conservative MPs, he warned, 'confer on me no personal obligation in having placed me in this office'.[23] It was precisely this Statesmanly disinterestedness – Peel's determination to pursue an independent course for the sake of the country, even if it made him unpopular with his own party – which encouraged Victoria and Albert to place so much confidence in their Prime Minister.[24] Accordingly, they were strongly supportive of the policies he chose to adopt. In the case of the income tax, introduced in 1842, they not only gave their approval but indicated that they were prepared to be made liable to it themselves; Peel's plan for the Maynooth grant in 1845, was, the Queen declared, 'so great and good a one, that people must open their eyes, and will not oppose it'; and, when Peel finally resolved to do away with the Corn Laws, Victoria expressed her appreciation of Sir Robert's 'high-minded conduct, courage and loyalty, which ... cannot fail to meet with success, and the ultimate grateful acknowledgement on the part of the Country'.[25]

As we shall see, Peel's reluctance to allow his policies in government to be shaped by the interests and prejudices of the Conservative party, despite the fact that he owed his position as Prime Minister to the support of the Conservative majority in the House of Commons, eventually led to a catastrophic schism in 1846. There proved to be an unbridgeable gap between Peel's high-minded theory of his constitutional role, and the awkward reality that party allegiances, and party commitments, were coming to play an indispensable part in the creation and maintenance of governments. Increasingly, Peel would be provoked into displaying the professional administrator's impatience and contempt for the ignorance and amateurishness of rank-and-file Conservatives whose votes he needed: 'How can those, who spend their time in hunting and shooting and eating and drinking, know what were the motives of those who are responsible for the public security, who have access to the best information, and have no other object under Heaven but to provide against danger, and consult the general interests of all classes?'[26] In the summer of 1841, however, these troubles were still some way in the future, and to an open-minded Whig observer, such as Charles Greville, it seemed that if Peel was true to his declared intentions, and governed upon 'liberal and popular principles', for the good of the whole nation, he might yet succeed in reconciling 'Conservatism with Reform' and thereby prove himself to be a great minister.[27]

The Condition of England

It quickly became clear that Peel's objective was indeed to show that Conservatism and reform were not incompatible. Rooted as it was in the 'liberal' Tory practices of the 1820s, as well as in his 'executive' notions of government, Peel's Conservatism was never merely a defensive strategy, content to react against threats to cherished national institutions if and when they arose. From the Prime Minister's perspective, the safety of such institutions was best secured through the pursuit of active and constructive policies, designed to seize the initiative on behalf of those forces committed to the existing social order.

The immediate practical issue confronting Peel and his colleagues, on their accession to office, was how to deal with the persistent budgetary deficits which had blighted the last years of Whig rule. Since 1837–8, government expenditure had regularly exceeded revenue from taxation, and in 1840–1 the deficit reached £1,851,000. For the year ending 5 April 1842, Peel calculated that total expenditure, standing at almost exactly £50 million (approximately £30 million of which went on servicing the national debt, and £15 million was for the armed forces), meant an even worse deficit of around £2,350,000, and in the following year this was going to reach £2,469,000, even before the exceptional costs of the China and Afghan wars were taken into account. The aggregate budgetary deficit for the six year period 1837–43 was therefore set to exceed £10 million, equivalent to one-fifth of one year's spending.

These deficits were a symptom of the depressed state of the British economy in the late 1830s and early 1840s. With over 80 per cent of government revenue deriving from customs and excise duties, a sharp drop in the level of trading activity in the country inevitably affected tax receipts to the Exchequer. It is impossible to measure the depth of the depression in terms of unemployment figures, but conditions in the manufacturing towns were certainly at their worst since the depression of the immediate post-war period, and 1842 may well have been the worst year in the whole of the nineteenth century to be an industrial worker. Unfortunately, the cyclical downturn in the manufacturing sector was greatly exacerbated by a succession of bad harvests, due to the weather, which meant that bread prices were kept high. From the government's point of view, the problem was not simply one of lost revenue, but of the social and political unrest generated by the dire state of the economy. Indeed, it was around this time that the term 'the condition of England question' came into fashion amongst the thinking classes. The late 1830s had witnessed a resurgence of agitation for radical reform, in the shape of the Chartist movement, with its demands for universal manhood suffrage and other measures designed to make parliament democratically accountable. Chartist activity reached its peak in 1842, and Peel and the Home Secretary, Graham, were obliged to remain in London for much of the hot summer co-ordinating the steps being taken at the local level to deal with possible outbreaks of working-class violence. Perhaps the greater political threat to the government, however, came from the Manchester-based Anti-Corn Law League's campaign for the abolition of agricultural protection. This organisation, founded in 1839, received much of its financial backing from factory owners in the cotton textile districts of Lancashire, and it articulated a 'middle-class' sense of grievance against a political establishment allegedly committed to protecting the selfish interests of the aristocratic and landed élite. The ability of the League and its supporters to wield influence through the *existing* electoral system – at the 1841 general election, Anti-Corn Law League candidates won seats at Manchester, Stockport and Walsall, and there was obvious potential for future gains – as well as by conventional pressure group methods, suggested that they presented a long-term challenge to the political establishment which could not easily be ignored.[28]

It is evident from Peel's private correspondence, during the summer and autumn of 1841, that he already had a clear idea of how he intended to tackle the growing budget deficit and the economic problems which had brought it about.[29] There was no point in simply raising the level of indirect taxes still further: the Whigs had resorted to this in 1840, but the worsening trade depression meant that government revenue did not increase as a result. A far better approach was the one tentatively adopted by the Whigs in 1841, but which Peel believed had to be pursued in a more systematic way, in other words, the *reduction* of indirect taxes in order to cut the cost of raw materials for industry and of foodstuffs and other items for the consumer. Such a policy, according to advocates of Free Trade like Joseph Hume, the Radical MP who chaired a commission of inquiry into tariffs in 1840, would help to stimulate production and consumption, and thus lead to a recovery of government revenues. However, these desirable effects were bound to take some years to work their way through, and, in the short-term, cuts in tariffs would cause the budget deficit to widen even further. Peel concluded that, if an experiment in Free Trade was to be attempted, he had no alternative but to introduce a temporary income tax so as to raise additional revenue and cover the deficit. In embracing these fiscal and commercial solutions to the country's predicament, it should be noted that Peel was reverting to ideas which he had advocated as a member of Wellington's government, early in 1830, and which were inspired by Huskisson's 'liberal' tariff reforms of the mid-1820s (see Chapter 2). But while the policy prescription was not new, the introduction of an income tax in peacetime remained politically controversial, and was something that the Whigs had never dared to propose.

Peel detailed his plans to the House of Commons in a financial statement on 11 March 1842.[30] An income tax was to be levied at the rate of 7d (3p) in the pound on incomes of over £150 (well above the level of earnings of manual workers), for an initial period of three years, raising an estimated £3.7 millions for the Exchequer. This, along with certain other imposts, would provide a substantial budget surplus and thus facilitate a major overhaul of the complex tariff structure. Of the 1200 or so dutiable items, Peel proposed to lower the level of tax on around 750 – 'all those articles which enter into manufactures as chief constituent materials' – at a cost of £270,000 in lost revenue. The general principle was that imported raw materials should be taxed at no more than 5 per cent, partly manufactured items at no more than 12 per cent, and fully manufactured items at no more than 20 per cent. In addition, the duty on coffee was reduced, at a loss to the Exchequer of £171,000, and, most importantly of all, £600,000 was sacrificed by cutting the duties on timber. All export duties on manufactured goods were to be completely abolished. 'The real way', Peel advised the House, 'in which we can benefit the working and manufacturing classes is, unquestionably, by removing the burden that presses on the springs of manufactures and commerce.' He therefore urged MPs to rise to the crisis facing the country by supporting proposals which the government had brought forward in the belief that they were 'conducive to the public welfare'.

Another key component in Peel's general scheme for reforming Britain's tariff system had been announced to the House of Commons a month earlier. The sliding scale of import duties on wheat and other cereals (the Corn Laws), introduced in 1828, had manifestly failed in its object of promoting greater price stability – as the Anti-Corn Law League's agitation testified. And though the Conservative party, when in opposition, had asserted the principle of protection for agriculture in the most uncompromising terms, it was noticeable that Peel never committed himself to the specific defence of the existing arrangements. Internal discussions within the new government, in the autumn of 1841, reveal that Peel was convinced the sliding scale provided an excessive level of protection for British agricultural producers.[31] Working on the basis that a domestic price of 56 shillings for a quarter bushel of wheat ought to ensure an adequate remuneration for farmers (the average price had been 67s 2d, during the period 1838–40, thanks in part to the tariff), Peel decided that it was possible to revise substantially downwards the duty imposed at each step on the scale without harming agrarian interests. If anything, Peel erred on the side of generosity in drawing up his new sliding scale: when the domestic price of wheat stood at 56s, for example, the duty would be 16s even though his own calculations suggested that 11s should suffice to protect British farmers from being undercut by cheaper foreign produce. Nevertheless, Peel's adjustment of the sliding scale did offer significant reductions in the amount of protection afforded to home producers, so that when wheat was priced at between 59s and 60s per quarter, for instance, the import duty payable was 13s instead of 27s 8d. Presenting his plan to MPs, in February 1842, Peel argued that it would achieve greater price stability while at the same time maintaining a reasonable level of protection for farmers (after all, it was acknowledged that the country must not become over-dependent on foreign supplies of food, for strategic reasons). The revised sliding scale was reportedly greeted with cold indifference by most Conservative back-benchers, and the Duke of Buckingham resigned from the Cabinet in protest, but it seemed to one Conservative observer that, on the whole, Peel's proposal was 'of a lenient nature, not likely to frighten the agriculturalists'.[32]

From a general political perspective, Peel was in no doubt that his package of Free Trade reforms was necessary for the sake of social stability. In a letter to Croker, he expressed the opinion that 'property ... must submit to taxation, in order to release industry and the millions from it; [and] that the doing so voluntarily and with a good grace, will be a cheap purchase of future security'. Throughout the 1840s, in fact, Peel's policies were informed by the belief that the survival of the ruling elite depended on his ability to cultivate public confidence in the fairness and impartiality of the nation's system of government. Following in the footsteps of Pitt the Younger, Peel sought to convince the British people that the State which ruled over them was supremely neutral and virtuous, inspired by principles of the strictest probity and frugality, and that it disdained to promote the selfish interests of sectional groups. In this way, the attacks routinely made by demagogic radicals on government 'extravagance', and the alleged parasitism of the elite which controlled it, could be easily deflected. It is important to recognise that, in the political and intellectual climate of early Victorian Britain, a system of government that was perceived as being fair and, above all, cheap, was likely to commend itself to all sections of society, as there was little desire for widespread State interference in peoples' lives. Minimal government was thought to be the best kind of government, and it was automatically equated with 'progressive' political development.[33]

Contemporary commentators were certainly agreed that Peel's masterly conduct in 1842 had enhanced his public reputation and consolidated the position of his government in the process.[34] Lord Aberdeen, the Foreign Secretary, declared that 'we are triumphant in Parliament; and we shall carry our great financial measures with ease. Peel shows that he is really the Minister of the Country, and that his experience, talent, courage, and honesty, deserve support.'[35] Peel's own belief in the correctness of his course of action was conveyed to his colleague in India, Lord Ellenborough, with that tone of self-satisfaction which was one of his more unattractive character traits:

> I feel that confidence in the result which must always accompany the consciousness of acting from pure and honourable motives, and the deep conviction that the course taken is a just and wise one.
>
> I should feel much less confidence than I do if I had acted as a mere instrument in the hands of a powerful majority, and had conciliated their temporary, undivided support, by deference to their wishes and opinions.
>
> I have a firm persuasion that ultimate success will reward unflinching perseverence in that course which, having ample means of judging, you are convinced is the right course. But even if this be too sanguine a view, there is at any rate the consolation that failure itself, if you must fail, is honourable.[36]

The Free Trade budget of 1842 did not produce instant results in terms of reviving trade and improved employment prospects. It has already been mentioned that conditions in the manufacturing areas were particularly bad during the summer of 1842, *after* the budget, and while a fortuitously good harvest was of some help, the economy remained in a sluggish state through most of 1843. This explains the otherwise surprising impression, recorded by Charles Greville in August 1843, that the government seemed to be in the doldrums and Peel's own prestige on the wane.[37] By 1844, however, there was clear evidence that the economy was making a strong recovery, fortified by more good harvests and a boom in railway investment, and in these circumstances government revenue was buoyant despite the earlier tariff reductions. When Peel made his financial statement to the House of Commons in February 1845, he was able to report an estimated budget surplus, for 1845–6, of around £3.4 million, enough to permit the government to dispense with the income tax. However, he proposed instead that the income tax should be renewed for another three years, so that the budget surplus could be devoted to a further round of cuts in indirect taxes, which Peel claimed would promote even greater economic prosperity. All of the surviving export duties were thus abolished, the most important being that on coal, while of the 813 items liable to customs duties, 430 yielding small amounts of revenue disappeared.

These included silk, hemp, flax, iron, zinc, dyestuffs and furniture timber. More spectacularly, Peel announced that he was removing altogether the import duty on raw cotton – the Lancashire cotton textile industry, of course, was totally dependent on foreign supplies of its basic raw material – at a cost to the Exchequer of £680,000. The duties on sugar, a major item of consumption for working people, were reduced, by sacrificing £1.3 million of revenue, and the excise on glass (worth £642,000) and the auction duty (£300,000) were abandoned. Peel's hope was that, by extending his financial experiment, 'the direct and instant effect will be increased consumption of many articles now subject to duty, invigorating the industry and extending the commercial enterprise of the Country through other channels, and supplying the void we cannot hope to fill up by direct taxation.' Placing his confidence in 'the elasticity of the resources of this Empire', Peel predicted that in three years' time the government's revenue from the remaining indirect taxes would be so high that the income tax might then be disposed of.[38]

Peel's endeavours to stimulate manufacturing and trade, and so improve the material well-being of many working people, were an acknowledgement of the indispensable contribution made to the nation's economic strength by those non-agrarian sectors which had advanced so rapidly in recent decades. 'If you had to constitute new societies', he reflected to Croker in the summer of 1842, 'you might on moral and social grounds prefer cornfields to cotton factories, an agricultural to a manufacturing population. But our lot is cast and we cannot recede.' Significantly, though, Peel does not seem to have envisaged an indefinite expansion of the industrial base. His letter to Croker mentioned the need for effective measures 'to *revive* the languishing commerce and manufacturing industry' of the country, because the concentration of large numbers of people in the industrial towns meant that any *'retrograde* in manufactures' would have disastrous social consequences.[39] Britain, in other words, could not go back to being an agrarian nation, but it did not follow that Peel expected the newer wealth-creating sectors to eventually outstrip agriculture in importance to the national economy. His commitment to preserving the political rule of the aristocracy, which depended for much of its economic and social power on landownership, suggests that he had no conception of a perpetually expanding industrial community destined to finally subjugate the agrarian classes. The purpose of Peel's Free Trade policies, therefore, was simply to restore prosperity to the existing manufacturing sector, and so promote social tranquillity.

Boyd Hilton has argued that Peel in fact held an 'essentially static vision' of the economy, which he tended to think of as a self-regulating machine, in contrast to the 'growth oriented' ideas of men such as Richard Cobden of the Anti-Corn Law League. This point can be illustrated by reference to one of the most famous measures associated with Peel's government, the Bank Charter Act of 1844. The object of this legislation was to establish more stable foundations for the English banking system, which had been prone to periodic crises in the past, by preventing the excessive supply of paper money. Henceforth, the Bank of England was allowed to issue notes to the value of its gold reserves plus a fiduciary limit of £14 million, while no new provincial banks were permitted to issue notes at all. If Peel's measure had operated according to his intentions, the effects would have been deflationary, limiting the scope for banks to finance economic growth and diversification. But for the new gold discoveries, from the late 1840s onwards (a substantial proportion of which found their way into the Bank of England's reserves, enabling the note supply to be increased), and the development of alternative forms of 'money', such as cheques and bills of exchange, the expansionary economic conditions of the 1850s and 1860s, which Peel is usually credited with fostering, could not have occurred.[40]

Beyond this purely economic response to the 'condition of England question', Peel looked above all else to the Established Church to fulfil its national mission by inculcating Christian values into the minds of the urban masses. 'The state of the population in the manufacturing districts', he declared to his former Home Office colleague, Henry Hobhouse, in 1843, 'is such, with reference to spiritual instruction, that it is impossible to defer the consideration of a remedy of social evils fraught with imminent danger.'[41] Clearly, there was an urgent need for the Church to extend its physical presence in the towns, and compensate for decades of failure to adapt to the geographical shift of population. Progress in this field was hampered, though, by the growing power and assertiveness of the nonconformist sects, whose jealousy of the privileged status of the Anglican Church made it politically impossible, as Peel realised, for the State to do what some Conservative MPs were still demanding, and provide public funds for the purpose of building new churches (the last grants were made in 1818 and 1824). Such a step was now guaranteed to engulf the Church in further damaging sectarian conflict with its nonconformist rivals. A Populous Parishes Act was passed in 1843, empowering the Ecclesiastical Commissioners to create new parishes and provide the necessary stipends out of Church funds, but it was evident to Peel that the cost of building new churches could only be covered by a more efficient use of the Church of England's existing resources together with charitable donations. Peel himself, as a private individual, subscribed £4000 for use in London and the industrial areas of Staffordshire, Warwickshire and Lancashire. This contribution formed part of an impressive, but ultimately unavailing, money-raising campaign to retrieve the Church's position, which led to a total of £25 million being spent on building and restoration work between 1840 and 1876.

Nonconformist antipathy towards the Established Church also wrecked Sir James Graham's plan for the education of factory children, incorporated into his Factory Bill of 1843. Graham proposed that factory schools should be run by committees chaired by the local Anglican priests, but the favoured status thus accorded to the Church provoked an angry response from nonconformists, who organised public demonstrations and petitions to parliament denouncing the Home Secretary's scheme. The government was finally compelled to retreat, abandoning Graham's Bill, although Peel considered this to be a 'sorry and lamentable triumph that Dissent has achieved'.[42] Once again, it proved necessary to look to the voluntary efforts of the Church and its supporters to provide for what the State could not enforce by law, and Peel gave £1000 of his own money to the special fund raised by the Anglican National Society to establish schools in manufacturing and mining districts.

If there were certain areas of 'social' policy where the denominational rivalries in the country made it politically hazardous for the State to attempt to do more, in other cases Peel was ideologically inclined to the view that it would be improper for State intervention to proceed any further. For instance, as leader of the opposition, in 1834, he had endorsed the Whig government's Poor Law Amendment Act, and he resisted subsequent demands for the new poor relief system to be modified or replaced. Some Conservative candidates gave prominence to the Poor Law issue in their 1841 general election contests, condemning the inhumanity of a regime inspired by the utilitarian principles of the workhouse test and 'less eligibility'. Peel, however, had argued in the House of Commons in 1840 that the old practice, of giving a rate-in-aid of wages, effectively subsidised low wages and tended to lower the 'moral and social condition of the poor', leaving them in a state of permanent dependency. It was therefore an act of 'real friendship' towards the poor to establish a more rational and efficient method of relieving poverty which would ultimately 'raise the character and elevate the position of the poor in the social scale'.[43] As Prime Minister, he continued to defend the Poor Law against attacks from back-bench Conservatives, the most colourful of whom were the 'Young England' group, including Lord John Manners and Benjamin Disraeli, who espoused a revivified aristocratic paternalism dedicated to protecting the interests of the poor. While Peel accepted that there were specific instances where poor relief was administered harshly by those in control at the local level, he did not believe that the principles behind the 1834 Act were thereby discredited. He was able to point out, during a debate in February 1843, that the Poor Law operated in a much more flexible way than its critics allowed: 221,000 people had been admitted to workhouses, in the previous year, but 1,207,000 had received outdoor relief (of course, in the depressed manufacturing towns it was simply impossible to accommodate all the claimants in workhouses). Peel also maintained that the standard of poor relief was generous, compared to other countries, and that the system was generally fair to those in need of help without placing an excessive financial burden on the industrious portion of the community.[44]

It is probably true to say that Conservative paternalist sentiments were expressed more forcibly in the 1840s than in the previous decade, when the bulk of the party seemed ready enough to follow Peel's lead in voting for the Poor Law Amendment Act. At that time, there was widespread concern about the rising cost of poor relief and the failure of the old system to prevent rural unrest. The strength of the popular agitation against the implementation of the 1834 Act no doubt encouraged some Conservatives to take up the issue, as a useful stick with which to beat the Whig government. Another reason why paternalism later gained in political force was that it provided the Conservative country gentlemen with a powerful riposte to the attacks being made upon them by the middle-class radicals of the Anti-Corn Law League. If landowners were to be accused of selfishly protecting their own incomes, at the expense of urban consumers of bread, through the maintenance of the Corn Laws, they could reasonably retaliate by pointing to the scandalous working conditions, appalling job insecurity, and urban squalor endured by those who laboured in the factories owned by supporters of the League. Consequently, when Peel's government re-introduced its Factory Bill (minus the controversial education clauses) in 1844, which proposed a $6\frac{1}{2}$-hour limit on the working day for children aged between nine and fourteen in textile mills, and the extension of the existing 12 hour limit for children under eighteen to cover adult women, ninety-five Conservative MPs supported Lord Ashley's amendment lowering the 12 hour limit to 10 hours. 'A great body of the agricultural members' had voted against ministers, as Peel reported to the Queen, 'partly out of hostility to the Anti-Corn Law League, partly from the influence of humane feelings', and Ashley's amendment was carried by a majority of nine.[45] At the premier's insistence, however, the House of Commons rescinded this vote a few nights later, and a subsequent attempt by Ashley to reinsert his amendment was heavily defeated (297:159), thanks to the exertions of the government whips.

Peel's objection to the Ashley amendment was not simply that it violated the laws of political economy, but that it would materially harm the interests of those whom it was supposedly trying to protect. Always the master of plausible arguments, he managed to conceal his distaste for over-zealous State intervention behind a wall of practical difficulties and concerns. It was clear, for a start, that the amendment effectively restricted men to a 10-hour day, as well as women and children, since the latter comprised the majority of the workforce in the textile mills. In Peel's view, this was going far beyond the legitimate scope of interference by the State. Furthermore, he warned that a shorter working day was bound to result in lost production, as output levels in the textile industry were determined (so he claimed) chiefly by the machinery in use, and the inevitable consequence would be a loss of earnings for the workers, amounting to 'an income tax upon the poor man'. The proposed restrictions on labour would also reduce the competitiveness of British manufactures in overseas markets, at a time when textiles accounted for £35 million out of the country's total exports of £51 million, and provided employment for 450,000 people. Peel's judgement was that the dangers posed to the success of the textile industry, and the livelihoods of those who depended on it, far exceeded any benefits to society derived from women working shorter hours, however desirable that might be in principle. Moral considerations, in his opinion, afforded 'no safe rule for legislation'. The country, Peel reminded MPs, was just recovering from a severe economic depression, which had itself produced great 'moral and social evils', and nothing should be done to jeopardise the improving state of affairs.[46] While it would be inaccurate to describe Peel's attitude towards the factory question as being founded on a pure doctrine of *laissez-faire* – some degree of State interference had already been accepted, on behalf of women and children, who were not considered to be free negotiating agents, and it was really now a matter of how far this interference should be extended – it is nevertheless obvious that he wished restrictive legislation to be minimised as far as possible.[47] *Laissez-faire* principles were always more fully applicable in the sphere of commercial policy than in matters affecting the welfare of individuals.[48] In the case of the 10 hour amendment, moreover, there is a strong suspicion that the rigidity of Peel's opposition had as much, and possibly more, to do with annoyance at the way the House of Commons was trying to dictate the details of his government's legislation.

Similar conflicts of opinion between Peel and back-bench Conservatives arose on a number of issues touching upon the principle of protectionism. Those who advocated 'paternalistic' State intervention in defence of textile workers, after all, were also likely to be favourably disposed towards State regulation of trade. Conservative loyalty to the Prime Minister did prove strong enough to withstand the strains imposed by the modified Corn Laws of 1842, but later in the same parliamentary session eighty-five MPs voted against the reduction of the import duty on cattle. The following year, over sixty Conservatives opposed the Canada Corn Bill, which allowed this item into the country at a very low duty. In 1844, a more serious back-bench revolt was provoked by the government's plan to slash the tariff on foreign sugar grown by free labour, from the exorbitant level of 63s per hundredweight to 34s plus 5 per cent, while leaving the duty on colonial sugar unchanged at 25s 3d. Ostensibly, the question at stake, for Conservative dissidents, was that of maintaining imperial preference for sugar grown in the West Indies, but there was also an underlying worry about the depth of Peel's commitment to protectionism in general, which had obvious implications for the landed interest in Britain. Many Conservative MPs feared that their leader was leaning further and further in the direction of the urban Free Trade radicals, and that he accordingly approached the 'condition of England question' exclusively from the viewpoint of cheap food, regardless of its consequences for rural society and the old political order. Philip Miles, the member for Bristol, moved a shrewd amendment to the government's Bill, proposing that the tariff differential between foreign and colonial sugar should be widened by reducing the duty on colonial sugar to 20s. This attracted the support of many Whig and Radical free-traders, as well as sixty-two Conservatives, and Miles thus inflicted a defeat on ministers by twenty votes.

Peel's reaction to this show of Conservative defiance was identical to his conduct during the 10 hours crisis, earlier in the session: he threatened to resign unless the House of Commons reversed its decision. A meeting of some 200 thoroughly alarmed MPs at the Carlton Club, on 17 June, expressed its appreciation of Peel's services to the nation, and his demand was duly complied with after forty-three absentees from the original division attended for the second vote and ten of the rebels stayed away. Nevertheless, Charles Greville wrote in his diary that the Prime Minister's tone in the Commons had been 'offensive and dictatorial, and people of all parties were exasperated and disgusted with it'. Peel, in Greville's view, was guilty of 'a morbid sensitiveness unworthy of a great man'.[49] Even Gladstone, one of Peel's young disciples, was dismayed by his chief's uncompromising stance, which appeared to be the product of personal disgust at the wayward behaviour of Conservative MPs. Unnecessary damage, Gladstone therefore feared, was being done to the relations between ministers and back-benchers: 'a deep wound [has] been inflicted upon the spirit and harmony of the party... a great man [has] committed a great error'.[50] In fact, Peel had been advised by the Conservative party managers that only about twenty MPs were true malcontents – men such as Disraeli, who wished to bring the government down – and this assessment has been confirmed by the findings of modern research.[51]

The sugar duties episode, coming so soon after the Factory Bill dispute, highlighted the difficulties in reconciling Peel's 'executive' ideals of government with Conservative back-bencher's claims to be allowed their 'independence'. Although the parliamentary rank-and-file were prepared to give their general confidence to Peel and his colleagues, in the sense that they wished them to remain in office, the reality was that MPs in this period did not owe their seats to a party machine and were therefore difficult to discipline. Back-benchers genuinely were in a position to exercise their independent judgement on specific issues. Peel, on the other hand, expected MPs' allegiance to ministers to override their personal opinions. Arguably, he was asking for rather more obedience than he had a right to demand, given the looseness of party ties in the early-Victorian House of Commons.[52] When one of the sugar duties rebels, Lord Sandon, wrote to assure Peel that the Conservative party remained loyal to him, the Prime Minister's tart reply was that 'declarations of general confidence will not, I fear, compensate for that loss of authority and efficiency which is sustained by a Government not enabled to carry into effect the practical measures of legislation which it feels it to be its duty to submit to Parliament'.[53]

Care must be taken, however, not to exaggerate the seriousness of Conservative disunion, which in 1844 had yet to develop into a terminal condition. There were signs that Peel and his party had managed to patch up their quarrels, before the end of the session, and that a better feeling prevailed.[54] The Premier was persuaded to use more conciliatory language at the conclusion of the sugar duties affair, and towards the end of June he enthused Conservative back-benchers with a powerful speech affirming that his government had no intention of diminishing the level of protection to agriculture secured by the Corn Laws.[55] He was unrepentant, though, about his basic style of leadership, even going so far as to claim, in March 1845, that 'people like a certain degree of obstinacy and presumption in a Minister. They abuse him for dictation and arrogance, but they like being governed.'[56] The 'condition of England question', in its many forms, undoubtedly caused considerable friction in the relations between ministers and back-benchers, but it was the government's handling of the situation in Ireland which provided a more severe test of Conservative MPs' loyalty to their leaders.

The Condition of Ireland

Peel's approach to the governing of Ireland, after 1841, presents a remarkable contrast to the early part of his career, and shows how far he had travelled, politically, since his days as the champion of the Protestant Constitution in the 1810s and 1820s. The circumstances surrounding the extraction of Catholic Emancipation from Wellington's government, which were discussed in Chapter 2, had forced a reappraisal of Peel's thinking about the nature of the Irish problem, leading him towards a more 'liberal' perspective founded on the principle of allowing free-play between the forces of Protestantism and Catholicism. Subsequent events, however, mostly occurring while Peel was out of office, made it clear that Ireland was still not reconciled to the Union with Britain. Daniel O'Connell, the hero of the emancipation movement, put himself at the head of a new campaign for the repeal of the Act of Union, to which end he sought to exploit Irish agrarian grievances and the resentment of the Catholic majority towards the Established, Protestant, Church of Ireland. In conversation with Gladstone, early in 1836, Peel expressed a sense of hopelessness over the state of Ireland, a country in which it seemed impossible even to maintain the basic administration of justice, such was the lack of identification between the interests of citizens, called upon to serve as jurors, and the interests of the State.[57] It may have been true that the Whig government of Lord Melbourne temporarily succeeded in containing the situation, establishing a working political relationship with O'Connell, but by 1841 the imminent prospect of a Conservative regime prompted the renewal of the agitation for repeal.

The spirit in which the new government wished to deal with Ireland was described in a letter to Peel from the Home Secretary, Sir James Graham, dated October 1841. Graham believed that it was essential for ministers to pursue 'an impartial and liberal policy... equal justice administered to Roman Catholics – in a word, the policy which you enjoin'.[58] Irish society would benefit more than anything else from a period of quiet and stability, and if this could be achieved the repeal fever would surely soon 'subside'.[59] One vital practical step was to ensure that Catholics received a reasonable share of the Crown patronage available in Ireland. Peel was, indeed, anxious to demonstrate the material advantages of Catholic Emancipation by encouraging the recruitment of 'moderate' and 'respectable' Catholics into the magistracy, the police, the armed forces, the legal profession and other walks of life. (As was so often the case, Peel sought to justify his policies by reference to the alleged existence of a well-disposed mass of people who would be amenable to conciliatory measures.) No longer was he prepared to subscribe to the old Protestant Ascendancy doctrine that conciliation of the Catholics was a futile policy, since they did not want to be conciliated, and that a Protestant monopoly of key offices was therefore indispensable for the sake of the Union.[60] Given his earlier association with the Protestant cause, Peel was now extraordinarily dismissive of the complaints made about his resolute impartiality by former admirers.[61] In order to help redress the present religious imbalance, Peel was even willing to accept that merit need not be the sole criterion for making public appointments, reminding the Lord Lieutenant that 'considerations of policy, and also of justice, demand a liberal and indulgent estimate of the claims of such Roman Catholics as abstain from political agitation'. To follow a policy of exclusion risked turning these people into enemies of the Crown.[62] It was a regrettable mistake, on Peel's part, that the man he chose as Lord Lieutenant, Lord de Grey, was a Protestant sympathiser who systematically refused to co-operate with this conciliatory approach and even dismissed a number of Catholics from the magistracy. Lord Heytesbury, who succeeded de Grey in 1844, was more sensitive to Peel's wish for transparent impartiality in the distribution of patronage, with a view to distancing 'the great body of wealthy and intelligent Roman Catholics' from the repeal movement.[63] Unfortunately, it was far too late by this stage for Peel's strategy to have any chance of producing the desired results.

Far from fading away, O'Connell's campaign acquired added momentum during the course of 1843. Mass meetings were held all over the Catholic areas of Ireland, and the repeal movement broadened the social basis of its support to include members of the Catholic gentry and the urban middle classes – precisely the groups whom Peel was trying to prevent being drawn into the agitation. More worryingly still, the Catholic bishops and clergy also put their formidable influence behind O'Connell. The British government's initial response was confined to passing an Arms Bill, requiring the registration of firearms, and prohibiting the sale of other lethal weapons and gunpowder. With the agitation in Ireland continuing to mount, and as O'Connell's language became more violent and militaristic, ministers finally decided to ban a monster demonstration planned at Clontarf for October, and to launch a prosecution of the nationalist leader on the charge of treasonable conspiracy. O'Connell was convicted the following February and jailed, before the verdict was overturned on the grounds that the jury had been packed with Protestants. Despite this setback, the government could be said to have scored a partial victory, in the sense that O'Connell's unwillingness to bring about a confrontation with the authorities, at the time of the Clontarf ban, undermined his reputation with some of the younger Irish nationalists (although this had serious consequences thereafter, allowing the repeal movement to fall into more radical hands). Looking no further than the immediate future, it at least seemed possible that the blow dealt to O'Connell's authority had cleared the path for Peel's government to press ahead with constructive measures of conciliation in Ireland.

In a series of memoranda presented to the Cabinet in February 1844, Peel summarised his thinking on the condition of Ireland and his government's response to it.[64] Recent events had demonstrated that the Irish Catholic majority remained disaffected from British rule, and this was a state of affairs which might well expose Britain to military danger, if Irish discontent were ever to be exploited by a foreign power for hostile purposes (France was uppermost in Peel's mind, in this respect). The Prime Minister reiterated his view that it was expedient to seek to accommodate the more respectable elements within the

Catholic population, by creating equal employment opportunities for them in the service of the State, and by conceding an enhanced status to the Roman Catholic Church. Only in this way could moderate Catholics be persuaded to assist the authorities in upholding law and order, especially through their participation on juries. And only by attaching moderate Catholics to the interests of the State was there a possibility of reconciling them to the existence of the Established Church in Ireland, and of the Union with Britain.

When parliament debated the state of Ireland, at the beginning of the 1844 session, Peel was able to announce that the government had already set-up a Commission of Inquiry, chaired by the Earl of Devon, to investigate the question of land tenure. The Devon Commission's voluminous report was published in 1845, and it prompted ministers to bring forward a Compensation to Tenants Bill in the House of Lords, in June of that year. This Bill would have provided tenant farmers, evicted by their landlords, with a right to compensation for unexhausted improvements – buildings, fences or drainage – made by them to their holdings. It was also intended that a Commissioner of Improvements should be appointed to supervise applications by tenant farmers for improvements they wished to make to the land they were renting. By encouraging farmers to invest money in their holdings, the government's aim was to promote an entrepreneurial spirit amongst an important section of the Catholic 'middle class', who ought naturally to be bulwarks of social order. Predictably, the ministerial plan met with strong opposition, in a landlord-dominated assembly, where objections were voiced to any interference in the freedom of landowners to remove their tenants and to control what improvements were made to their property. Just a month after its introduction, the Bill had to be withdrawn. Realistically, there was never any hope of passing a controversial measure so late in the session, and by the time parliament met again the famine crisis in Ireland had transformed the situation.

Peel's government enjoyed limited success in its endeavour to improve the provision of higher education in Ireland. The Academical Institutions Bill, introduced and carried in 1845, established colleges at Cork, Galway and Belfast, where no religious tests were to be applied to entrants and no theology taught. At Cork and Galway, the majority of students were likely to come from the Catholic laity of southern and western Ireland, and while Peel did not seriously expect better education to convert these students into Protestants, he at least believed that they might be 'wean[ed] . . . from vicious habits', and given knowledge in place of 'idleness and profligacy'.[65] Sir James Graham was more blunt in expressing the hope that the new colleges would 'emancipate the rising generations from the thraldom of priestly domination'.[66] It was precisely the fear that this was the British government's objective which caused the Catholic Church to boycott the colleges at Cork and Galway, preventing them from attracting the desired numbers of Catholic students.

Even more forbidding obstacles were encountered by those government measures devised to promote greater harmony in the relationship between the British State and the Roman Catholic Church in Ireland.[67] One of the problems identified by Peel, in his Cabinet memoranda of February 1844, was the fact that Catholic priests were largely dependent for financial support upon the poorer classes in Irish society, notably the peasantry, which increased the likelihood of priests being drawn into the agitation against the Act of Union. Ideally, the solution would have been for the State to pay salaries to the priests, and thus gain some political leverage over them, but such a policy was certain to be anathema to many supporters of the Established Churches of England and Ireland, and also to Protestant nonconformists. The best alternative, in Peel's judgment, was to strengthen the link between members of the Catholic gentry and their Church by facilitating religious endowments from real property. In this way, theoretically, the Catholic priesthood might be induced to behave responsibly, if their interests were more closely tied to those of the landowning class, and they would certainly be less inclined to stoke up inflammatory thoughts in the minds of their peasant flocks. The Charitable Bequests Bill of 1844 accordingly proposed to relax the law of mortmain, so as to allow the private endowment of Catholic chapels and benefices, and it also replaced the existing Board for Charitable Trusts in Ireland – an exclusively Protestant body, despite the fact that three-quarters of the trusts it administered were for Catholics – with a Board of mixed denomination. There was little parliamentary opposition to the Bill, and the government's main battle was to secure the involvement of Catholic bishops on the new Board, which was finally achieved in December.

Peel's Cabinet memoranda of February 1844 also considered the shortcomings in the training of Catholic priests, and the question of what could be done to improve their social character. It appeared to the Prime Minister that the Catholic Seminary at Maynooth in County Kildare, which received an annually voted parliamentary grant of £9000, was inadequately funded, and that its poor standards had the tendency of deterring entrants from respectable gentry families. Instead, it was young men from the lower ranks of Irish society who were taking holy orders, and this merely served to reinforce the connection between Catholic priests and nationalist agitators. The Maynooth Bill of 1845 therefore sought to improve the quality – educationally and socially – of those entering the priesthood, by increasing the annual parliamentary grant to £26,360 and making it permanent, while providing an additional one-off grant of £30,000 for new buildings. As the government's scheme was in the course of preparation, Graham declared to Peel that 'It is the key which will open to the Queen's Government influence over the Roman Catholic priesthood, if it still be possible to obtain it.'[68]

Whereas, from Peel's and Graham's point of view, the Maynooth Bill was a pragmatic attempt to undermine support for the nationalist movement, from within the ranks of the Catholic Church, and obtain a better understanding between that Church and the British State, for many back-bench Conservative MPs it represented a flagrant betrayal of those Protestant principles which the Conservative party was supposed to uphold. In Britain as a whole, there was a sense of outrage at the prospect of more generous funding for a Catholic training college by a State which was still regarded as essentially 'Protestant' in its character. The Central Anti-Maynooth Committee, a remarkable interdenominational organisation including Anglicans and nonconformists, quickly emerged, and parliament was deluged with some 10,000 petitions, signed by over $1\frac{1}{4}$ million people, condemning the Maynooth plan. When the Bill came to be debated in the House of Commons, the Whig diarist Charles Greville recorded that 'The Carlton Club was in a state of insurrection afterwards and full of sound and fury.... The disgust of the Conservatives and their hatred of Peel keep swelling every day.'[69] It was at this point that a maverick back-bencher, named Benjamin Disraeli, emerged as a dangerous critic of Peel's style of leadership, denouncing the Prime Minister as an unscrupulous middleman whose shameless borrowing of his opponents' policies demonstrated a total lack of commitment to fixed political principles. Sir James Graham reported gloomily to the Lord Lieutenant in Dublin that the Maynooth Bill had 'destroyed' the Conservative party: 'A large body of our supporters is mortally offended.' On the other hand, it was comforting to reflect that 'Sir Robert Peel has a strong hold on the public mind, and on the House of Commons, without distinction of parties; and at no time was the Crown more willing and ready to give a cordial support to a favoured Minister.'[70] Ultimately, the Bill was carried, thanks to the support of the Whig opposition, but at the third reading stage Conservative MPs divided 149 to 148 against their own Prime Minister.

Peel's remedy for the threat posed to the Union by O'Connell's repeal campaign involved constructing an alliance between the British State and the Catholic gentry and middle classes of Ireland. To this end, he strove to ensure that Catholics obtained a fair share of Crown patronage, that their opportunities for a secular higher education were improved, and that business attitudes were inculcated amongst the tenant farmers. Similarly, he aimed to strengthen both the government's and the Catholic gentry's influence over the Roman Catholic Church, trusting that this would make the latter a more amenable body, less prone to subversive activity. Whatever chance of success these policies may be thought to have had, they were simply denied the time they obviously needed to work on Irish social and cultural attitudes – for reasons that are about to become clear. Difficulties also arose because the attempt to build up certain religious and social groups, whose co-operation with the British State might make Ireland a more stable and governable country, meant that it was imperative for Peel and his colleagues to be seen to be impartial in their dealings with Catholics and Protestants. But an even-handed approach always ran the risk of offending both sides and pleasing neither, and Peel himself recognised that this had been the result in a consoling letter to the despondent Home Secretary, written in October 1845: 'My views of Ireland and its prospects have long been very gloomy. It is in a state which seems to preclude honest and impartial government. To conduct the Government on party principles ensures the support of one party at least; to administer it on any other than party principles is to forfeit the confidence of both.'[71] The quest for a dispassionate, 'executive' system of government was hard enough in the case of Britain, but in Ireland it proved totally impossible.

The Repeal of the Corn Laws

By the early autumn of 1845 additional grounds were emerging to justify ministerial pessimism about the Irish condition, and these were also to have a profound impact upon the course of politics at Westminster. It became known in August–September that the potato blight, a fungoid disease attacking crops on the continent of Europe, had spread to Britain and Ireland. Wet weather conspired to aggravate an already perilous situation and, towards the end of October, reports were reaching Peel that at least one-half of the Irish potato crop had been ruined. This was bound to have devastating consequences in a country where there were large numbers of subsistence farmers entirely dependent on the fortunes of the potato harvest.

Faced with the prospect of an imminent famine crisis in Ireland, Peel urged upon his Cabinet colleagues the policy of throwing open United Kingdom ports immediately, admitting foreign grain and all other foodstuffs without importation duties. Rather than proposing a temporary solution to a (hopefully) short-term emergency, however, Peel was adamant that there must be a 'total and absolute repeal for ever of all duties on all articles of subsistence'. Once the Corn Laws and other tariffs on foodstuffs were removed, he argued, it would be impossible to reconcile public opinion to their re-imposition at a future date.[72]

Peel's readiness, at this point, to advocate the complete abandonment of protectionism, raises important questions about his motives and intentions. Desperate as the plight of the Irish population undoubtedly was, a policy of Free Trade had no obvious relevance to the situation, because the failure of the potato crop meant that peasant farmers lacked the means of earning money to pay for other foodstuffs, even if they were made somewhat cheaper. The £750,000 subsequently spent by Peel's government on public works projects, the purchase of cheap maize from America, and other relief measures, was of far more practical use than the repeal of the Corn Laws. Furthermore, since the Corn Laws were in no way responsible for the Irish famine, and the years from 1842 to 1844 had seen a series of good grain harvests in Britain, keeping down the price of bread, it is curious that Peel should have been so determined to force through repeal before his own sliding scale of 1842 had had a chance to show whether or not it worked effectively in times of scarcity.[73]

If, as appears likely, Peel was seizing the opportunity provided by the Irish potato famine to implement a Free Trade policy upon which his mind was already made up, the real question we need to consider is at what point did he become converted to the ideas espoused by the middle-class radicals of the Anti-Corn Law League? While it is impossible to provide a definitive answer, Boyd Hilton may well be right to suggest that Peel had absorbed the intellectual case for Free Trade in corn long before the League came into existence. In the 1820s, as a minister in Lord Liverpool's government, Peel supported the commercial reforms promoted by William Huskisson, and his later thinking was apparently shaped by Huskisson's argument that the continued rapid growth of population (at rates well in excess of 10 per cent each decade, in the early nineteenth century), would eventually make it impossible for British farmers to supply the nation's needs, rendering the repeal of the Corn Laws inevitable. There is a striking similarity, as Hilton points out, between the options discussed by Peel in his Cabinet memoranda on the Corn Laws, composed shortly after taking office in 1841, and those outlined by Huskisson in the late 1820s.[74] It is also noteworthy that in his speeches defending the Corn Laws, as leader of the opposition, Peel was careful to allow himself an escape clause, asserting that while he did not accept the claim that protectionism was to blame for the distressed condition of the labouring classes, *if* he could ever be persuaded otherwise, then matters would be quite different.[75] In April 1840, he was prepared to acknowledge that the policy of repeal might be 'theoretically correct', in the sense that the general Free Trade argument – that each country should specialise in producing those things it could make most efficiently, and then exchange those goods for the products of other countries, without tariff restrictions – was sound in principle. However, 'He doubted the possibility of applying this principle to the external commerce of this Country, in a state of society so artificial, with relations so complicated, and with such enormous interests at stake, which had grown up under another principle, however defective it might be – namely, the principle of protection in certain cases.' Peel therefore declined to support an experiment which, fine as it sounded in theory, was based on an untried principle, the adoption of which could jeopardise the country's commercial prosperity fostered under the protectionist system.[76]

At an intellectual level, then, Peel probably accepted that the Corn Laws would have to go, sooner or later, before he became Prime Minister in 1841. Observing, in a letter to Croker the following year, how a lowering of the price of wheat tended to bring down other prices, he nevertheless added that 'We do not push this argument to its logical consequences. . . . We take into account vested interests, engaged capital, the importance of independent supply, the social benefits of flourishing agriculture, &c.'[77] The question that remains to be addressed, of course, is at what stage did Peel become convinced that repeal was politically practicable, and worth the upset it was bound to cause to the vested interests involved? Judging from Gladstone's memoranda, recording conversations with his chief in 1842–3, it seems clear that from the outset Peel considered the level of protection incorporated in his revised sliding scale to be too high, although this had been necessary in order to secure political support from his Cabinet colleagues and the House of Lords. He even specified the lower rates of duty which he would have preferred to implement.[78] By December 1843, on the other hand, Peel went much further, expressing 'a strong opinion that the next change in the Corn Laws would be to total repeal'.[79] A plausible suggestion might be that his silent shift away from the sliding scale, and towards the alternative policy of repeal, was connected to the early signs that his wider Free Trade measures, introduced in the budget of 1842, were yielding positive results. In other words, as soon as it became apparent that the reduction in tariff levels was having a beneficial effect on the economy, stimulating production and increasing employment, Peel was finally satisfied that he could safely dispense with protection without doing any great harm to British agriculture.[80]

During the 1845 session of parliament, Peel's speeches on the Corn Law question had been as ambiguous as ever, simultaneously admitting that protective tariffs were bad in principle, but denying that he had any intention of altering the sliding scale again, yet also hinting at a gradual approach towards the adoption of sound commercial principles.[81] Perhaps the nearest thing to explicit evidence that Peel was indeed nurturing a plan for the repeal of the Corn Laws before the Irish famine crisis occurred, and that this crisis merely accelerated the timetable for action, is provided by Prince Albert's account of a conversation with Peel on Christmas Eve, 1845. This cannot be taken as conclusive proof of Peel's intentions, as he was speaking to the Prince shortly *after* the decision to proceed with Corn Law repeal had been taken, but it is probably a good indication of what he had in mind:

> He said he had been determined not to go to a general election with the fetters the last election had imposed upon him, and he had meant at the end of the next session to call the whole Conservative Party together and to declare this to them, that he would not meet another Parliament pledged to the maintenance of the Corn Laws, which could be maintained no longer, and that he would make a public declaration to this effect before another general election came on. This had been defeated by events coming too suddenly upon him, and he had no alternative but to deal with the Corn Laws before a national calamity would *force* it on.[82]

The Conservative party, according to this version of Peel's original plan, was going to be persuaded to abandon its commitment to agricultural protection before the general election due in 1847 or 1848, with repeal following on sometime during the next parliament – say, in the early 1850s.

Peel's conversation with Prince Albert indicates that his decision to press ahead immediately with Free Trade in corn was motivated not so much by the crisis in Ireland itself, but by fear of how this crisis might be exploited by the radical proponents of repeal in Britain. In the course of 1844–5, the campaign by the Anti-Corn Law League had entered a new, and politically more threatening, phase, in which urban supporters of Free Trade were encouraged to purchase freehold property in county constituencies so as to qualify themselves for the vote in parliamentary elections. This deliberate manufacturing of voters was concentrated in South Lancashire, North Cheshire, the West Riding of Yorkshire and Middlesex, but by November 1845 there were plans for a wider geographic effort aimed at challenging landed MPs in their county strongholds.[83] At the same time, the League responded to the impending famine in Ireland by renewing its demand for the immediate repeal of the Corn Laws, a move which Peel evidently feared would succeed in persuading the British public that the protectionist system was somehow responsible for Ireland's plight. No matter how illogical or dishonest such a claim might be, if it gained ground in people's minds the government risked being depicted as callously defending the interests of landowners while Ireland starved. As Sir James Graham warned Peel in October, 'The Anti-Corn Law League pressure is about to commence, and it will be the most formidable movement in modern times. Everything depends on the skill, promptitude, and decision with which it is met.'[84] Peel was therefore anxious, he informed Prince Albert on Christmas Eve, to prevent radical agitators from using the current crisis to launch a class-spirited attack on landowners, by promoting a wider settlement of the Free Trade issue which would appeal to the whole nation:

> Sir Robert has *an immense scheme in view*; he thinks he shall be able to remove the contest entirely from the dangerous ground upon which it has got – that of a war between the manufacturers, the hungry and the poor against the landed proprietors, the aristocracy, which can only end in the ruin of the latter; he will not bring forward a measure upon the Corn Laws, but a much more comprehensive one. He will

deal with the whole commercial system of the Country... not in favour of one class and as a triumph over another, but to the benefit of the nation, farmers as well as manufacturers.[85]

In other words, he envisaged a pre-emptive strike designed to take the initiative away from middle-class agitators, and thus help to perpetuate the landed élite's customary domination of the system of government in Britain.

This characteristically 'national' approach to the situation by Peel, had been encouraged by the outcome of the recent ministerial crisis. Unable to obtain Cabinet backing for his proposal to dispense with the Corn Laws,[86] Peel tendered his resignation in early December so that the Whig leader, Lord John Russell, who had recently announced his support for total repeal, might be allowed to form a government and settle the matter. Divisions within the ranks of the Whig hierarchy, however, where by no means everyone was converted to Russell's view, meant that they were unable to construct a viable alternative ministry, and the attempt had to be abandoned. Peel was thereupon invited to resume the premiership, and he was now able to secure the acquiescence of his more sceptical colleagues in the policy of repeal, with the single exception of Lord Stanley, who declined to take office. The fact was that, with both party leaders committed to repeal, this solution looked to be politically inevitable, and the Whigs' failure to provide an alternative ministry placed executive-minded Conservatives such as Wellington under a moral obligation to serve again with Peel for the sake of carrying-on the Queen's government.[87] Having been summoned once more by his monarch, in the circumstances described, Peel felt a heightened sense of duty to act as a national rather than a mere party leader, and he was more than ever resolved to produce a measure calculated to reconcile the various classes in British society.

On 27 January 1846, Peel unveiled to the House of Commons his comprehensive Free Trade budget.[88] He proceeded on the assumption that protective duties were objectionable in principle, unless there was some specific justification for them, and he reminded his audience that the Free Trade measures of recent years had been accompanied by growing commercial prosperity, increased demand for labour, and a buoyant government revenue. In short, 'there has been increased comfort, contentment, and peace in this Country'. Peel therefore called upon all sections of society to relinquish the protection they still enjoyed, so that Free Trade might be firmly enthroned as the guiding principle of British commercial policy in all areas. For instance, there were very few tariffs left on raw materials for industry, but two significant ones remained, affecting tallow and timber, and Peel was prepared to reduce them both. In return, he asked the manufacturing interests to sacrifice a large portion of the protection they still received from imported manufactured goods, proposing that the coarser items of cotton and silk produced abroad should be admitted to the country without any duty, and the tariff on similar woollens halved to 10 per cent. The beneficiaries of this change were going to be the British people, especially the poorer classes, who would have the opportunity to purchase cheaper clothing. A wide range of other imported goods, including candles, soap, hats, boots and shoes, processed sugar and tobacco, were also to be allowed in at substantially reduced levels of duty.

Peel's object was to emphasise the extent to which his tariff revisions applied to the manufacturing class, before entering the more treacherous territory of tariffs affecting the agriculturalists. Both interest groups, he maintained, were being treated in accordance with the same principles. He now proposed that the import duties on all meats, and on live animals, should be abolished forthwith, while those on butter, cheese, hops and cured fish were halved. The British consumer, once again, was the chief beneficiary of Peel's budget. Coming finally to the Corn Laws (i.e. the tariffs on wheat, barley and oats), the Prime Minister announced that, determined as he was to remove them altogether, he nevertheless wished to give the agriculturalists time to adjust to a Free Trade system. Import duties would therefore continue to be levied, but at substantially reduced rates (a maximum tariff of 10s on wheat, when the domestic price was less than 48s, diminishing to 4s when the price reached 53s), until 1 February 1849, when 'repeal' would follow.[89] This three year phasing-out period permitted by Peel, strongly confirms the view expressed earlier that the repeal of the Corn Laws had little relevance to the emergency facing the people of Ireland.[90]

It can be argued that Peel was performing an elaborate conjuring trick, designed to convince the House of Commons that a financial statement primarily concerned with the repeal of the Corn Laws acually embodied a more ambitious and even-handed scheme. By presenting his budget in this light, he could urge the vested interests affected by it to consider the package as a whole, rather than dwelling on specific aspects disagreeable to themselves. The truth was, however, that the total loss of revenue resulting from the abolition or reduction of import duties was about £1 million, considerably less than the amounts involved in 1842 and 1845. Peel would have liked to go further, but increased defence expenditure made this impossible. His statement did include a number of ideas for relieving the financial burdens falling upon the land, such as a more efficient organisation of local highway authorities, modifications to the law of settlement, and the transfer of certain poor law and prison costs to the Treasury. But, in the event, none of these proposals had been enacted before the fall of Peel's ministry, and in any case the projected savings for ratepayers were fairly modest – perhaps around £500,000.[91] Another interesting sop to the landed interest, which never finally materialised, was a scheme for State loans to landowners (repayable with interest), in certain circumstances, to facilitate improvements to their property, notably through the laying down of drainage systems under the soil. In this way, Peel claimed that he was trying to help British agriculture become more efficient, and better equipped to cope with foreign competition.

Prior to the meeting of parliament, it seems that Peel felt confident of his ability to obtain the support necessary for repealing the Corn Laws.[92] The Conservative front-bench, after all, was solidly behind him, and Lord John Russell and the Whigs would find it difficult to vote against the government if they wished to preserve any semblence of political integrity. Whether Peel thought that he could carry most of his own back-benchers with him is much less certain. It is quite possible that he no longer cared what happened to the Conservative party, after his earlier difficulties with them culminating in the Maynooth revolt. The only evidence that Peel did believe he could hold his party together, forcing all but a hard-core of irreconcilables to fall into line with the policy of repeal, comes from a memorandum written by Gladstone several years after the event, which for this reason cannot be treated as an entirely reliable source.[93] If there was any lingering notion that back-bench Conservative resistance to repeal might yet be overcome, the parliamentary reception given to Peel's proposals made it obvious that he faced a bitter and unrelenting opposition, fortified by the depth of feeling in the agricultural constituencies. A network of County Protection Societies had emerged in recent years, co-ordinated by the Central Agricultural Protection Society (known as the 'Anti-League'), founded in February 1844. These organisations ensured that, during the winter of 1845–6, when Peel's intentions towards the Corn Laws became clear, formidable pressure was kept up on MPs to reflect their constituents' sense of outrage. In the House of Commons, towards the end of March 1846, the 'Protectionist' Conservative MPs formed their own committee, under the chairmanship of Lord George Bentinck, and their anger and resentment at Peel's conduct were brilliantly articulated by Disraeli, who mocked and condemned both the character and the intellect of the Prime Minister.[94]

Charles Greville, the Whig diarist, was struck by the vehemence of the Conservatives' opposition to their own leader's policy. On 29 March, for example, he wrote that:

> The Protectionists are bent upon turning Peel out, and if possible grow more, rather than less bitter. On Friday this was especially apparent; no Prime Minister was ever treated as Peel was by them that night, when he rose to speak. The Marquis of Granby rose at the same time, and for five minutes they would not have Peel, and tried to force their man on the House, and to make the Prime Minister sit down. The Speaker alone decided it, and called on Peel. When he said he knew they would turn him out, they all cheered *savagely*.[95]

In back-bench eyes, Peel was proposing to surrender the fundamental interests of the landowning class, and asking Conservative MPs to abandon the main principle on which they had been elected in 1841. All of this was apparently being done in a misguided attempt to satisfy the demands of aggressive radicals such as Cobden and Bright, who represented only the narrow interests of manufacturers. More provoking still was the suspicion that Peel was simply using the Irish famine to justify repealing the Corn Laws, which suggested that his 'betrayal' of the Conservative party had long been contemplated – possibly for years. This was one of the main charges levelled against the premier by Disraeli, and when the Corn Bill reached its third reading stage in May, even Greville was shocked by the intense hatred displayed towards Peel:

> Last week the debate in the House of Commons came to a close at last, wound up by a speech of Disraeli's, very clever, in which he hacked and mangled Peel with the most unsparing severity, and positively tortured his victim. It was a miserable and degrading spectacle. The whole mass of the Protectionists cheered him with vociferous delight, making the roof ring again; and when Peel spoke, they screamed and hooted at him in the most brutal manner. When he vindicated

himself, and talked of honour and conscience, they assailed him with shouts of derision and gestures of contempt. Such treatment in a House of Commons where for years he had been an object of deference and respect, nearly overcame him. The Speaker told me that for a minute and more he was obliged to stop, and for the first time in his life, probably, he lost his self-possession, and the Speaker thought he would have been obliged to sit down, and expected him to burst into tears. They hunt him like a fox, and they are eager to run him down and kill him in the open.... To see the Prime Minister and leader in the House of Commons thus beaten and degraded, treated with contumely by three-fourths of the party he has been used to lead, is a sorry sight, and very prejudicial to the public weal.[96]

The Corn and Customs Bills were passed by the House of Commons in May, and endorsed in the House of Lords the following month, thanks to the assistance of the Whig opposition and the personal authority of the Duke of Wellington. Peel had achieved his objective, however, at the expense of a catastrophic schism in the Conservative party. Only 106 Conservative MPs voted with the government for the third reading, with eight more paired in favour and three known supporters absent, whereas 222 opposed their own leader. Breaking down these figures, it emerges that 86 per cent of MPs sitting for county or university constituencies resisted repeal, as did 63 per cent of those representing boroughs with electorates of less than 500, while the rest of the borough members were more-or-less evenly divided on the issue.[97] Fatally, Peel had lost his hold over the hearts and minds of the agrarian interest, which still constituted the bedrock of support for Conservatism. So bitter was the Protectionist antagonism towards the Prime Minister that when his government's Irish Arms Bill was considered by the Commons, in late June, just hours after the passage of the Corn and Customs Bills had been secured, sixty-nine estranged Conservative MPs joined with the opposition for the purpose of defeating a measure which they would normally have supported automatically. On 29 June, Peel duly announced his resignation,[98] in a defiant speech containing the famous, melodramatic assertion that 'I shall leave a name execrated by every Monopolist...but it may be that I shall leave a name sometimes remembered with expressions of good-will in the abodes of those whose lot it is to labour...when they shall recruit their exhausted strength with abundant and untaxed food, the sweeter because it is no longer leavened by a sense of injustice.'[99]

Tempting as it may be to interpret the Conservative schism of 1846 as the inevitable culmination of a long-term process of disenchantment with Peel's leadership, the reality is more complicated than this. For some Conservatives, no doubt, Peel had been an object of suspicion ever since his earlier 'betrayal' of the Protestant cause in 1829. In the more immediate past, it is right to point out that of the eighty-five MPs who rebelled against Peel on the 10 hours question in 1844, and who also voted on the Corn Laws, the division of opinion in 1846 was fifty-nine to twenty-six against repeal; and of the 153 Conservatives who opposed the Maynooth grant, at some stage in 1845, and also voted on the Corn Laws, 133 voted against repeal and only twenty supported Peel.[100] The connection between opposition to the Maynooth grant and opposition to Corn Law repeal is therefore beyond dispute. But it is pertinent to add that *before* the Maynooth revolt, displays of 'independence' on the part of back-benchers were not indicative of a widespread desire to destroy Peel's government. Instead, it was a normal and regular feature of parliamentary politics for MPs to vote against their leaders on issues that were not considered to be of first-rate importance: eighty-five Conservatives had thus opposed the reduction of the cattle duties in 1842, sixty-five voted against the Ecclesiastical Courts Bill of 1843, and 106 opposed the Dissenters' Chapels Bill of 1844. None of these gestures signified the repudiation by MPs of Peel's leadership.[101] It was the strain imposed on Conservative loyalties by the Maynooth grant of 1845, followed by the even greater shock of Corn Law repeal the following year, which really destroyed the party's cohesion.

The case of Thomas Sotheron, MP for Devizes from 1835 until 1844, and thereafter a representative for North Wiltshire, provides a useful illustration of one back-bencher's attitude towards Peel's leadership. When the Prime Minister made his budget statement in March 1842, Sotheron hailed what he described in his diary as a 'wonderful speech'; yet this did not stop him from voting against the government on the cattle duties, later in the same session.[102] Sotheron's loyalty in the division lobbies remained firm over the 10 hours question, in 1844, though he shared the anger of many other Conservatives at Peel's dictatorial tone during the sugar duties crisis.[103] Disregarding pressure from his constituents, Sotheron also voted in favour of the Maynooth grant.[104] It is particularly interesting that, in the summer of 1845, Sotheron made a speech to his constituents in which he warned them that he 'feared Free Trade in corn was not very distant', and advised that 'we should prepare for it, by requiring certain taxes & Burdens on land to be removed as a preliminary'.[105] He was dismayed, though, by Peel's statement of intent in January 1846: 'Free Trade in Corn – no compensation – but a miserable three years of a reduced sliding scale and some trifling articles of pretended Relief to Agriculturalists. Miserable Disappointment.'[106] One feels that if Peel had been able to adhere to his original plan (as described to Prince Albert), and prepared the Conservative party for the idea of eventual repeal in several year's time, and perhaps done more to redress landowners' grievances over the burden of local rates, he might have had considerably more success in carrying back-bench MPs with him. Sotheron was not one of the irreconcilables who brought down Peel's government over the Irish Arms Bill, but he described the Prime Minister's resignation speech, which included a tribute to the efforts of the Anti-Corn Law League campaigner, Richard Cobden, as one 'which cuts him off for ever from his old Party'.[107]

Peel himself remained unrepentant about the course he had adopted. Shortly after his removal from office, he wrote to Sir James Graham that he was 'firmly convinced that the permanent adjustment of the Corn Laws has rescued the Country, and the whole frame of society, from the hazard of very serious convulsion'.[108] Despite fierce denunciations from the country gentlemen, Peel preferred to view his actions as those of a true Conservative who, through timely concession, had prevented circumstances from arising which might have posed a grave threat to the social and political authority of the ruling élite. He was scathing in his comments about the ingratitude of 'a set of men with great possessions and little foresight, who call themselves Conservatives and Protectionists, and whose only chance of safety is that their counsels should not be followed'. Involuntarily freed from the burdens of high office, but also tired and unwell, he was determined never again to put himself at the head of a political party, when, as seemed to be the case in the modern world, it was expected that the rank-and-file's 'passions and sordid interests should be the rule of a Minister's conduct'.[109]

5

PEEL'S ACHIEVEMENT

Peel and the Peelites, 1846–50

The Conservative schism over the Corn Law question, and the fall of Peel's ministry, inaugurated a period of confusion and instability in British party politics which extended well beyond Peel's death in July 1850. For the last four years of his life, Peel's determination to occupy an independent position, free from party associations and obligations, did more than anything else to perpetuate the incoherence of the political scene at Westminster. Some contemporaries, indeed, felt that he was guilty of inconsistency in the way he behaved. On the one hand, Peel repeatedly asserted to his friends that he had no wish to return to office, and yet, on the other hand, he evidently had no intention of retiring from political life, as he retained his seat in the House of Commons and regularly attended and spoke in the debates.[1] Complete uncertainty therefore surrounded the intentions of Peel and his Free Trade Conservative followers: would they seek a rapprochement with the main body of Conservatives, or else gravitate towards Lord John Russell's Whig government (which had replaced Peel's ministry in June 1846), or at least organise themselves into a proper third party, until their political destiny became clearer? In practice, Peel was unwilling to countenance any of these courses of action, and this guaranteed that no government could possibly be formed on secure parliamentary foundations.

Events after 1846 fulfilled the worst fears of the veteran Conservative politician, Charles Arbuthnot, that if Peel remained active in public life this must preclude any chance of Conservative reunion, because the

Protectionists would never trust him again as their leader. In effect, Peel's decision to hold himself in reserve was condemning his old party to a prolonged period of political impotence.[2] As things stood, almost every member of the former Conservative front-bench was estranged from the parliamentary rank-and-file. Several initiatives were undertaken by intermediaries anxious to improve relations between the Peelites and the Protectionist leaders, Lord Stanley and Lord George Bentinck, with a view to eventually reconciling the two bodies of Conservatives, but these moves were invariably rebuffed by Peel and his friends. In Peel's opinion, such well-intentioned proposals seriously underestimated the 'difficulty of cordially reuniting the Conservative party', more especially as he was now inclined to regard the schism of 1846 as the product of more deep-seated differences than those occasioned by the Corn Law dispute.[3] Although the resignation and subsequent death of Bentinck removed one personal obstacle to Conservative unity, the emergence of Benjamin Disraeli as the new Protectionist leader in the House of Commons simply erected a fresh barrier against better mutual feelings. It is difficult to see how anything short of the recantation by the Protectionists of their beliefs, and acceptance of Peel's Free Trade system as a permanent settlement, could have healed the rift between the Conservative sections. While Stanley and his colleagues adhered to their Protectionist heresies, Peel was resolved to do everything in his power to prevent them from forming a government. So strongly was the opinion of the country in favour of Free Trade, according to Peel, that the accession of a Protectionist administration was totally out of the question.[4]

The logic of Peel's thinking dictated that he must be prepared to uphold the existing Whig government – which, for all its faults, was committed to the defence of Free Trade – so long as the only alternative was a Protectionist government dedicated to restoring the Corn Laws. Matters were complicated, however, by the fact that Lord John Russell did not control a majority in the House of Commons. Worse still, the non-Conservative MPs were not even a homogeneous body, including as they did an assorted group of some sixty radicals whose antagonism towards the aristocratic Whigs meant that they could never be counted as reliable allies. Consequently, Russell's government was always in a potentially vulnerable parliamentary position, especially when issues arose on which the radicals could vote with the Protectionists, and it was therefore necessary for Peel to avoid doing anything to weaken ministers any further. Early in 1849, he wrote to Sir James Graham that 'It seems to me that the position of parties – or rather of the relics of ancient parties – is now more complicated and embarrassing than ever. The weakness of the Government, and the disunion of all opponents except the Radical party, will still constitute its strength. But strength resting on such a foundation cannot be very satisfactory, and implies nothing but continued tenure of office.'[5] And yet, Peel's friends refused to help reinforce the Whigs' position by accepting any of the offers made to them, at various times, to join Russell's Cabinet. Instead, ministers had to be content with advice dispensed to them in private, the most famous case involving the Chancellor of the Exchequer, Sir Charles Wood, who regularly consulted Peel on commercial and financial matters.[6] Russell's government, it seemed, was fated to be kept in a permanent state of weakness, so that the Peelites could preserve their independence, but not allowed to die, because the Peelites saw no acceptable substitute for them.

To add to the chaotic situation in the House of Commons, Peel never encouraged the creation of anything that could properly be described as a 'Peelite party'. There were some 119 Conservative MPs who had supported the repeal of the Corn Laws at the second or third reading stages, in 1846, and even after the general election in the summer of 1847 almost the same number of 'Free Trade Conservatives' remained – around thirty-five of whom were newly elected members.[7] Clearly, the potential existed for the organisation of a powerful third force in the Commons, but Peel's unhappy experiences in the past, as the leader of a political party, meant that he was unwilling to assume that role again. He sat on the opposition front-bench (though he was supporting the government) and consulted occasionally with a few of his former Cabinet colleagues, notably Graham, Gladstone, Herbert and Lincoln, but the bulk of the Free Trade Conservatives received no lead from Peel, each being left to determine his own individual course. John Young, who had served as Peel's chief whip from 1844 to 1846, was keen that some effort should be made to hold the Free Trade Conservatives together, but when he sent out circulars to MPs, prior to the opening of the 1847 session, informing them of the date on which parliament was due to meet and requesting their attendance, Peel would not permit this to be done in his name. Young responded by warning Peel of the dangers inherent in his resolutely independent stance:

if you stand aloof, and let people know and see you mean to do so permanently, by degrees the Conservatives who adhered to you will drop off, all but a score, and unite with Lord Stanley, and give him a decided majority to turn out the present Government, take, and keep their places. And then, though he will not dare or attempt to subvert, or reverse, your commercial policy, he and his men will cramp and confine it, and not let it have fair play.[8]

Despite Young's expression of concern that, by failing to act as the leader of the Free Trade Conservatives, Peel risked letting them drift back towards the main body of Conservatives (which is precisely what happened, in a great many cases, during the 1850s), nothing more was done to build up a Peelite organisation – not even a repeat of the 1847 pre-session circular.

The practical result of Peel's remoteness from his Free Trade Conservative supporters was that, in voting terms, no effective Peelite bloc operated in the House of Commons. It is true that on certain occasions, when issues arose directly threatening the Free Trade edifice, those Conservatives loyal to the cause could be expected to rally to the government's support. For instance, when Radical MPs (with some Protectionist help) challenged Sir Charles Wood's proposal to renew the income tax, in 1848, seventy-five Conservatives voted with ministers on the grounds that the income tax was an integral part of the Free Trade experiment. Similarly, at the start of the 1849 session, Free Trade Conservatives voted heavily against a motion by Disraeli, on the state of the nation, which had Protectionist implications. On many other major questions, though, whereas Peel faithfully voted with the government, more Free Trade Conservatives opposed than supported ministers. Thus, they divided forty-three to twenty-nine against Jewish emancipation, in 1847, and sixty-five to twenty-seven in favour of a protectionist motion by Sir John Pakington, in 1848, relating to the West Indies. A cleverly contrived motion could sometimes put the Free Trade Conservatives in an awkward spot, and when, in February 1850, Disraeli raised the subject of relief to the landed interest from the burden of local taxation (rather than referring directly to protectionism), Peel's friends were left in a quandry: twenty-two backed the government, but fifty-six voted with Disraeli, some of them for constituency reasons. Curiously enough, the only time that Peel spoke and voted against Russell's government was in his very last appearance in the Commons, the day before his fatal accident, when he condemned the conduct of the Foreign Secretary, Lord Palmerston, over the 'Don Pacifico' affair. Even so, Peel was privately relieved that the ministry survived this debate, and while sixty-seven Free Trade Conservatives voted to censure Palmerston, he was still supported by twenty-two.[9] J. B. Conacher's analysis of division lists for the 1847–50 period shows that of the near-120 nominal Free Trade Conservatives, only forty-eight (including fourteen former office holders) can be defined as fairly consistent supporters of Peel, to whom we might add a further twenty-four voting with him more often than not on critical issues.[10]

Charles Greville expressed the view, in the autumn of 1847, that 'nothing was ever so strange or anomalous' as the position occupied by Peel. Politically speaking, the stark fact was that, leaving aside Peel's Free Trade Conservative friends, 'he is liked by nobody. The Conservatives detest him with unquenched hatred, and abuse him with unmitigated virulence. The Whigs regard him with a mixture of fear, suspicion, and dislike, but treat him with great deference and respect.' In the eyes of the public, on the other hand, Peel was seen as the man best qualified to lead a government, and as the obvious choice to be called to the helm and rescue the country in a time of crisis. 'The consequence of all this is that his *prestige* and influence are enormous.'[11] No doubt it was gratifying for Peel to find himself accepted in the role he had always wished to cast himself in, as a national leader, above the petty considerations of party politics. But this domestic equivalent of 'spendid isolation', however much it suited Peel temperamentally, placed tremendous strain on the loyalty of some of his younger followers, such as Gladstone, whose careers were still ahead of them. Indeed, there were signs of intense frustration at Peel's refusal to offer any encouragement to those who still looked to him for leadership.[12]

It is interesting to find that Prince Albert, one of Peel's greatest admirers, felt that his death in July 1850 came at the right time, politically speaking. Until the last, he fulfilled his intention of working as a mediatory figure, effectively 'directing the government of the Country', and his reputation with the public had never been higher. Nevertheless, his final intervention in the House of Commons, during the Don Pacifico debate, had highlighted the problems with this independent stance. It was hardly convincing to voice disapproval of the government's foreign policy when it was all too obvious that he had no desire to remove the Whigs from power, for fear that he might clear the path for a Protectionist ministry which would be 'dangerous to the Country.' Had he lived to pursue this strategy indefinitely, Prince Albert doubted whether Peel's friends could have continued to support him.[13]

One can only speculate, of course, as to what might have happened if Peel had not died suddenly, as the result of an accident, at the age of sixty-two. It is easily forgotten that he was four years *younger* than both Lord Aberdeen, who headed the Peelite–Whig coalition government of 1852–5, and Lord Palmerston, who dominated the political scene for a decade after 1855. Despite his persistent avowal that he had no ambition to return to office, it is not inconceivable that his view might have changed if the Russell ministry had collapsed, as it regularly threatened to do, and the only choice was between leading a Free Trade coalition government or allowing the Protectionists into power. Perhaps Peel would have been the beneficiary of a royally engineered coalition, in much the same way that Aberdeen was in December 1852. Before we go too far down this speculative path, however, it also has to be borne in mind that, after 1850, the relations between leading Peelites, such as Gladstone, Lincoln and Herbert, and prominent Whigs like Russell and Palmerston, were notoriously unharmonious, and that it eventually proved beyond the conciliatory powers of the mild-mannered Aberdeen to hold them together. Not until June 1859 was a durable coalition of the Free Trade parties finally established, under Palmerston's auspices. With the benefit of hindsight, therefore, it is difficult to believe that a strong-willed leader like Peel would have enjoyed greater success in uniting the Peelites with the Whigs, and rather more probable that any such attempt would have broken down in circumstances of the greatest acrimony. Another point to consider is that Peel's health might not have been robust enough to cope with the burdens of high office, which had taken a considerable toll on his strength during the ministry of 1841–6, and was undoubtedly one of the reasons why he declared that he no longer aspired to the premiership.

The danger for Peel, if he had lived longer, was that he risked leaving himself in an increasingly isolated position, from which his hold on the public's imagination must inevitably have diminished over the years. It would have been a sad ending to a long and distinguished career for Peel to be reduced to a dim light, on the margins of the political world, deserted by followers who felt they had no option but to come to terms with the Whigs or else make their peace with the Protectionists. As it was, Peel's public work was complete, and it seems fitting that he should have been removed from the scene while his fame was still at its height.

Peel and the British People

On the morning of Saturday 30 June 1850, Peel attended a meeting of the commissioners responsible for organising what came to be known as the Great Exhibition, held in Hyde Park the following year. In the afternoon, he went out for a ride on a horse which he had recently acquired, but, stopping to greet some acquaintances on Constitution Hill, he was thrown off by his new mount. As Peel hit the ground, the animal's knees came down on his back, fracturing his ribs and collar-bone, and causing internal injuries. He was removed to his house in Whitehall Gardens where, after three days of great suffering, he died on 2 July.

Francis Wey, a French visitor to England, recounted how the news of Peel's accident prompted a remarkable manifestation of public concern:

> London lived through three days of intense anxiety. People went as often as six times a day to inquire, the little garden at White Hall was thronged with a silent dejected crowd.
>
> I called there myself one evening. Night was falling in heavy Shadows; respectful groups stood about in front of the railings, looking across the small garden at a dim light glowing in a ground floor window. Without really knowing why, I also waited. A few moments later a policeman came out of the house, approached the gate, and as the people pressed forward he said in even tones: 'He is dead'.
>
> By my watch it was ten minutes to eleven. Not a word was spoken, the crowd just melted into the night. An hour later all London had heard the news and was mourning the loss of her greatest Statesman.[14]

On the day of Peel's funeral at Drayton, many businesses in the City and the West End of London were closed, and church bells were rung in places all over the country. Queen Victoria wrote to her uncle, King Leopold of the Belgians, that 'The sorrow and grief at his death are most touching, and the country mourns over him as over a father. Everyone seems to have lost a personal friend.'[15] Not since Pitt the Younger, in 1806, had there been such a display of anguish at the death of a political leader.

In the hearts and minds of the mid-Victorian public, Peel's reputation was now secure. He was the wise Statesman who had risen above the selfish interests of classes and parties to deliver cheap food and prosperity to the whole of the British people. The sudden and shocking manner of his death lent added poignancy to the belief that here was a man who had willingly sacrificed his career for the good of others. Tributes to Peel's memory were paid by all sections of British society.[16] Provincial newspapers committed to the Free Trade cause, such as the *Manchester Guardian*, *Leeds Mercury*, *Preston Chronicle* and *Liverpool Mercury*, which had often been grudging in their praise of Peel at the time he repealed the Corn Laws, now eulogised him in black-bordered columns. Admiration for Peel's work was equally expressed by publications such as *Chambers's Papers for the People*, which devoted a special edition to him, and even by Feargus O'Connor's *Northern Star*, the leading Chartist organ. The radically inclined satirical magazine *Punch* produced a cartoon entitled 'Monument to Peel', depicting a pyramid of loaves with the inscription 'Cheap Bread', and a working-class family happily eating their meal. Many newspapers carried advertisements for mementoes of the deceased Statesman, including portraits, busts, medals, biographies and chinaware. Street ballads were also produced, such as 'The Poor Men's Lamentation for the Death of Sir Robert Peel', and the following composition, issued from Seven Dials, one of the roughest districts in London:

> The Poor long has praised and bless'd him,
> Now tears wet each eye, while in sorrow they sigh,
> He is gone, is Sir Robert, God rest him.
>
> * * * *
>
> He'd by no one be led, he'd by no one be said,
> No Government feared to trust him.
> In every way he carried the sway
> For the good of his Country, God rest him.

Parliament voted money for the erection of a statue in Westminster Abbey, to honour Peel, and the dead man's friends paid for another one which was finally sited, after long delays, in Parliament Square. Statues were meantime put up in most of the big provincial towns, including Manchester (where a public subscription raised over £5000 – enough to pay for a colossal bronze monument), Birmingham, Liverpool, Leeds, Bradford and Glasgow, along with smaller urban centres such as Bury, Peel's birthplace, where in addition to a statue a 120 feet high column was placed on a hill. At Cheapside, the statue of Peel faced, appropriately enough, towards the Bank of England and the City of London.

One particularly interesting initiative was the 'Poor Man's Testimonial to Sir Robert Peel', organised by the prominent Radical MP Joseph Hume, and supported by Cobden and Bright, among others. The idea was to raise penny subscriptions from ordinary people, and 167 local collection committees were formed to assist in the work. It was eventually disclosed that a total of £1736 0s 6d had been collected, equivalent to 416,886 penny subscriptions, and the money was handed over to University College London for use in promoting working-class education – for instance, through the donation of books to public libraries and mechanics' institutes. Entries in the subscription book show how 1102 people employed by the London and Brighton and South Coast railway raised £19 1s 0d (indicating an average donation of 3–4d each), 804 letter carriers from the London district sent in £3 17s 0d (roughly 1d each), 424 working men of Pontefract collected £1 15s 4d, and 752 Sheerness dockyard workers raised £5 8s 3d, while an astonishing 30,902 subscriptions from the Manchester area amounted to £128 15s 2d (an average of slightly over 1d each).

The tremendous outpouring of public grief at the time of Peel's death, and the subsequent monuments to his memory, are all the more remarkable when we consider that few of the individuals involved would ever have seen Peel, let alone met him. Nevertheless, it is obvious that large numbers of people did have a powerful mental image of what they supposed Peel to be like, and of what he stood for. Francis Wey wrote that 'What Peel's death meant for the entire country was the disappearance of a trusted pilot, a glory extinguished, a burnt-out torch. The depth and unanimity of such a feeling is a strange spectacle for a Frenchman, and gives one a high idea of the political conscience and the essential solidarity of the different elements of English Society.'[17] If this judgement seems a little too bland, it remains the case that there was a collective folk memory of Peel, shared by people of various social classes, whatever their differences might be in other respects. For a politician who had lived through the turbulence of the Peterloo years, the Parliamentary Reform crisis and the Chartist demonstrations, the common feeling displayed towards Peel when he died was a significant tribute to his achievement. Arguably, the public sorrow expressed in 1850 was a testament to the way that Peel, through his general Free Trade policies, and above all through the abandonment of the Corn Laws, had helped the country to adjust, psychologically, to the idea that it was now an industrial nation as much as anything else. Of course, the Great Exhibition at the Crystal Palace in 1851, which Peel had been working to promote on the day of his fatal accident, was an extraordinary symbol of Britain's new-found industrial awareness. By the middle of the nineteenth century, it seemed as if the country had survived the ordeal of industrialisation without suffering a social collapse, and that, thanks to Peel's Free Trade legacy, the people were now reaping the material rewards after decades of instability and fear. In the manner of his death, Peel stood out as a great moral force in a nation which liked to equate economic progress with moral progress.

Peel and the Politicians

Naturally, it was the policies associated with Peel's name which left such a powerful impression on the popular imagination, but the way in which he presented himself and his work was an equally important facet of his national appeal. This must have been particularly true in the case of the political class at Westminster, as well as the educated, newspaper-reading public. From an early stage in his career, Peel had developed a highly effective parliamentary manner which marked him out as a potential future leader, even if it did grate on the nerves of some hostile critics, for whom his 'premature worldly wisdom' made Peel a 'peculiarly odious' figure.[18] After Canning's death in 1827, there was no doubting Peel's status as the foremost debater on the Tory benches, and it was as leader of the opposition, in the 1830s, that he succeeded in establishing himself as *the* pre-eminent parliamentarian, a man whose reputation extended beyond the narrow world of Westminster and into the minds of an increasingly politically conscious nation. The journalist D. O. Maddyn, writing after Peel's death, recalled that the 1830s were:

> the period...when his eloquence was most matured, and when a loftier tone, a more genuine dignity, and greater classical polish, adorned his speeches.... Sir Robert Peel was the most practically persuasive speaker I ever heard. Though not an orator of the highest class, his talents in addressing a public assembly were extraordinary. His voice was like a lute, pleasing, resonant, and not too loud; his words came clearly from his lips, without any pedantic formalism; his fluency was unbroken, and he had high histrionic powers of delivery. This able man, who in private life was often so awkward, and almost rude, assumed an air of graceful amenity and of bland insinuation,

when addressing the House of Commons; and it was difficult to listen to his melodious tones, and dexterous play of parliamentary logic, without being gradually biassed. . . . No man could approach an audience with more art; no one could better choose the tone right for employing, and he was seldom thrown off his guard.[19]

One of the most detailed contemporary descriptions of Peel's physical appearance and debating mannerisms comes from the pen of another journalist, James Grant, and dates from the mid-1830s, precisely the period that Maddyn had referred to. It is well worth reproducing some lengthy extracts:

He is a remarkably good looking man, rather above the usual size, and finely proportioned. He is of a clear complexion, full round face, and red-haired. His usual dress is a green surtout, a light waistcoat, and dark trowsers. He generally displays a watch-chain on his breast, with a bunch of gold seals of unusually large dimensions and great splendour. He can scarcely be called a dandy, and yet he sacrifices a good deal to the graces. I hardly know a public man who dresses in better taste. He is in the prime of life, being forty-seven years of age. His whole appearance indicates health. His constitution is excellent, and his temperate habits have seconded the kindly purposes of Nature. . . .

There never was a more complete master of the plausibilities than Sir Robert Peel. He is apparently all candour and sincerity. He invariably appeals to his honour for the truth of what he says. He not only urges the best arguments which can be advanced in favour of the cause which he espouses, but there is such an appearance of honesty and fair-dealing about him, that it is with great difficulty those who are most opposed to his politics can guard against being led away by his winning manner. He is a most consummate special pleader: had he been destined for the bar, he would long since have been one of its most distinguished ornaments.

In his manner Sir Robert is highly dignified, and his delivery is generally graceful. He usually commences his most important speeches with his left hand resting on his side. His utterance on such occasions is slow and solemn in the outset; but when he advances to the heart of his subject he becomes animated and speaks with some rapidity, but always with much distinctness. His enunciation is clear; and few speakers possess a greater power over their voice. He can modulate its soft and musical tones at pleasure. He is sometimes humorous, on which occasions his manner has an irresistibly comic effect. His jokes, when he does indulge in them, are almost invariably good, though often too refined to tell with effect on any other than an intellectual audience. It is, however, but comparatively seldom that he makes any effort at wit. His *forte* manifestly lies in the serious mode of address. He excels all men I ever knew in deep tragedy: in that he is quite at home. No man in the House can appeal with a tittle of the effect which he can, to the fears of his audience; and he is too good a tactician not to know, that a great deal more may be accomplished by addressing in this strain an audience who have rank and property to lose, than by cold argumentative orations. Hence the staple of his principal speeches consists of a forcible and skilful exhibition of the alleged frightful consequences which will inevitably flow from the adoption of a course of policy different from that which he recom-mends.... The deepest stillness pervades the House while he is speak-ing. Even in the gallery, where there is generally a great deal of noise from the exits and the entrances of strangers, the falling of a pin might be heard. All eyes are fixed on Sir Robert. Honourable Mem-bers, of all parties, are, for the time, spell-bound. Their reason is taken prisoner.... The solemnity of the speaker is communicated to the hearers....

One feature in the oratory of Sir Robert, which every one who ever heard him must have observed, is the practice he has, when speaking on any great question, of striking the box which lies on the table, at regular intervals, with his right hand. On an average, he gives it two strokes in a minute; and as these are given with great force, and the box is remarkable for its acoustic properties, the sound is distinctly heard in every part of the house, and considerably aids the effect which his speech would otherwise produce.[20]

G. H. Francis's account of Peel, published in 1847, confirms that he was 'indeed the master-spirit of the House of Commons', but also agrees with the other writers cited in emphasising that Peel was not the most eloquent or brilliant or intellectual of speakers. On the contrary, the authority he exercised over his fellow MPs was based on a practical, commonsensical tone, which was usually pitched at 'the level of the average understanding of the House'. Francis considered that Peel's style of address was ideally suited to the businesslike atmosphere in the post-Reform Act House of Commons, and he even suspected that

Peel might have been forced to conceal something of his real passion in order to achieve the influence he desired. Commonplace thoughts expressed in commonplace language were what MPs required, and oratorical genius of the kind associated with Fox, Pitt and Sheridan, would actually have been out of place, in Francis's opinion. The unfortunate result of parliamentary necessity was that Peel's speeches were characterised by 'vagueness', 'empty pomposity' and 'verbose inconclusiveness'. Confronted with a direct question, Peel was slippery and eel-like, having mastered the art of appearing to intend a frank answer while in fact skilfully diverting his audience's attention from the real issue: 'Ten to one he sits down "amidst loud cheers", having uttered much, but avowed nothing.' Only on rare occasions in his later years, notably during the Corn Law debates of 1846, did Peel adopt a more lofty tone, displaying some flashes of genuine spirit. But the impact of his oratory was always marred, according to Francis, by the idiosyncratic postures and gestures to which he was prone, including having his 'elbow resting on the table before him, while his pointed finger shakes ominously at his opponents', or 'his thumbs buried in the pockets of his capacious waistcoat, while his coat is thrown back ostentatiously', or, most commonly of all, with 'his hands hidden under his coat-tails, while he stands much as he might with his back to a fire'. In sum, Francis found Peel to be a man who commanded respect for 'his ease and self-possession, the thorough knowledge he has, even to the minutest details, of every subjects he undertakes', although a stranger to the House of Commons was likely to be disappointed by the absence of 'vivid imagination or profound thought'.[21]

A puzzling contradiction exists between the official face which Peel presented to his audience and the private exterior familiar to his parliamentary colleagues. Charles Arbuthnot exclaimed, at one point during the minority government of 1834–5, that 'Peel is certainly a most extraordinary being. He keeps all his ill temper for his friends, for in debate one does not know which to admire the most – his calmness – his clear expositions – or the consummate tact and ability with which he treats every question.'[22] The earlier chapters of this book record many of the complaints made by contemporaries about Peel's morose and forbidding character. Charles Wynn, who joined Lord Liverpool's Cabinet at around the same time as Peel, remarked upon the latter's 'coldness and reserve of…manner towards me', though he added that it was some consolation to know that Peel treated others in the same way.[23] From the opposite end of the Tory spectrum, in the 1820s,

Lord Ellenborough felt that Peel's temperament rendered him unsuitable for the task of party leadership, while in his dealings with his Cabinet colleagues he was 'certainly... not an agreeable person to transact business with', despite his obvious competence.[24] Harriet Arbuthnot, who was close to the Duke of Wellington, often made somewhat bemused observations about Peel in her journal. In March 1830, for instance, when commenting on reports that Peel was improving in his management of the House of Commons, she added that:

> It is a pity he makes himself so unpopular, for he can be very agreeable when he likes it, & he is really very good & amiable but his manners are quite odious. He asks immense parties of the H. of Commons to dinner every week & treats them so *de haut en bas* & is so haughty & silent that they come away swearing they will never go to his house again, so that his civilities do him harm rather than otherwise.[25]

No glib explanation can be offered for why Peel was so cold and reserved in his private manner. In all probability, it was partly a case of innate shyness, although we do not know a great deal about his childhood.[26] One superficially tempting argument would be that the key to Peel's prickliness and frigidity lay in a sense of social inferiority arising from his family's industrial origins, but this can almost certainly be rejected. In fact, Peel took great pride in his background, and was rather fond of reminding MPs about it during debates. He seems, moreover, to have been well-integrated into the lifestyle of the old ruling élite, not only through his public school and university education, but also because he enjoyed country pursuits such as riding and shooting. It is true that he always spoke with a regional accent, but this was not unusual for peers and MPs in this period, before the public schools imposed a uniform 'received pronunciation' on their students. Within the Tory ministerial ranks, Peel's *industrial* lineage did make him unique, but there were other men from middle-class backgrounds, such as Henry Addington (Lord Sidmouth) and Lord Chancellor Eldon, and few of those with aristocratic and landed connections were actually great territorial magnates or possessors of ancient hereditary titles. Lord Liverpool, to take one example, inherited a peerage awarded to his father for services to the Crown during the late eighteenth century, and his landed property in Oxfordshire was quite modest in size. There is little reason, then, to suppose that Peel was socially crippled by being considered a vulgar parvenu, and the occasional snide references to 'spinning jenny' came, more often than otherwise, from the snobbishly exclusive ranks of the Whig party.[27]

Peel's experiences as a Tory minister may, nevertheless, be of some relevance for understanding his attitude towards fellow members of the ruling élite. When he took office in 1810, Peel entered into a Pittite tradition of administration which prided itself on its devotion to the interests of the State and the nation – which were engaged, of course, in a struggle for existence against Napoleonic France – rather than indulging the selfish claims of the aristocratic and landed class. It was for this reason that even men like Pitt, Liverpool and Canning were emotionally somewhat distanced from the élite to which they undoubtedly belonged. Peel came to manifest these Pittite values of disinterestedness, and administrative efficiency and rectitude, to an exaggerated degree, and the result was a formidable disdain for those who failed to come up to his own pure and high standards. The sordid realities of politics and government often disgusted him, and shortly after the Tories fell from power in 1830, he confessed to one of his few close colleagues, Henry Goulburn, that 'I feel a want of many essential qualifications which are requisite in party leaders, among the rest personal gratification in the game of politics, and patience to listen to the sentiments of individuals whom it is equally imprudent to neglect and an intolerable bore to consult.'[28] From this perspective, it can be said that Peel's problem was not that he felt inferior to those he was politically associated with, but that he felt convinced of his own superior high-mindedness. So proud was he of his reputation for integrity, that on several occasions when his honour was questioned by an opponent, Peel responded by challenging that person to a duel – or else threatened to.[29]

If his Pittite heritage may have served to reinforce a natural tendency towards pride and haughtiness in Peel's character, it is similarly possible that the six years spent in governing Ireland contributed something to his personal development. Appointed to the Irish Chief Secretaryship, at the age of just twenty-four, it is easy to see how Peel might have found it necessary to build a thick outer shell. There can be little doubt that the wide-ranging responsibilities thrown upon him induced an excessive reliance on his own administrative skills, and he was forever afterwards reluctant to delegate work or consult with others. But the trauma of being regularly besieged by hungry applicants for patronage may also have left a permanent mark on Peel's personality, encouraging him to acquire a habit of extreme caution in what he said to other people.

The suggestion that Peel's notoriously stiff and remote manner may have been something that, part-consciously, he allowed to grow on himself, and was related to the political circumstances in which his career progressed, is supported by evidence of the very different way in which he treated some of his colleagues during the ministry of 1841–6. Towards young protégés such as Gladstone, Lord Lincoln and Sidney Herbert, whom Peel sought to inspire with the same noble ethics of administration as those in which he had been trained, he exhibited a personal warmth and openness which belies his usual reputation. Peel also found a trustworthy confidant in his Home Secretary, Sir James Graham, a Whig convert and near-contemporary. Evidently, by the 1840s, Peel felt sufficiently secure to be able to relax his guard in a way that he had not previously dared to do.

Those contemporaries who were never able, or never allowed, to penetrate Peel's outer shell, were deprived of the knowledge that an interesting and, in certain respects, attractive human personality existed beneath it. Peel seems to have been genuinely devoted to his wife, Julia, and wrote daily letters to her when they were apart. He was also fond of children, and had a large family of his own. The inspiration he found in the wild scenery of the Scottish Highlands, where he spent several long holidays, indicates that there was a romantic side to Peel's nature, and is worthy of remark because the Highlands had not yet become a fashionable place for English tourists. Peel was a man of culture, well-read in the classics, theology and history – he was fascinated by the French Revolution, a subject on which he possessed a fine library of books. From time to time, he invited men from various branches of learning, including the sciences, to gatherings at Drayton in order to discuss the latest ideas and discoveries. In artistic terms, Peel's great love was for paintings, and he not only collected old masters but commissioned portraits of some of his colleagues. Lord Ellenborough, who seldom found Peel an easy man to communicate with, managed to get through to him on one occasion when he was hosting a Cabinet dinner: 'I asked Peel to drink a glass of wine, and showed him two or three pictures. The consequence was a cordiality of manner. I really believe he is only rather a proud, touchy man, and that the least attempt at management would make him very cordial.'[30] Peel could also be compassionate, as is shown by his private acts of charity, notably the assistance he gave to ease the tragic plight of the painter Benjamin Robert Haydon.[31]

Ostensibly, at least, Peel's austere exterior and obsession with dry administrative detail is not suggestive of a man with strong religious feelings, but this would be a misleading impression to convey. He was certainly not doctrinaire in matters of theology, and he therefore had little sympathy with groups like the Tractarians, whose antics created serious divisions within the Church of England during the 1830s and 1840s. Peel regretted that such controversies weakened the ability of the Established Church to perform its essential duty to the nation, of spreading Christian knowledge and values among the mass of the people, the urbanised portion of whom were becoming dangerously estranged from any kind of organised religion. His own faith was that of a moderate evangelical, and there were times when he allowed religious emotions to enter into his political language, especially during the Corn Law debates of 1846. When Peel spoke to vindicate his Free Trade system, in 1849, a year after the European revolutions and the failure of the last Chartist demonstration, he affirmed that 'That which was done was no act of a sagacious Minister. . . . It was no lucky accident. It is my firm belief that it pleased Almighty God to hearken to your prayers. It pleased him to turn "your dearth and scarcity" into "cheapness and plenty".' Divine Providence had led the British parliament to abandon protectionism and rest its policy on the principle of justice, and the country had reaped its just reward: 'You have passed unscathed through the sternest trials to which the institutions of nations were ever subjected. You have stood erect amid the convulsions of Europe.'[32]

Peel and the Historians

Considering the extraordinary display of emotion by the British public, at the time of Peel's death, it is a surprising fact that, in political and intellectual circles, his reputation diminished quite rapidly thereafter. In some ways, this was a mark of the success of his Free Trade system, which became so securely established as the basis of government policy, for the remainder of the nineteenth century, that it was easy to lose sight of just how great Peel's achievement had been. As Gladstone extended his master's principles still further, dismantling much of the remaining tariff structure in his budgets of the 1850s and 1860s, and as the Liberal party (including the leading Peelites) enjoyed their long political supremacy, what had originally been a bold experiment in economic policy appeared instead as a rather tentative step towards an orthodox position. Looking back from the vantage point of the mid-Victorian era, with its comparative social and political tranquillity, Liberal writers such as Walter Bagehot were unable to discern in Peel anything more than an unquestionably able, but overly cautious administrator, possessed of a very ordinary intellect which meant that his ideas developed at about the same pace as the average person's. Peel was judged to have been lacking in powers of foresight, and, by the 1890s, biographers like Justin McCarthy and J. R. Thursfield depicted him as little more than a half-hearted Liberal – an honorary one at best – who had spent his life pursuing modest measures of reform from within a political party which was obviously unsuited to the task.[33]

Since the 1920s, however, Peel has been the beneficiary of a process of scholarly rehabilitation, beginning with the work of Anna Ramsay and George Kitson Clark.[34] This new trend culminated in the major two-volume biographical treatment of Peel by Norman Gash, published in 1961 and 1972.[35] From Gash's account, Peel emerges as a pragmatic, empirical administrator, and an instinctively consensual politician, whose great achievement was to lay down the basic principles of modern Conservatism. (Peel's career was now assuming a greater historical significance, given the demise of the Liberal party and the impressive record of the Conservatives as the dominant party of government in the twentieth century.) The Tamworth Manifesto, in Gash's view, was the key document in the evolution of Conservative ideas, embodying as it did Peel's perception that his party must accept the need for gradual change in order to become a viable party of government. If ancient institutions such as the Church and the aristocracy were to survive against radical attack, their interests had to be reconciled with the values and expectations of a society experiencing rapid and profound change. By implementing moderate reforms, where these were shown to be justified, and thus occupying the middle ground in British politics, Gash argued that Peel helped the Conservatives to broaden the social basis of their support, appealing to urban middle-class voters as well as landowners and farmers. His object was to preserve the role of the traditional ruling élite, by earning the trust of other sections of society, and this required a government devoted to promoting the national interest rather than the narrow interests of one particular class. Peel was uniquely qualified to perform this work, according to Gash, because he personally straddled the old and the new forces in society, having been born into a business dynasty but educated and trained within the ranks of the traditional élite. Through the success of his policies, Peel was in fact the true architect of the mid-Victorian 'age of equipoise'.

Even the Conservative party, which repudiated his leadership in 1846, was soon forced to learn the hard lesson that there was no alternative but to adopt a Peelite approach to politics. Ironically, Disraeli, the man who did so much to destroy Peel's government, subsequently embraced Peelite practices himself, and most other Conservative leaders have followed the same path since then. Thus, Gash concluded that it was right to describe Peel as the 'founder of modern Conservatism',[36] and the period between 1830 and 1850, in British history, has become known to students as 'The Age of Peel'.[37]

This assessment of Peel's achievement has been called into question by a number of historians approaching the subject from various directions. One obvious problem is that Peel's allegedly pragmatic style of administration is not easily squared with the resolutely anti-reformist stance which he took on many major issues early in his career. The granting of Catholic Emancipation in 1829, for instance, came after more than a decade in which Peel had been the foremost critic of such a policy, and its concession was only made because of the fear that the British government might otherwise lose control over Ireland. In the case of the Whigs' Parliamentary Reform Bill, Peel opposed this measure until the bitter end. He also resisted the extension of religious equality to cover Jews, in 1830, and, while he never explicitly opposed the abolition of slavery in British colonies, his speeches in the late 1820s and early 1830s did nothing but find obstacles in the way of decisive action.[38]

Any claim that Peel might have to recognition as a *consistent* proponent of reform therefore rests upon his record at the Home Office in the 1820s. His efforts to consolidate the criminal law statutes, abolishing many capital offences in the process, were indeed presented by Gash as proof of Peel's humanitarian concerns. Derek Beales, however, in a review article published in 1974, demonstrated that Peel's rationalisation of the statutes had only a limited effect on the number of executions carried out, and that credit was really due to the Whig ministers of the 1830s for substantially reducing the use of the death penalty.[39] More recently, V. A. C. Gatrell has passionately argued that Peel has no right to be regarded as a humanitarian Home Secretary at all, as his instinct was to strongly resist appeals for clemency, on behalf of those convicted of capital offences, and to allow the law to take its course.[40] The inspiration behind Peel's measures, it now seems, was not so much a desire for more leniency in the application of the criminal law, but a determination to achieve greater consistency by ensuring that anyone committing a felony knew the penalty they could expect to suffer if caught.[41]

If it is difficult to accept that, prior to 1832, Peel was a great reformer, helping to calm the many tensions in British society, it might reasonably be said, in his defence, that the true test of Peel's credentials comes with the examination of his career after the Reform Act. The validity of Gash's argument that Peel realised he had to persuade the Conservative party to be more adaptable, so that it might come to terms with the new political dispensation created by the Whigs, has never been questioned. However, it is less clear that Peel succeeded in transforming his party into a truly national entity capable of embracing urban middle-class voters. Robert Stewart and Ian Newbould have both shown that, in terms of the geographical distribution of its electoral support and the kinds of issues on which its candidates campaigned, the Conservative party had not altered very much by 1841. The general election triumph of that year was won mainly in the counties and small boroughs of England, and the issue which dominated the contest was agricultural protection.[42] Bearing this in mind, it is hardly surprising that the constructive reforms, which Peel undeniably did promote as Prime Minister between 1841 and 1846, should have encountered growing opposition from back-bench Conservative MPs, and that the story ended with a disastrous schism over the Corn Law question.

Without doubt, the most fundamental challenge to Gash's understanding of Peel has come from Boyd Hilton, in a seminal article which appeared in 1979.[43] Far from seeing Peel as a natural mediator, who always looked for the middle ground in politics, Hilton presents him as a rigid and dogmatic leader who was unwilling to compromise on his views. This analysis relates mainly to Peel's thinking on questions of economic policy, which betrayed the signs of his training in mathematics while at Oxford. According to Hilton, Peel's intellect was readily susceptible to the charms of a system, and, once convinced of the theoretical correctness of a proposition, it was necessary for him to fit everything else into that model, like elements in a mathematical equation. If a 'fact', or a statistic, contradicted the model which Peel had already embraced, his reaction was likely to be that the 'fact' or statistic must be wrong, for he lacked the creative imagination with which to adjust the model. Hilton shows how Peel's 'schematic intellect' explains his inflexible and obsessional attitude towards the resumption of cash payments, in and after 1819, and he suggests that Peel was probably converted to the principle of Corn Law repeal by the end of the 1820s. Peel's doctrinaire adherence to *laissez-faire* ideas meant, for instance, that in the 1840s an opportunity was missed for the government to establish regulatory control over the construction of the railway network. Hilton therefore concludes that Peel's legacy was not to modern Conservatism, but that he can properly be described as 'the progenitor of Gladstonian Liberalism'. The 'moral energy' created by his supreme gesture of self-sacrifice, in 1846, was eventually transfused into the Liberal political tradition by his young disciples.

Peel's stature as a great Statesman has clearly been reduced to a significant extent by recent historical writing. One symptom of this historiographical reaction against Peel is the long-overdue attention currently being given to the Whig governments of the early Victorian years, which can no longer be treated as dismissively as they were by Gash.[44] The notion of an 'Age of Peel' frankly seems insufficient as a descriptive title for the period 1830–50. But there is a danger that the re-evaluation of Peel could be taken too far, and his political accomplishments undervalued. The fact remains that Peel established a system of commercial and financial policy which endured for almost a century, and, though the immediate political beneficiaries of this were the Liberals, within a few years the Protectionist leaders, Stanley (the Earl of Derby) and Disraeli, had been obliged to jettison their policy of tariffs and accept the new Peelite orthodoxies. Belatedly, the Protectionists seem to have realised the truth of Lord Hardinge's observation, in 1845, that 'a Conservative party after the Reform Bill can only govern on Peel principles'.[45] It can therefore be argued that Peel's career has a wider significance in that he compelled the whole of the British ruling élite, Liberals and Conservatives, to be more responsive to the needs of the urban population, and this influence was surely vital in terms of maintaining social stability, in 1848 and beyond. Peel may be said to have laid the foundations of the mid-Victorian 'age of equipoise', precisely for the reason that this depended on the endorsement of his Free Trade settlement across the political spectrum. If it is misleading to describe Peel simply as a consensual politician, the policies he pursued as Prime Minister, and the tragic circumstances of his death, helped to create a consensus for the generation to come.

NOTES

1 The Tory Administrations, 1809–30

1. See Norman Gash, *Mr Secretary Peel: The Life of Sir Robert Peel to 1830* (London, 1961), chs 1–3, for the whole of this section.
2. For the politics of this period, see A. D. Harvey, *Britain in the Early Nineteenth Century* (London, 1978).
3. Eldon to his wife, 13 September 1809, in Horace Twiss, *The Life of Lord Chancellor Eldon* (London, 1844), vol. 2, pp. 90–1.
4. Abbot's diary, 18 January 1810, in *The Diary and Correspondence of Charles Abbot, Lord Colchester* (London, 1861), vol. 2, p. 225.
5. 23 January 1810, in *The Speeches of the Late Right Honourable Sir Robert Peel, Delivered in the House of Commons* (London, 1853), vol. 1, pp. 5–7.
6. Creevey to his wife, 23 January 1810, in Sir Herbert Maxwell, *The Creevey Papers* (London, 1903), vol. 1, p. 122.
7. 18 March 1811, *Peel Speeches*, vol. 1, pp. 8–11.
8. Perceval to the Prince, 19 March 1811, in Arthur Aspinall (ed.), *The Correspondence of George, Prince of Wales, 1770–1812*, 8 vols (London, 1963–71), vol. 7, p. 280; Ward's diary, 18 March 1811, in Edmund Phipps, *Memoirs of Robert Plumer Ward, Esq.* (London, 1850), vol. 1, pp. 406–7.
9. For a detailed account of Peel's Chief Secretaryship, see R. C. Shipkey, *Robert Peel's Irish Policy, 1812–1846* (New York, 1987), chs 1–3.
10. Peel wrote to his friend Croker, from Dublin on 8 August 1815, that

> I had a passage of thirty-three hours from Holyhead – two nights and a day. Wretched beyond description...a completely foul wind. The packet was full of passengers. The men were all sick, and the women and children thought they were going to the bottom, and filled up the intervals of sickness with a chorus of lamentation, and cries of 'Steward, are we sinking?'
>
> (Louis J. Jennings (ed.), *The Correspondence and Diaries of John Wilson Croker* (London, 1884), vol. 1, pp. 75–6)

11. See, for example, Peel's own subsequent admission on this point, in a letter to Lord Liverpool, 24 December 1825, in C. S. Parker (ed.), *Sir Robert Peel: From his Private Correspondence*, 3 vols (London, 1891–9), vol. 1, pp. 388–9.

12. Peel to William Gregory [early 1816], and the reply from one magistrate, Willcocks, 17 April 1816, in Lady Gregory (ed.), *Mr Gregory's Letter-Box, 1813–1835* (London, 1898), pp. 95–103.

13. For the political situation at this time, see Sidmouth to his brother, 23 May 1812, in George Pellew, *The Life and Correspondence of the First Viscount Sidmouth* (London, 1847), vol. 3, p. 77.

14. Although they agreed on the Catholic question, there were serious differences over the conduct of the war, which Canning and Wellesley wished to prosecute with more vigour.

15. Peel to Croker, 30 October 1812, in *Croker Correspondence*, vol. 1, pp. 46–7.

16. Liverpool to Peel, 1 November 1812, in *Peel Correspondence*, vol. 1, pp. 44–5. Cf. Peel to Vesey Fitzgerald, 5 December 1812, ibid., vol. 1, p. 64.

17. 3 February 1812, *Peel Speeches*, vol. 1, pp 11–12.

18. 19 May 1813, ibid., vol. 1, pp. 21–6.

19. Peel to the Duke of Richmond, 26 May 1813, in *Peel Correspondence*, vol. 1, p. 86.

20. 9 May 1817, *Peel Speeches*, vol. 1, pp. 74–84.

21. *Letters, of the Earl of Dudley to the Bishop of Llandaff* (London, 1841), pp. 166–7 (10 May 1817).

22. See *Peel Correspondence*, vol. 1, pp. 249–50.

23. W. H. Lyttelton to Sir Charles Bagot, 1 June 1817, in Josceline Bagot, *George Canning and his Friends* (London, 1909), vol. 2, pp. 50–1.

24. 26 April 1816, *Peel Speeches*, vol. 1, pp. 56–64.

25. Ibid.

26. Peel to Speaker Abbot, 30 September 1814, in *Peel Correspondence*, vol. 1, pp. 154–7. In January 1816 the Insurrection Act was in force in four counties: Peel to Liverpool, 24 January 1816, *ibid.*, vol. 1, pp. 206–7.

27. Peel to the Rev. Trench, 27 April 1816, ibid., vol. 1, pp. 232–3; Peel to Liverpool, 24 June 1816, in C. D. Yonge, *The Life and Administration of Robert Banks, Second Earl of Liverpool* (London, 1868), vol. 2, pp. 279–80.

28. Peel to Sir Charles Flint, n.d., and Peel to Gregory, 20 April 1818, in *Peel Correspondence*, vol. 1, pp. 119–20, 264.

29. Peel to Beckett, 5 December 1816, ibid., vol. 1, p. 235.

30. Peel to Speaker Abbot, 25 December 1816, ibid., vol. 1, p. 236.

31. Peel to Gregory, n.d., ibid., vol. 1, p. 161.

32. See, for example, the material printed in ibid., vol. 1, pp. 270–84, showing also that corrupt practices were rife within the Irish administration.

33. Peel to Croker, October 1818, in ibid., vol. 1, pp. 287–8.

34. Arbuthnot to Castlereagh, 14 March 1819, in Arthur Aspinall (ed.), *The Correspondence of Charles Arbuthnot* (Royal Historical Society, Camden 3rd Series, LXV, 1941), pp. 13–18.

35. George III died in January 1820. The Prince of Wales, who had acted as Regent since 1811, now succeeded to the throne as King George IV.

36. W. H. Fremantle to Buckingham, 15 July 1818, in Duke of Buckingham and Chandos, *Memoirs of the Court of England, During the Regency, 1811–1820* (London, 1856), vol. 2, pp. 267–8.

37. It is in this sense that the label 'Tories' is applicable to them.

38. R. G. Thorne (ed.), *The History of Parliament, 1790–1820* (London, 1986), vol. 1, pp. 297–8.

39. See Charles Wynn to Buckingham, 9 February 1819, in *Memoirs of the Regency*, vol. 2, pp. 302–3, for the distinction between the government's 'friends' and the 'country gentlemen'.

40. For a full account of the government's problems, see J. E. Cookson, *Lord Liverpool's Administration, 1815–22* (Edinburgh, 1975).

41. See Fremantle to Buckingham, 16 February 1819, in *Memoirs of the Regency*, vol. 2, p. 308, and Fremantle to Buckingham, 11 March 1822, in Duke of Buckingham and Chandos, *Memoirs of the Court of George IV, 1820–1830* (London, 1859), vol. 1, pp. 295–8. Cf. *Letters of Dudley*, pp. 274–5 (29 January 1821): 'the opposition out-debated the Ministry – and the Ministry out-voted the opposition – and that will be the history of the session. I regard the majority as a majority against the Foxites.'

42. *Letters of Dudley*, pp. 223–4 (June 1819).

43. Henry Bankes to Lord Colchester, 3 December 1819, in *Diary and Correspondence of Colchester*, vol. 3, p. 95. Cf. *Memoirs of Plumer Ward*, vol. 2, pp. 39–40 (diary, 2 December 1819).

44. Arbuthnot to Castlereagh, 14 March 1819, in *Arbuthnot Correspondence*, pp. 13–18. Cf. Vesey Fitzgerald to Gregory, February 1819, in *Mr Gregory's Letter-Box*, p. 46.

45. Wynn to Buckingham, 31 December 1820, in *Memoirs of the Court of George IV*, vol. 1, pp. 102–3. The Grenville connection had broken with the Whigs in 1817, supporting as they did the government's policy of suspending Habeas Corpus.

46. Lyttelton to Bagot, 27 February 1819, in *Canning and Friends*, vol. 2, p. 92.

47. E. Bootle Wilbraham to Lord Colchester, 24 February 1819, in *Diary and Correspondence of Colchester*, vol. 3, pp. 70–1; Wynn to Buckingham, 'Wednesday', in *Memoirs of the Regency*, vol. 2, pp. 324–5.

48. Lord Colchester's diary, 3 June 1819, in *Diary and Correspondence of Colchester*, vol. 3, p. 79. It is ironic, of course, that the Pitt Club should have been celebrating Protestant principles when Pitt himself had favoured Catholic Emancipation.

49. See the letters from December 1820 in *Memoirs of the Court of George IV*, vol. 1, pp. 93–100.

50. Peel's memorandum, December 1820, in *Peel Correspondence*, vol. 1, p. 298. Peel's earlier letter to Croker, 10 August 1820, in *Croker Correspondence*, vol. 1, pp. 176–7, shows that his criticisms of the government were genuine.

51. Sidmouth to Bragge Bathurst, 20 December 1820, in *Life of Sidmouth*, vol. 3, p. 338.

52. Wynn to Buckingham, n.d. [early 1821], in *Memoirs of the Court of George IV*, vol. 1, pp. 130–2.

53. Francis Bamford and the Duke of Wellington (eds), *The Journal of Mrs Arbuthnot, 1820–1832* (London, 1950), vol. 1, pp. 82, 89–90 (17 March and 3 May 1821).

54. Liverpool to George IV, 10 June 1821, in *Peel Correspondence*, vol. 1, pp. 299–300.

55. Arbuthnot to his wife, 2 September 1822, in *Arbuthnot Correspondence*, p. 31.

56. See Wynn to Buckingham, 15 May 1822, in *Memoirs of the Court of George IV*, vol. 1, pp. 326–7, for comments about Peel's supposed ambitions.

57. Michael Ignatieff, *A Just Measure of Pain: The Penitentiary in the Industrial Revolution, 1750–1850*, (London, 1978), p. 179.

58. V. A. C. Gatrell, *The Hanging Tree: Execution and the English People, 1770–1868* (Oxford, 1994), pp. 568–9.

59. Ibid., p. 575.

60. Derek Beales, 'Peel, Russell and Reform', *Historical Journal*, XVII (1974), pp. 879–80.

61. Boyd Hilton, 'The Gallows and Mr Peel', in T. Blanning and D. Cannadine (eds), *History and Biography* (Cambridge, 1996), pp. 92–7.

62. Gatrell, *The Hanging Tree*, pp. 554–65.

63. Ignatieff, *A Just Measure of Pain*, pp. 168–9, 187–93.

64. 29 April 1823, *Peel Speeches*, vol. 1, pp. 239–40.

65. Gatrell, *The Hanging Tree*, pp. 576–8.

66. Hilton, 'The Gallows and Mr Peel', pp. 109–10.

67. Peel to Rev. Sydney Smith, 24 March 1826, in *Peel Correspondence*, vol. 1, pp. 401–2.

68. Peel to Hobhouse, 8 December 1826, ibid., vol. 1, pp. 432–3.

69. 28 February 1828, *Peel Speeches*, vol. 1, pp. 556–64.

70. 15 April 1829, *Hansard's Parliamentary Debates*, 3rd Series, XXI, 867–84.

71. Peel to Wellington, 5 November 1829, in *Peel Correspondence*, vol. 2, p. 115. Ignatieff, *A Just Measure of Pain*, p. 185, notes that 85 per cent of arrests in the 1830s were for vagrancy, prostitution, drunkenness, disorderly behaviour and common assault.

72. Peel to Hobhouse, 4 February 1828, in *Peel Correspondence*, vol. 2, p. 37. See also Peel to Hobhouse, 9 July 1826, ibid., vol. 1, p. 405, on the need for police forces in the industrial districts.

73. Canning to George IV, 9 March 1826, in Arthur Aspinall (ed.), *The Letters of King George IV, 1812–1830* (Cambridge, 1938), vol. 3, pp. 141–2.

74. Peel to Liverpool, 12 October 1822, in *Life of Liverpool*, vol. 3, pp. 215–17.

75. Peel to Bentham, 4 April 1826, cited by Ruth Richardson, *Death, Dissection and the Destitute* (London, 1987), p. 111.

76. Peel to Goulburn, 6 December 1828, in *Peel Correspondence*, vol. 2, pp. 44–5.

77. 12 March 1829, *Peel Speeches*, vol. 1, p. 733.

2 The Crisis in Church and State

1. Nicholas Vansittart was relegated upwards to a peerage (Lord Bexley) and an honorific Cabinet post, while Bragge Bathurst retired from the govern-

ment. Lord Sidmouth himself made way for Peel at the Home Office, becoming Lord President of the Council before his retirement in 1824.

2. For the older view that there was a clear dividing line between the Liverpool ministry's 'repressive' and 'Liberal' phases, see E. Halévy, *A History of the English People, 1815–1830* (London, 1926), and W. R. Brock, *Lord Liverpool and Liberal Toryism, 1820–1827* (Cambridge, 1941).

3. For the current textbook view, see Eric J. Evans, *The Forging of the Modern State, 1783–1870*, 2nd edn (London, 1996), pp. 200–5.

4. Canning had been a member of the Cabinet from 1816 until 1820, when he resigned over the Queen Caroline affair. Robinson and Huskisson were junior ministers throughout the post-war 'repression'. Peel's retirement from the government in 1818, as we saw in Chapter 1, had nothing to do with policy disagreements, and he backed his former colleagues at the time of the Peterloo massacre.

5. See the definitions in the *Oxford English Dictionary*. It was only gradually, during the 1830s and 1840s, that 'Liberal' came to be adopted as a *party* label.

6. On this subject generally, see Boyd Hilton, *Corn, Cash, Commerce: The Economic Policies of the Tory Governments, 1815–30* (Oxford, 1977).

7. Norman Gash, *Mr Secretary Peel: The Life of Sir Robert Peel to 1830* (London, 1961), pp. 439–40, 473, 639–40.

8. Ibid., pp. 364–5, 428.

9. It was a characteristic device of Liverpool's to use committees of inquiry as a means of engineering a consensus of opinion behind policy changes which he was already, privately, resolved to implement. In this way, he sought to keep potentially divisive policy decisions out of the Cabinet: Boyd Hilton, 'The Political Arts of Lord Liverpool', *Transactions of the Royal Historical Society*, 5th Series, XXXVIII (1988), pp. 147–70.

10. Boyd Hilton, *The Age of Atonement: The Influence of Evangelicalism on Social and Economic Thought, 1785–1865* (Oxford, 1988), pp. 218–31, for this paragraph.

11. Boyd Hilton, 'Peel: A Reappraisal', *Historical Journal*, XXII (1979), pp. 607–8.

12. Peel to Huskisson, 7 February 1827, in Lewis Melville (ed.), *The Huskisson Papers* (London, 1931), pp. 213–14.

13. Peel to Leonard Horner, 29 November 1825, in C. S. Parker (ed.), *Sir Robert Peel: From his Private Correspondence*, 3 vols (London, 1891–9), vol. 1, pp. 379–80.

14. Creevey to Miss Ord, 3 May 1826, in Sir Herbert Maxwell, *The Creevey Papers* (London, 1903), vol. 2, p. 100.

15. Charles Wynn to Buckingham, 28 April 1826, in Duke of Buckingham and Chandos, *Memoirs of the Court of George IV, 1820–1830* (London, 1859), vol. 2, pp. 300–1.

16. Dr Hilton's 'High' Tories were all 'Protestants', with the exception of Castlereagh. Of the 'liberal' Tories, though, Liverpool and Peel were opposed to Catholic Emancipation.

17. Peel to William Gregory, 5 April 1823, in *Peel Correspondence*, vol. 1, p. 341. 'Prescription' was a Burkean term used to describe the inherited wisdom of ancient institutions. Peel's pejorative reference to 'liberal doctrine', in this context, was no doubt prompted by its association with democratic measures of reform.

18. Wellington to Peel, 23 November 1824, in *Peel Correspondence*, vol. 1, pp. 350–1.

19. W. H. Fremantle to Buckingham, 4 and 29 February 1824, in *Memoirs of Court of George IV*, vol. 2, pp. 42–3, 50. Cf. Wynn to Buckingham, 21 July 1823, ibid., vol. 1, pp. 478–9: 'Peel continues very glum and sulky.'

20. Francis Bamford and the Duke of Wellington (eds), *The Journal of Mrs Arbuthnot, 1820–1832* (London, 1950), vol. 1, p. 321 (10 June 1824), referring to a letter received from Wellington.

21. Ibid., vol. 1, p. 271 (29 October 1823).

22. Arthur Aspinall (ed.), *The Diary of Henry Hobhouse, 1820–1827* (London, 1947), pp. 101–2 (22 January 1823).

23. Charles Arbuthnot to Lord Bathurst, 29 August 1823, reporting a conversation with Peel, in *Report on the Manuscripts of Earl Bathurst* (Historical Manuscripts Commission 1923), vol. 76, p. 543.

24. *Journal of Mrs Arbuthnot*, vol. 2, p. 29 (4 June 1826). Similarly, ibid., vol. 2, pp. 21–2 (23 April 1826).

25. Ibid., vol 2, pp. 69–70 (25 December 1826).

26. Charles Arbuthnot to Bathurst, 22 January 1827, in *Bathurst Manuscripts*, p. 627.

27. Gash, *Mr Secretary Peel*, pp. 413–20.

28. *Journal of Mrs Arbuthnot*, vol. 2, p. 79 (15 February 1827), reports that Liverpool and Peel were talking of resigning.

29. See Eldon to Lord Encombe, 20 February 1827, in Horace Twiss, *The Life of Lord Chancellor Eldon* (London, 1844), vol. 2, p. 584, for the significance of the two events.

30. Eldon to Lady F. J. Bankes, April 1827, ibid., vol. 2, p. 588. For a detailed documentary account of this period, see Arthur Aspinall (ed.), *The Formation of Canning's Ministry February to August 1827*, Royal Historical Society, Camden 3rd Series, LIX (1937).

31. King George IV to Peel, 31 March 1827, in *Peel Correspondence*, vol. 1, p. 458.

32. Peel to Eldon, two letters dated 9 April 1827, ibid., vol. 1, pp. 460–3.

33. Peel to Canning, 17 April 1827, Peel to his father, 12 April 1827, ibid., vol. 1, pp. 466–8, 474–5.

34. Eldon to Lady F. J. Bankes, n.d. [1825], in *Life of Eldon*, vol. 2, pp. 555–6.

35. Peel to Leslie Foster, 3 November 1826, 16 July 1826, in *Peel Correspondence*, vol. 1, pp. 422–3, 414.

36. Peel to Arbuthnot, 17 August 1827, in Arthur Aspinall (ed.), *The Correspondence of Charles Arbuthnot* (Royal Historical Society, Camden 3rd Series, LXV, 1941), pp. 90–1.

37. Peel's memorandum, January 1828, in *Peel Correspondence*, vol. 2, pp. 28–9.

38. Peel to Bishop Lloyd, 15 January 1828, ibid., vol. 2, pp. 30–1.

39. See Peel to Huskisson, 25 March 1828, in *Huskisson Papers*, pp. 300–1, urging conciliation.

40. Lord Colchester (ed.), *A Political Diary, 1828–1830: By Edward Law Lord Ellenborough* (London, 1881), vol. 1, p. 64 (19 March 1828). Cf. *Journal of Mrs Arbuthnot*, vol. 2, pp. 174–5 (24 March 1828).

41. *Journal of Mrs Arbuthnot*, vol. 2, pp. 172, 185 (17 March and 2 May 1828).

42. Ibid., vol. 2, p. 187 (20 May 1828).

43. *Ellenborough Diary*, vol. 1, p. 154 (27 June 1828). A journalist writing after Peel's death recalled that his 'manners were peculiarly stilted and repellent' during his early years as Leader of the House of Commons: D. O. Maddyn, *Chiefs of Parties*, (London, 1859), vol. 2, p. 52.

44. Bathurst to Arbuthnot, 15 August 1828, in *Arbuthnot Correspondence*, pp. 105–6.

45. *Journal of Mrs Arbuthnot*, vol. 2, p. 196 (29 June 1828). See also ibid., vol. 2, p. 230 (5 January 1828).

46. Colchester's diary, 30 April 1828, in *The Diary and Correspondence of Charles Abbot, Lord Colchester* (London, 1861), vol. 3, p. 558.

47. One Irish source reckoned that at the next general election as many as sixty O'Connellite MPs could be returned: Leslie Foster to Peel, 6 November 1826, in *Peel Correspondence*, vol. 1, pp. 423–4.

48. In a letter to Peel, dated 12 September 1828, Wellington stated that he had been gradually drawn to this conclusion by the election results in Ireland since 1826: *Despatches and Memoranda of Field Marshal Arthur Duke of Wellington, KG, ed. by his son* (London, 1867–80), vol. 5, pp. 42–3.

49. Bathurst to Arbuthnot, 15 August 1828, in *Arbuthnot Correspondence*, pp. 105–6.

50. Peel to Wellington, 11 August 1828, in *Peel Correspondence*, vol. 2, pp. 54–7.

51. Peel to Wellington, 12 January 1829, ibid., vol. 2, pp. 79–80.

52. *Ellenborough Diary*, vol. 1, p. 380 (6 March 1829); *Journal of Mrs Arbuthnot*, vol. 2, p. 249 (8 March 1829).

53. Lord Mahon and Edward Cardwell (eds), *Memoirs of the Right Honourable Sir Robert Peel* (London, 1856–7), vol. 1, pp. 116–17; see ibid., pp. 112–27, for Peel's correspondence on the situation in Ireland during the summer of 1828. For the significance of Peel's speech in the Commons, see Boyd Hilton, 'The Ripening of Robert Peel', in Michael Bentley (ed.), *Public and Private Doctrine* (Cambridge, 1993), pp. 69–72.

54. Henry Reeve (ed.), *The Greville Memoirs* (London, 1899 edn), vol. 1, pp. 187–8 (6 March 1829).

55. Peel to Gregory, 1 February 1829, Peel to Colonel Yates, 18 February 1829, in *Peel Correspondence*, vol. 2, pp. 86–8, 94–5.

56. Hilton, 'The Ripening of Robert Peel', pp. 72–8.

57. Colchester's diary, 28 February 1829, in *Diary and Correspondence of Lord Colchester*, vol. 3, p. 602; *Greville Memoirs*, vol. 1, p. 181 (27 February 1829).

58. *Ellenborough Diary*, vol. 1, p. 366 (28 February 1829).

59. Even at Westbury, though, Peel may have been fortunate that a 'Protestant' candidate arrived too late to contest the election: *Peel Memoirs*, vol. 1, p. 342.

60. *Ellenborough Diary*, vol. 2, pp. 198–9 (17 February 1830).
61. *Journal of Mrs Arbuthnot*, vol. 2, pp. 344–5 (15 March 1830).
62. Arbuthnot to Lord Cowley, 11 April 1830, in *Arbuthnot Correspondence*, pp. 125–8.
63. *Journal of Mrs Arbuthnot*, vol. 2, p. 343 (12 March 1830). The Duke of Wellington was among those hostile to the plan.
64. Ibid., vol. 2, pp. 316, 331 (14 November 1829, 5 February 1830), partly reflecting Wellington's view.
65. *Ellenborough Diary*, vol. 2, p. 221 (16 April 1830).
66. *Journal of Mrs Arbuthnot*, vol. 2, pp. 358–9 (24 May 1830).
67. *Ellenborough Diary*, vol. 2, pp. 270–1, 288, (16 and 29 June 1830).
68. The memorandum is printed in *Wellington Despatches*, vol. 7, pp. 106–8.
69. *Ellenborough Diary*, vol. 2, pp. 220, 315–16 (12 April and 17 July 1830); *Journal of Mrs Arbuthnot*, vol. 2, pp. 372–3 (16 July 1830).
70. Arthur Aspinall (ed.), *Three Early-Nineteenth Century Diaries* (London, 1952), pp. xvi–xxii.
71. Arbuthnot to Peel, 1 November 1830, in *Peel Correspondence*, vol. 2, pp. 163–6.
72. *Three Diaries*, p. xxv. Aspinall took to be Ultras those who had voted against Catholic Emancipation in 1829. Their numbers in November 1830 suggest that Planta's estimate of their strength (see note 70) was too low.
73. Peel to Croker, 23 March 1820, in Louis J. Jennings (ed.), *The Correspondence and Diaries of John Wilson Croker* (London, 1884), vol. 1, p. 170.
74. *Ellenborough Diary*, vol. 2, pp. 432–3 (14 November 1830); Ellenborough's diary, 27 November 1830, in *Three Diaries*, p. 27.
75. Denis Le Marchant's diary, 1 March 1831, in *Three Diaries*, p. 13.
76. 3 March 1831, in *The Speeches of the Late Right Honourable Sir Robert Peel, Bart, Delivered in the House of Commons* (London, 1853), vol. 2, pp. 276–88.
77. Peel to Croker, 15 April 1831, in *Croker Correspondence*, vol. 2, pp. 114–15.
78. Ellenborough's diary, 20 April 1831, in *Three Diaries*, p. 82.
79. See the letters in *Peel Correspondence*, vol. 2, pp. 193–6.
80. Peel to Harrowby, 5 February 1832, ibid., vol. 2, pp. 199–202.
81. Peel to Croker, 12 May 1832, ibid., vol. 2, pp. 205–6.
82. Ellenborough's diary, 14–15 May 1832, *Three Diaries*, pp. 253–4, 258.
83. John Brooke and Mary Sorensen (eds), *The Prime Minister's Papers: W. E. Gladstone* (Historical Manuscripts Commission, 1971–82), vol. 3, pp. 78–9 (October 1851).

3 The New Conservatism

1. Peel to Henry Goulburn, 3 January 1833, in C. S. Parker (ed.), *Sir Robert Peel: From his Private Correspondence* (London, 1891–9), vol. 2, pp. 212–14.
2. Lord Mahon to Peel, 8 January 1833, ibid., vol. 2, pp. 209–11.
3. Arbuthnot to his son, 9 March 1833, Lord Rosslyn to Mrs Arbuthnot, 24 July 1833, in Arthur Aspinall (ed.), *The Correspondence of Charles Arbuthnot* (Royal Historical Society, Camden 3rd Series, LXV, 1941), pp. 167, 172–3.

4. Hardinge to Arbuthnot, 19 February 1834, Arbuthnot to his son, 7 May 1834, ibid., pp. 178, 186.
5. Peel to Croker, 5 March 1833, in *Peel Correspondence*, vol. 2, pp. 215–16.
6. Peel to Herries, n.d. [early 1833], in Edward Herries, *Memoir of the Public Life of the Right Hon. John Charles Herries* (London, 1880), vol. 2, pp. 165–6.
7. Hardinge to Mrs Arbuthnot, 10 February 1833, in *Arbuthnot Correspondence*, pp. 166–7.
8. *A Portion of the Journal kept by Thomas Raikes, Esq., from 1831 to 1847* (London, 1856), vol. 1, pp. 159–61 (14 February 1833). See also Henry Reeve (ed.), *The Greville Memoirs* (London, 1899 ed.), vol. 2, pp. 362–4 (14 February 1833), for similar comments.
9. Peel to Croker, 28 May 1831, Peel to Goulburn, 5 June and 26 August 1831, in *Peel Correspondence*, vol. 2, pp. 186–8.
10. Ian Newbould, 'Sir Robert Peel and the Conservative Party, 1832–1841: A Study in Failure?', *English Historical Review*, XCVIII (1983), pp. 531–7.
11. Peel to Goulburn, 25 May 1834, in *Peel Correspondence*, vol. 2, pp. 243–4. Similarly, Peel to Arbuthnot, 27 May 1834, ibid., p. 247.
12. Peel to Goulburn, 24 June 1833, ibid., vol. 2, pp. 222–4.
13. Wellington to Peel, 23 July 1833, ibid., vol. 2, p. 218.
14. See the material in ibid., vol. 2, pp. 227–42, for this paragraph.
15. *Raikes Journal*, vol. 1, p. 157 (3 February 1833).
16. *Greville Memoirs*, vol. 3, pp. 65–6 (22 February 1834).
17. Peel to Edmund Peel, 10 December 1834, in *Peel Correspondence*, vol. 2, p. 263.
18. Creevey to Miss Ord, 22 November 1834, in Sir Herbert Maxwell, *The Creevey Papers* (London, 1903), vol. 2, pp. 298–9.
19. Stanley to Peel, 11 December 1834, in *Peel Correspondence*, vol. 2, pp. 257–9.
20. *Greville Memoirs*, vol. 3, pp. 199–200 (12 January 1835).
21. The full text of the manifesto is printed in Lord Mahon and Edward Cardwell (eds), *Memoirs of the Right Honourable Sir Robert Peel* (London, 1856–7), vol. 2, pp. 58–67. There is a valuable essay on the background to the manifesto by Norman Gash, 'The Historical Significance of the Tamworth Manifesto', in his *Pillars of Government* (London, 1986), pp. 98–107.
22. *Raikes Journal*, vol. 1, p. 312 (22 December 1834); *Greville Memoirs*, vol. 3, pp. 183–4 (20 December 1834).
23. See Norman Gash, 'The Crisis of the Anglican Establishment in the early-19th century', in his *Pillars of Government*, pp. 16–25.
24. Peel to Croker, 2 February 1835, in Louis J. Jennings (ed.), *The Correspondence and Diaries of John Wilson Croker* (London, 1884), vol. 2, pp. 264–5; Peel to Goulburn, 29 January 1835, in *Peel Correspondence*, vol. 2, p. 283.
25. Peel to the Bishop of Exeter, 22 December 1834, in *Peel Correspondence*, vol. 2, pp. 265–6.
26. See Owen Chadwick, *The Victorian Church*, Part I (London, 1966), pp. 126–41.
27. See the material in *Peel Correspondence*, vol. 2, pp. 292–8.
28. Peel to King William IV, 29 March 1835, Peel to Wellington, 4 April 1835, ibid., vol. 2, pp. 298–300, 302–3.

29. *Greville Memoirs*, vol. 3, pp. 250–1 (5 April 1835). See also, ibid., pp. 269–70 (14 June 1835).
30. Peel to Wellington, 10 February 1836, in *Peel Correspondence*, vol. 2, pp. 322–3.
31. 5 June 1835, *The Speeches of the Late Right Honourable Sir Robert Peel, Bart, Delivered in the House of Commons* (London, 1853), vol. 3, pp. 137–48.
32. Peel to his wife, 3 and 6 June 1835, in George Peel (ed.), *Private Letters of Sir Robert Peel* (London, 1920), pp. 153–4, 157.
33. Peel to Goulburn, August 1835, in *Peel Correspondence*, vol. 2, pp. 314–15.
34. Newbould, 'Peel and the Conservative Party', pp. 539–40.
35. *Annual Register*, 1837, p. 126.
36. Peel to Croker, 14 April 1837, in *Croker Correspondence*, vol. 2, pp. 306–7.
37. Peel to Croker, 12 January 1836, ibid., vol. 2, pp. 303–6. Cf. Peel to Goulburn, 3 January 1836, in *Peel Correspondence*, vol. 2, p. 318.
38. *Raikes Journal*, vol. 2, p. 315 (6 February 1836).
39. Arbuthnot to his son, 20 June 1836, 21 July 1836, 1 November 1836 and 29 April 1837, in *Arbuthnot Correspondence*, pp. 192–5.
40. Abraham D. Kriegal (ed.), *The Holland House Diaries* (London, 1977), p. 340 (August 1836).
41. Robert Stewart, *The Foundation of the Conservative Party, 1830–1867* (London, 1978), pp. 109, 117.
42. Peel's memorandum, 4 July 1837, in *Peel Correspondence*, vol. 2, pp. 336–8.
43. Arbuthnot to his son, 13 February 1838, in *Arbuthnot Correspondence*, pp. 196–7.
44. See the letters printed in *Peel Correspondence*, vol. 2, pp. 355–65, and John Brooke and Mary Sorensen (eds), *The Prime Minister's Papers: W. E. Gladstone* (Historical Manuscripts Commission, 1971–82), vol. 2, pp. 91–100, for memoranda relating to the various Conservative meetings.
45. See T. A. Jenkins, *Parliament, Party and Politics in Victorian Britain* (Manchester, 1996), pp. 157–8.
46. Newbould, 'Peel and the Conservative Party', pp. 544–5.
47. *Peel Correspondence*, vol. 2, pp. 390–2. See also Norman Gash, *Sir Robert Peel: The Life of Sir Robert Peel after 1830* (London, 1972), pp. 220–7.
48. Indeed, relations were so bad that in January 1840 the Conservatives carried an amendment to reduce the annual parliamentary grant settled on Prince Albert, the Queen's prospective husband, from £50,000 to £30,000. As Arbuthnot observed to Peel, on 29 January, this vote would be 'a useful lesson to the Queen' (*Peel Correspondence*, vol. 2, p. 433).
49. Peel to Arbuthnot, 4 November 1839, ibid., vol. 2, pp. 409–10.
50. See the letters printed in ibid., vol. 2, pp. 415–29.
51. 31 January 1840, *Peel Speeches*, vol. 3, pp. 687–703.
52. Graham to Peel, 9 June 1840, in *Peel Correspondence*, vol. 2, pp. 438–40.
53. See the letters printed in ibid., vol 2, pp. 433–51, for this paragraph.
54. Graham to Arbuthnot, 3 May 1841, in C. S. Parker, *Life and Letters of Sir James Graham* (London, 1907), vol. 1, pp. 301–2.
55. For what follows, see Stewart, *Foundation of Conservative Party*, pp. 151–65; Newbould, 'Peel and the Conservative Party', pp. 547–57.

56. *Annual Register*, 1837, pp. 16–17, 1838, pp. 115–19. Cf. Peel to Graham, 29 November 1836, in *Life of Graham*, vol. 1, p. 246.
57. See G. I. T. Machin, *Politics and the Churches in Great Britain, 1832–1868* (Oxford, 1977), pp. 64–9.
58. Newbould, 'Peel and the Conservative Party', p. 550.
59. See Stewart, *Foundation of Conservative Party*, pp. 136–46.
60. Ibid., pp. 128–36.
61. Peel to Arbuthnot, 8 November 1838 [*sic* 1839], in *Peel Correspondence*, vol. 2, p. 368.
62. Graham to Arbuthnot, 12 September 1839, in *Arbuthnot Correspondence*, pp. 207–9.
63. Graham to Peel, 26 December 1839, in *Peel Correspondence*, vol. 2, pp. 427–9.
64. Croker to Peel, 20 July 1841, ibid., vol. 2, pp. 475–6.

4   Prime Minister, 1841–6

1. See, for example, John Brooke and Mary Sorensen (eds), *The Prime Minister's Papers: W. E. Gladstone* (Historical Manuscripts Commission, 1971–82), vol. 2, pp. 41–3, for Gladstone's memorandum of a conversation with Peel, dated 26 January 1835; Lord Stanmore, *Sidney Herbert, Lord Herbert of Lea: A Memoir* (London, 1906), vol. 1, p. 20, for Peel's letter to 'My Dear Sidney', 1 January 1835; John Martineau, *The Life of Henry Pelham, Fifth Duke of Newcastle* (London, 1908), pp. 52–3, 63, including a remarkably boyish letter from Peel to Lincoln written in 1846.
2. Gladstone's memorandum, 26 February 1842, *Prime Minister's Papers*, vol. 2, p. 172.
3. Peel to Graham, 20 October 1842, in C. S. Parker (ed.), *Sir Robert Peel: From his Private Correspondence* (London, 1891–9), vol. 3, p. 39.
4. For this paragraph, see Norman Gash, *Sir Robert Peel: The Life of Sir Robert Peel after 1830* (London, 1972), pp. 482–525.
5. Peel to Ashley, 16 June 1842, in *Peel Correspondence*, vol. 2, p. 534.
6. Peel to Croker, 3 August 1842, in Louis J. Jennings (ed.), *The Correspondence and Diaries of John Wilson Croker* (London, 1884), vol. 3, pp. 10–11.
7. Gladstone's memorandum, 12 July 1845, in *Prime Minister's Papers*, vol. 2, pp. 279–80.
8. Peel to Arbuthnot, 14 August 1845, in Arthur Aspinall (ed.), *The Correspondence of Charles Arbuthnot* (Royal Historical Society, Camden 3rd Series, LXV, 1941), p. 237.
9. Peel to Graham, 3 July 1846, in *Peel Correspondence*, vol. 3, pp. 456–7 and note; Gladstone's memorandum, July 1846, in *Prime Minister's Papers*, vol. 3, p. 30.
10. See Peel's memorandum, 11 May 1841, in *Peel Correspondence*, vol. 2, pp. 455–8.
11. Peel to Henry Hobhouse, 18 September 1841, ibid., vol. 2, pp. 484–5.
12. Sir Theodore Martin, *The Life of His Royal Highness the Prince Consort* (London, 1875–80), vol. 1, pp. 119–25, 166–7.

13. Peel to Lord Ellenborough, 6 April 1842, in *Peel Correspondence*, vol. 2, p. 584.
14. *Life of the Prince Consort*, vol. 1, pp. 142–3.
15. See the letters in *Peel Correspondence*, vol. 2, pp. 542–5.
16. Albert to Stockmar, 17 December 1843, in *Life of the Prince Consort*, vol. 1, pp. 195–6.
17. Peel to Queen Victoria, 20 October 1844, in *Peel Correspondence*, vol. 3, p. 162.
18. Peel to Victoria, 25 March 1845, ibid., vol. 3, pp. 172–3.
19. Gladstone's memorandum, 20 May 1844, *Prime Minister's Papers*, vol. 2, p. 260.
20. Stockmar to Albert, 7 May 1841; also Stockmar to Albert, 18 May 1841 and Albert to Stockmar, November 1844, in *Life of the Prince Consort*, vol. 1, pp. 102–4, 109–11, 243–4. See also David Cannadine, 'The Last Hanoverian Sovereign? The Victorian Monarchy in Historical Perspective', in A. L. Beier *et al.* (eds), *The First Modern Society* (London, 1989), pp. 127–66.
21. Albert to Stockmar, 9 March 1845, in *Life of the Prince Consort*, vol. 1, pp. 258–9.
22. Peel to Croker, 5 July 1837, in *Croker Correspondence*, vol. 2, pp. 316–17.
23. 27 August and 17 September 1841, *Hansard's Parliamentary Debates*, 3rd Series, LXI, 400–29, 538–56.
24. *Life of the Prince Consort*, vol. 1, p. 163.
25. Ibid., vol. 1, p. 134; Victoria to Peel, 9 April 1845 and 21 December 1845, in *Peel Correspondence*, vol. 3, pp. 173, 285.
26. Peel to his wife, 16 December 1845, in George Peel (ed.), *Private Letters of Sir Robert Peel* (London, 1920), p. 274.
27. Henry Reeve (ed.), *The Greville Memoirs* (London, 1899 edn), vol. 5, pp. 24–5, 35–7 (10 August and 1 September 1841).
28. See Norman McCord, *The Anti-Corn Law League* (London, 1958).
29. For what follows, see Gash, *Sir Robert Peel*, pp. 295–329.
30. *The Speeches of the Late Right. Honourable Sir Robert Peel, Bart, Delivered in the House of Commons* (London, 1853), vol. 3, pp. 865–87.
31. Gash, *Sir Robert Peel*, pp. 306–18.
32. *A Portion of the Journal Kept by Thomas Raikes, Esq., from 1831 to 1847* (London, 1856), vol. 4, pp. 192–3 (9 and 11 February 1842). Cf. *Greville Memoirs*, vol. 5, pp. 84–5 (11 February 1842).
33. Peel to Croker, 21 February 1842, in *Croker Correspondence*, vol. 2, pp. 380–1. Philip Harling, *The Waning of 'Old Corruption': The Politics of Economical Reform in Britain, 1779–1846* (Oxford, 1996), pp. 228–54.
34. *Greville Memoirs*, vol. 5, pp. 89–90 (13 March 1842); *Raikes Journal*, vol. 4, p. 202 (23 April 1842).
35. Aberdeen to Princess Lieven, 25 March 1842, in Lady Frances Balfour, *The Life of George Fourth Earl of Aberdeen* (London, 1923), vol. 2, p. 140.
36. Peel to Ellenborough, 6 April 1842, in *Peel Correspondence*, vol. 2, p. 584.
37. *Greville Memoirs*, vol. 5, pp. 193–6 (1 and 6 August 1843).
38. 14 February 1845, *Peel Speeches*, vol. 4, pp. 436–57.

39. Peel to Croker, 27 July 1842, in *Croker Correspondence*, vol. 2, pp. 382–4. My italics.

40. Boyd Hilton, *The Age of Atonement: The Influence of Evangelicalism on Social and Economic Thought, 1785–1865* (Oxford, 1988), pp. 222–5.

41. Peel to Hobhouse, 21 January 1843, in *Peel Correspondence*, vol. 2, pp. 563–5. Similarly, Peel to Graham, 22 December 1842, ibid., pp. 550–1.

42. Peel to Ashley, 16 June 1843, ibid., vol. 2, p. 560.

43. 31 January 1840, *Peel Speeches*, vol. 3, p. 698.

44. 23 February 1843, ibid., vol. 4, pp. 180–4.

45. Peel to Queen Victoria, 19 March 1844, in *Peel Correspondence*, vol. 3, pp. 147–8.

46. 13 May 1844, *Peel Speeches*, vol. 4, pp. 366–74.

47. Thus, on the question of public health, Peel believed that 'it may be a law of civilisation that the extremes of wealth and poverty should increase together', but that, all the same, 'some effort must be made'. He favoured giving responsibility to local authorities for the improvement of conditions, while relying on the pressure of public opinion to ensure that these responsibilities were carried out. Gladstone's memorandum, 14 January 1845, in *Prime Minister's Papers*, vol. 2, pp. 272–3. In the event, of course, it fell to Russell's government to legislate on this subject.

48. Apart from commercial policy, Peel's *laissez faire* instincts are apparent in his hostility to state regulation of the railways: see Henry Parris, 'Railway Policy in Peel's Administration, 1841–1846', *Bulletin of the Institute of Historical Research*, XXXIII (1960), pp. 180–94.

49. *Greville Memoirs*, vol. 5, pp. 251–3 (21 June 1844).

50. Gladstone's memoranda, 15–20 June 1844, in *Prime Minister's Papers*, vol. 2, pp. 261–5.

51. D. R. Fisher, 'Peel and the Conservative Party: The Sugar Crisis of 1844 Reconsidered', *Historical Journal*, XVIII (1975), pp. 285–8.

52. See T. A. Jenkins, *Parliament, Party and Politics in Victorian Britain* (Manchester, 1996), pp. 28–50.

53. Sandon to Peel, 15 June 1844, Peel to Sandon, 17 June 1844, in *Peel Correspondence*, vol. 3, pp. 150–2.

54. *Greville Memoirs*, vol. 5, p. 254 (5 July 1844).

55. 26 June 1844, *Hansard*, 3rd Series, LXXV, 1522–39. One back-bench MP described this as an 'excellent speech': diary of Thomas Sotheron, 26 June 1844, Gloucestershire Record Office, D1571/F394.

56. Peel to Sir Henry Hardinge, 24 March 1845, in *Peel Correspondence*, vol. 3, pp. 269–70.

57. Gladstone's memorandum, 18 January 1836, in *Prime Minister's Papers*, vol. 2, p. 62.

58. Graham to Peel, 21 October 1841, in C. S. Parker, *Life and Letters of Sir James Graham* (London, 1907), vol. 1, pp. 350–1.

59. Graham to Peel, 6 November 1841, ibid., vol. 1, p. 351.

60. Peel to Graham, 16 June 1843, in *Peel Correspondence*, vol. 3, pp. 53–4.

61. Peel to Lord Lifford, 25 August 1845, ibid., vol. 3, p. 187.

62. Peel to de Grey, 22 August 1843, ibid., vol. 3, pp. 56–9.

63. Peel to Heytesbury, 1 August 1844, ibid., vol. 3, pp. 114–15.
64. See Gash, *Sir Robert Peel*, pp. 416–21. Two of the memorandums are printed in *Peel Correspondence*, vol. 3, pp. 101–3, 105–7.
65. Peel to Bulwer, 12 May 1845, in *Peel Correspondence*, vol. 3, p. 177.
66. Graham to Heytesbury, 10 May 1845, in *Life of Graham*, vol. 2, pp. 11–12.
67. On this subject generally, see Donal A. Kerr, *Peel, Priests and Politics: Sir Robert Peel's Administration and the Roman Catholic Church in Ireland, 1841– 1846* (Oxford, 1982).
68. Graham to Peel, 10 December 1844, in *Life of Graham*, vol. 1, p. 422.
69. *Greville Memoirs*, vol. 5, pp. 282–3 (5 April 1845).
70. Graham to Heytesbury, 12 April 1845, in *Life of Graham*, vol. 2, p. 10.
71. Peel to Graham, 5 October 1845, ibid., vol. 2, p. 19.
72. Peel to Heytesbury, 15 October 1845, Peel to Goulburn, 18 October 1845, in *Peel Correspondence*, vol. 3, pp. 224, 225–6.
73. Gladstone's memorandum of 18 December 1845 shows that even he had some doubts about the propriety of Peel's conduct on this score: *Prime Minister's Papers*, vol. 3, pp. 13–15.
74. Body Hilton, 'Peel: A Reappraisal', *Historical Journal*, XXII (1979), pp. 600–4. Peel's memorandums are printed in Lord Mahon and Edward Cardwell (eds), *Memoirs of the Right Honourable Sir Robert Peel* (London, 1856–7), vol. 2, pp. 327–57.
75. 15 March 1839, *Hansard*, 3rd Series, XLVI, 749–85.
76. 3 April 1840, *Peel Speeches*, vol. 3, pp. 709–21.
77. Peel to Croker, 3 August 1842, in *Croker Correspondence*, vol. 2, pp. 384–6.
78. Gladstone's memorandums, 26 February 1842, 17 August 1843, in *Prime Minister's Papers*, vol. 2, pp. 172, 220–1.
79. Gladstone's memorandum, 20 December 1843, ibid., p. 226.
80. The apparent link between lower duties and prosperous trading conditions was later emphasised by Peel in a conversation recorded in Prince Albert's memorandum, 25 December 1845, in E. F. Benson and Lord Esher (eds), *The Letters of Queen Victoria*, 1st Series (London, 1907), vol. 2, pp. 65–7.
81. 28 May 1845, *Hansard*, 3rd Series, LXXX, 989–98: 'From the principle . . . that protective duties are in themselves evils, I cannot withhold my assent; but I believe that the retrocession from any such course requires the utmost consideration. . . . I am not prepared to alter those laws. . . . I proposed them after due consideration, and I think nothing is so injurious as the constant alteration of a law of this nature.' Cf. 10 June 1845, ibid., LXXXI, 368–78: 'is it not more for the general interest that in returning to what I admit to be a better condition of society and the establishment of better principles, we should proceed with caution and deliberation – that our steps should be taken, not hastily, but with the fullest consideration of the interests which have grown up under a state of law which has endured for 150 years.' Readers are invited to draw their own conclusions.
82. Prince Albert's memorandum, 25 December 1845, in *Letters of Queen Victoria*, vol. 2, pp. 65–7.

83. See John Prest, *Politics in the Age of Cobden* (London, 1977), pp. 95–102. Of course, the fact that the League was disbanded in 1846 makes it impossible to assess with any certainty the possible electoral impact of the freehold campaign.

84. Graham to Peel, 27 October 1845, in *Peel Correspondence*, vol. 3, p. 224.

85. Prince Albert's memorandum, 25 December 1845, in *Letters of Queen Victoria*, vol. 2, pp. 65–7. See also, Peel to Goulburn, 27 December 1845, and Peel to Egerton, 6 January 1846, in *Peel Correspondence*, vol. 3, pp. 294, 323–4.

86. See the correspondence printed in *Peel Memoirs*, vol. 2, pp. 195–213.

87. Peel to Arbuthnot, 28 December 1845, in *Arbuthnot Correspondence*, p. 239.

88. *Peel Speeches*, vol. 4, pp. 582–604.

89. In fact, the Corn Laws were not completely repealed, as a one shilling registration duty continued to be levied until 1869. This proved to be a valuable source of revenue for governments, yielding average annual receipts of £629,602 between 1849 and 1868, more than had been raised under the old sliding scale. See John Prest, 'A Large Amount or a Small? Revenue and the 19th Century Corn Laws', *Historical Journal*, XXXIX (1996), pp. 467–78.

90. Earlier, in a Cabinet memorandum of 2 December 1845, he had even suggested an eight year phasing-out period: *Peel Memoirs*, vol. 2, pp. 214–20.

91. Peel to Wellington, 20 May 1846, ibid., vol. 2, pp. 284–6.

92. Peel to Arbuthnot, 7 January 1846, in *Arbuthnot Correspondence*, pp. 239–40.

93. Gladstone's memorandum, October 1851, in *Prime Minister's Papers*, vol. 3, pp. 77–9. But cf. Gash, *Sir Robert Peel*, pp. 566–7.

94. For the organisation of the Protectionists, see Robert Stewart, *The Foundation of the Conservative Party, 1830–1867* (London, 1978), pp. 205–15.

95. *Greville Memoirs*, vol. 5, p. 388 (29 March 1846).

96. Ibid., vol. 5, p. 400 (21 May 1846).

97. Stewart, *Foundation of Conservative Party*, p. 216.

98. In a memorandum dated 21 June 1846, Peel stated that he preferred to resign rather than dissolve parliament and fight a general election on the question of Irish coercion. The latter course of action, he argued, would only serve to inflame the situation in Ireland. Furthermore, if he requested a dissolution then logically he would have to act in alliance with other Free Trade politicians, like Cobden and Bright, whose views on general political issues Peel abhorred. *Peel Memoirs*, vol. 2, pp. 288–97.

99. 29 June 1846, *Peel Speeches*, vol. 4, pp. 709–17.

100. Stewart, *Foundation of Conservative Party*, p. 194.

101. Fisher, 'Peel and the Conservative Party', pp. 280–5.

102. Diary of Thomas Sotheron, 11 March and 25 May 1842, Gloucestershire Record Office, D1571/F392.

103. Sotheron's diary, 18 March and 17 June 1844, ibid., D1571/F394.

104. Sotheron's diary, 11–12 April 1845, ibid., D1571/F395.

105. Sotheron's diary, 23 July 1845, ibid.

106. Sotheron's diary, 27 January 1846, ibid., D1571/F396.

107. Sotheron's diary, 29 June 1846, ibid.
108. Peel to Graham, 2 September 1846, in *Peel Correspondence*, vol. 3, pp. 462–3.
109. Peel to Hardinge, 24 September 1846, ibid., vol. 3, pp. 472–4; Peel to Lord Justice Clerk, 3 August 1846, in *Private Letters*, pp. 280–2.

5 Peel's Achievement

1. See the comments in Henry Reeve (ed.), *The Greville Memoirs* (London, 1899 ed.), vol. 5, p. 441 (12 December 1846).
2. Arbuthnot to his son, 1 and 7 September 1846, in Arthur Aspinall (ed.), *The Correspondence of Charles Arbuthnot* (Royal Historical Society, Camden 3rd Series, LXV, 1941), pp. 240–1.
3. Peel to Graham, 3 April 1847, in C. S. Parker, *Life and Letters of Sir James Graham* (London, 1907), vol. 2, p. 54. Cf. Graham to Peel, 15 January 1848, ibid., pp. 63–4
4. Peel to Arbuthnot, 31 July 1849, in *Arbuthnot Correspondence*, p. 252.
5. Peel to Graham, 20 January 1849, in C. S. Parker (ed.), *Sir Robert Peel: From his Private Correspondence* (London, 1891–9), vol. 3, p. 502.
6. For Whig–Peelite relations, see J. B. Conacher, *The Peelites and the Party System, 1846–1852* (Newton Abbot, 1972), pp. 35–46.
7. Ibid., pp. 28–32.
8. Young to Peel, 14 January 1847, in *Peel Correspondence*, vol. 3, pp. 480–1.
9. All the voting figures in this paragraph are drawn from Conacher, *Peelites and Party System*, pp. 49–62.
10. Ibid., p. 65. Of these seventy-two MPs, six had either died or retired by the end of the 1850 session.
11. *Greville Memoirs*, vol. 6, pp. 103–4 (23 October 1847). Peel's reputation as a non-party politician even earned him the respect of the dyspeptic philosopher, Thomas Carlyle, who thought he discerned in Peel the potential for heroic leadership. This admiration was curious, because Carlyle was looking for a great leader who would preside over a government committed to interventionist social policies, whereas in fact Peel favoured a *laissez faire* approach: John Morrow, 'The Paradox of Peel as Carlylean hero', *Historical Journal*, XL (1997), pp. 97–110.
12. Conacher, *Peelites and Party System*, pp. 47–8.
13. Albert to Baron Stockmar, 22 July 1850, in Sir Theodore Martin, *The Life of His Royal Highness the Prince Consort* (London, 1875–80), vol. 2, pp. 296–7.
14. Valerie Pirie (adapted), *A Frenchman sees the English in the 'Fifties* (London, 1935), pp. 263–4.
15. Victoria to Leopold, 10 July 1850, in *Life of the Prince Consort*, vol. 2, p. 292.
16. The account that follows is drawn from Donald Read, *Peel and the Victorians* (Blackwell, 1987), pp. 266–304.
17. *A Frenchman sees the English*, pp. 264–5.
18. W. H. Lyttelton to Sir Charles Bagot, 18 October 1822, in Josceline Bagot, *George Canning and his Friends* (London, 1909), vol. 2, pp. 134–5.
19. D. O. Maddyn, *Chiefs of Parties* (London, 1859), vol. 2, pp. 26–31.

20. James Grant, *Random Recollections of the House of Commons* (London, 1836), pp. 105–22.

21. G. H. Francis, *Orators of the Age* (London, 1847), pp. 23–42.

22. Arbuthnot to Wellington, 26 March 1835, in R. J. Olney and Julia Melvin (eds), *Wellington II: Political Correspondence November 1834–April 1835* (Historical Manuscripts Commission, 1986), pp. 561–2.

23. Wynn to Buckingham, 15 and 20 July 1822, in Duke of Buckingham and Chandos, *Memoirs of the Court of George IV 1820–1830* (London, 1859), vol. 1, pp. 350–3. On the other hand, Wynn did write on 17 February 1823 that 'With Peel I have made much progress, and find him in general more fair, more manly, and more statesmanlike in his views than I had at all hoped' (ibid., vol. 1, pp. 431–2).

24. Lord Colchester (ed.), *A Political Diary 1828–1830 by Edward Law Lord Ellenborough* (London, 1881), vol. 1, p. 154 (27 June 1828), vol. 2, p. 288 (28 June 1830).

25. Francis Bamford and the Duke of Wellington (eds), *The Journal of Mrs Arbuthnot 1820–1832* (London, 1950), vol. 2, pp. 344–5 (15 March 1830). See also ibid., vol. 2, pp. 358–9 (24 May 1830).

26. But see the evidence in Norman Gash, *Mr Secretary Peel: The Life of Sir Robert Peel to 1830* (London, 1961), p. 36.

27. See, for example, Henry Brougham to Thomas Creevey, 19 and 21 August 1822, in Sir Herbert Maxwell, *The Creevey Papers* (London, 1903), vol. 2, pp. 44–5.

28. Peel to Goulburn, n.d., in *Peel Correspondence*, vol. 2, pp. 170–1.

29. See above, p. 16, for Peel's attempt to fight a duel with O'Connell in 1815. In 1837, he forced his election opponent at Tamworth to retract certain statements, by threatening a duel: *Peel Correspondence*, vol. 2, pp. 350–1.

30. *Ellenborough Diary*, vol. 1, p. 175 (23 July 1828).

31. See Norman Gash, *Sir Robert Peel: The Life of Sir Robert Peel after 1830* (London, 1972), pp. 666–9.

32. 6 July 1849, in *The Speeches of the Late Right Honourable Sir Robert Peel, Bart, Delivered in the House of Commons* (London, 1853), vol. 4, pp. 804–22.

33. Read, *Peel and the Victorians*, pp. 305–12.

34. A. A. W. Ramsay, *Sir Robert Peel* (London, 1928); G. Kitson Clark, *Peel and the Conservative Party: A Study in Party Politics, 1832–1841* (London, 1929).

35. Gash, *Mr Secretary Peel*, pp. 1–14; *Sir Robert Peel*, pp. 707–15.

36. See also Norman Gash, 'The Founder of Modern Conservatism', in his *Pillars of Government* (London, 1986), pp. 153–61.

37. Professor Gash's other books include *Politics in the Age of Peel* (London, 1953), and a collection of documents, *The Age of Peel* (London, 1968).

38. 17 May 1830, *Peel Speeches*, vol. 2, pp. 149–51, for Jewish Emancipation; 1 March 1826 and 13 July 1830, ibid., vol. 1, pp. 393–4, vol. 2, pp. 217–18, for the slave question.

39. Derek Beales, 'Peel, Russell and Reform', *Historical Journal*, XVII (1974), pp. 873–82.

40. V. A. C. Gatrell, *The Hanging Tree: Execution and the English People, 1770–1868* (Oxford, 1994), pp. 554–85.

41. Boyd Hilton, 'The Gallows and Mr Peel', in T. Blanning and D. Cannadine (eds), *History and Biography* (Cambridge, 1996), pp. 88–112.

42. Robert Stewart, *The Foundation of the Conservative Party, 1830–1867* (London, 1978), pp. 151–65; Ian Newbould, 'Sir Robert Peel and the Conservative Party, 1832–1841: A Study in Failure?', *English Historical Review*, XCVIII (1983), pp. 529–57.

43. Boyd Hilton, 'Peel: A Reappraisal', *Historical Journal*, XXII (1979), pp. 585–614.

44. Richard Brent, *Liberal Anglican Politics: Whiggery, Religion and Reform, 1830–1841* (Oxford, 1987); Peter Mandler, *Aristocratic Government in the Age of Reform: Whigs and Liberals, 1830–1852* (Oxford, 1990); Ian Newbould, *Whiggery and Reform, 1830–1841: The Politics of Government* (London, 1990); Jonathan Parry, *The Rise and Fall of Liberal Government in Victorian Britain* (Yale, 1993).

45. Hardinge to Peel, 12 June 1845, in *Peel Correspondence*, vol. 3, p. 274.

ANNOTATED BIBLIOGRAPHY

There is a full-scale modern biographical account of Peel by Norman Gash, *Mr Secretary Peel: The Life of Sir Robert Peel to 1830* (London, 1961, repr. 1985), and *Sir Robert Peel: The Life of Sir Robert Peel after 1830* (London, 1972, repr. 1986). An abridged, single-volume version of this work was published as *Peel* (London, 1977). Of the older biographies, A. A. W. Ramsay, *Sir Robert Peel* (London, 1928), is still useful. Eric J. Evans, *Sir Robert Peel: Statesmanship, Power and Party* (London, 1991), provides a brief introduction.

C. S. Parker (ed.), *Sir Robert Peel: From his Private Correspondence*, 3 vols (London, 1891–9), is an invaluable primary source. It can be supplemented by George Peel (ed.), *Private Letters of Sir Robert Peel* (London, 1920), which consists mainly of correspondence between Peel and his wife. Lord Mahon and Edward Cardwell (eds), *Memoirs of the Right Honourable Sir Robert Peel*, 2 vols (London, 1856–7), contains Peel's own accounts, with extensive documentary backing, of his conduct during the Catholic Emancipation crisis of 1828–9 and the Corn Law crisis of 1845–6. It also includes the full text of the Tamworth Manifesto of 1834. A large selection of Peel's parliamentary speeches was printed in *The Speeches of the Late Right Honourable Sir Robert Peel, Bart, Delivered in the House of Commons*, 4 vols (London, 1853), although this is by no means comprehensive.

There are many other volumes containing relevant primary material, and the following are particularly useful for their letters by Peel: Arthur Aspinall (ed.), *The Correspondence of Charles Arbuthnot* (Royal Historical Society, Camden 3rd Series, LXV, 1941); Louis J. Jennings (ed.), *The Correspondence and Diaries of John Wilson Croker*, 3 vols (London, 1884); C. S. Parker, *Life and Letters of Sir James Graham*, 2 vols (London, 1907); and E. F. Benson and Lord Esher (eds), *The Letters of Queen Victoria*, 1st Series, 3 vols (London, 1907). Several Tory/Conservative diaries are also available in print: Arthur Aspinall (ed.), *The Diary of Henry Hobhouse 1820–1827* (London, 1947); Francis Bamford and the Duke of Wellington (eds), *The Journal of Mrs Arbuthnot 1820–1832*, 2 vols (London, 1950); Lord Colchester (ed.), *A Political Diary 1828–1830. By Edward Law Lord Ellenborough*, 2 vols (London, 1881), and *A Portion of the Journal Kept by Thomas Raikes, Esq., from 1831 to 1847*, 4 vols (London, 1856). From the Whig side, of course, there is Henry Reeve (ed.), *The Greville Memoirs*, 8 vols (London, 1899, and other edns), an incomparable source. Arthur Aspinall (ed.), *Three Early-Nineteenth Century Diaries* (London, 1952), is useful for the Reform crisis of the early 1830s. For the post-1832 period, the memorandums written by one of Peel's young disciples can be found in John Brooke and Mary Sorensen (eds), *The Prime Minister's Papers: W. E. Gladstone*, 4 vols (Historical Manuscripts Commission, 1971–82).

The secondary literature on the Tory governments upto 1830 includes: A. D. Harvey, *Britain in the Early-Nineteenth Century* (London, 1978); J. E. Cookson, *Lord Liverpool's Administration, 1815–1822* (Edinburgh, 1975); and Boyd Hilton, *Corn, Cash, Commerce: The Economic Policies of the Tory Governments, 1815–1830* (Oxford, 1977). Eric J. Evans, *Britain before the Reform Act: Politics and Society, 1815–32* (London, 1989), is a useful introduction accompanied by documents. Biographies of leading Tories include: Norman Gash, *Lord Liverpool* (London, 1984); Elizabeth Longford, *Wellington: Pillar of State* (London, 1972); and Wendy Hinde's studies of *George Canning* (London, 1973) and *Castlereagh* (London, 1981). Peel's own record as Home Secretary has been critically examined by Derek Beales, 'Peel, Russell and Reform', *Historical Journal*, XVII (1974), pp. 873–82; V. A. C. Gatrell, *The Hanging Tree: Execution and the English People, 1770–1868* (Oxford, 1994); and Boyd Hilton, 'The Gallows and Mr Peel', in T. Blanning and D. Cannadine (eds), *History and Biography* (Cambridge, 1996), pp. 88–112. G. I. T. Machin, *The Catholic Question in English Politics, 1820–1830* (Oxford, 1964), provides a general account, while Wendy Hinde, *Catholic Emancipation: A Shake to Men's Minds* (Blackwell, 1992), concentrates on the events of 1828–9. The impact of the Catholic crisis on Peel's subsequent political development has been considered by R. W. Davis, 'Toryism to Tamworth: The Triumph of Reform, 1827–1835', *Albion*, XII (1980), pp. 132–46, and Boyd Hilton, 'The Ripening of Robert Peel', in Michael Bentley (ed.), *Public and Private Doctrine* (Cambridge, 1993), pp. 63–84.

For Peel and the Conservatives after 1830, there are excellent studies by Robert Stewart, *The Foundation of the Conservative Party, 1830–1867* (London, 1978), and Donald Read, *Peel and the Victorians* (Blackwell, 1987). Paul Adelman, *Peel and the Conservative Party, 1830–1850* (London, 1989), offers an introduction to the subject with some documents. Robert Stewart, *Party and Politics, 1830–52* (London, 1989), is an excellent concise account. Party organisation is the subject of two articles by Norman Gash, 'The Organisation of the Conservative Party, 1832–1846. Part 1: The Parliamentary Organisation. Part II: The Electoral Organisation', *Parliamentary History*, I (1982), pp. 137–59; II (1983), pp. 131–52. Professor Gash has also given us a splendid account of 'The Historical Significance of the Tamworth Manifesto', in his *Pillars of Government and other essays on State and Society, c.1770–c.1880* (London, 1986), pp. 98–107. George Kitson Clark, *Peel and the Conservative Party: A Study in Party Politics, 1832–1841*, 2nd edn (London, 1964), is a detailed examination of Peel's years in opposition, but for a more sceptical assessment, see Ian Newbould, 'Sir Robert Peel and the Conservative Party, 1832–1841: A Study in Failure?', *English Historical Review*, XCVIII (1983), pp. 529–57. Peel's attitude to party is also considered by Angus Hawkins, ' "Parliamentary Government" and Victorian Political Parties, c.1830–c.1880', *English Historical Review*, CIV (1989), pp. 638–69.

Travis L. Crosby has written a useful brief study of *Sir Robert Peel's Administration, 1841–1846* (Newton Abbot, 1976), while D. R. Fisher, 'Peel and the Conservative Party: The Sugar Crisis of 1844 Reconsidered', *Historical Journal*, XVIII (1975), pp. 279–302, looks at Peel's problems with his back-benchers. Norman McCord, *The Anti-Corn Law League* (London, 1958), deals with the Free Trade agitation in the country, while their opponents are the subject of Travis L. Crosby's *English Farmers and the Politics of Protection, 1815–52* (Harvester, 1977). Philip Harling, *The Waning of 'Old Corruption': The Politics of Economical Reform in Britain, 1779–1846* (Oxford, 1996), has an interesting chapter on the strategic political thinking behind Peel's fiscal and commercial reforms. The operation of the Corn Laws is examined by Susan Fairlie, 'The Nineteenth-Century Corn Law Reconsidered', *Economic History Review*, XVIII (1965), pp. 562–75, and Peel's motives for repealing them are discussed by Betty Kemp, 'Reflections on the Repeal of the Corn Laws', *Victorian Studies*, V (1961–2), pp. 189–204. This is also one of the issues covered in the major interpretative article by Boyd Hilton, 'Peel: A Reappraisal', *Historical Journal*, XXII (1979), pp. 585–614. J. B. Conacher, *The Peelites and the Party System, 1846–1852* (Newton Abbot, 1972), studies the last phase of Peel's career and the fate of his Free Trade supporters.

R. C. Shipkey, *Robert Peel's Irish Policy, 1812–1846* (New York, 1987), provides a general account of Peel's approach to the governing of Britain's sister isle, while there is a more specialised study by Donal A. Kerr, *Peel, Priests and Politics: Sir Robert Peel's Administration and the Roman Catholic Church in Ireland, 1841–1846* (Oxford, 1982).

INDEX

177